Pentecostal Sacraments

Encountering God at the Altar

To: Brian

Thanks for your
fellowship !

PENTECOSTAL SACRAMENTS

ENCOUNTERING GOD AT THE ALTAR

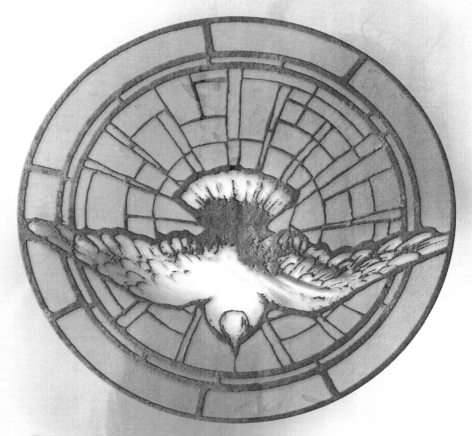

DANIEL TOMBERLIN
FOREWORD BY MARK WILLIAMS

For further information, contact:

Center for Pentecostal Leadership and Care
Pentecostal Theological Seminary

900 Walker Street, NE
P. O. Box 3330
Cleveland, Tennessee 37320-3330

Phone 423.478.7020 • Fax 423.478.7720
info@cplc.cc • www.cplc.cc

CONTENTS

FOREWORD

h is name was T.L. Phillips. He was affectionately known as "Pop."

Pop Phillips was something of a legend throughout the Church of God in Tennessee, having served as a prominent pastor in his day. He was regularly called upon to help with various denominational boards and committees, and he even ran the canteen during summer youth camps. Known for his love for Jesus and outspoken conservative beliefs, Pop was truly a joy to everyone who knew him.

When Sandra Kay and I assumed the pastorate of the South Cleveland Church of God, Pop was in his late 80s. I quickly noticed that every time I greeted him and inquired as to his well being, he always replied, "I'm happy!" On the back of his car was a bumper sticker with the same phrase: "I'm happy." On one occasion, I asked him, "Pop, how is it that you are always so happy?" He pointed to the ordinance of footwashing, quoting Jesus' words in John 13:17: "Happy are ye if you do them." Then, in classic Phillips humor, he quipped, "Brother Williams, people are just two feet away from happiness!"

I think Pop had it right.

Could it be that we are missing something in the Pentecostal church by treating Christ's established ordinances as ordinary? Could it be that we have focused so much on celebration that we have lost the blessing that comes through liturgy and practice?

Daniel Tomberlin, in his book, *Pentecostal Sacraments: Encountering God at the Altar*, dares to say that baptism, the Lord's Supper, footwashing, and anointing with oil are all sacramental means of grace enabling us to remember, experience, and anticipate the mysteries of salvation. Together they symbolize the Christian's journey from initiation to glorification and our need for continual cleansing along the way. Drawing from ecumenical dialogues, scholarly research, devotional reflections, and 30 years of pastoral experience, Tomberlin adds valuable insights to the discussion on what it means to be Pentecostal and how Spirit-filled believers view the practices Christ instituted.

I have tremendous respect for this author and the passion that drives him. He is a shepherd who takes seriously the call to care for souls.

It is a pleasure to commend this book to you for personal reflection, believing it will prove valuable in stimulating further discussion about the place and practice of sacraments in Pentecostal worship.

—Dr. Mark Williams
Assistant General Overseer
Church of God

PREFACE

I am unapologetically Pentecostal. By that I mean that I believe Christian faith is properly understood in terms of an *encounter* with God. My testimony is the story of one who encountered God in the person of Jesus Christ through the Holy Spirit. This encounter took place in the church—its members, teachers, and preachers. Yes, I accepted Jesus as Lord, but my encounter did not end there. I also encountered Spirit—I was baptized in the Holy Spirit with the initial evidence of speaking with other tongues. My study of the Scriptures, and the theological tradition of the church, has reaffirmed that encounter again and again. As a Pentecostal Christian, I am firmly committed to the premise that the mission and worship of the church must be empowered by an encounter with the Holy Spirit.

Also, I am unapologetically a man of the church. I love the church. By this, I do not mean the petty politics often associated with the church; nor do I mean that I naively embrace sinfulness and corruption within the church. I love the church—the body of Jesus Christ, the communion of the saints in the fellowship of the Spirit. I pray that I am properly submitted to Jesus Christ as the Head and Chief Bishop of the church. I am grateful for the opportunity to serve the church. I am convinced that one can come to church without knowing Jesus, but no one can come to Jesus without knowing the church.

I write as a pastor who is celebrating thirty years of ministry. As you read this material, I hope you will notice that my devotion to the church, and my Pentecostal convictions, have not dulled the critical edge of the message, but sharpened the edge. With a pastor's heart, I offer insights that may be painful, or misunderstood; but in my best judgment they are necessary.

I have told this story before, but it bears repeating. One of the more significant seasons of my spiritual journey was with a small group of pastors who met weekly to study the gospel text of the common lectionary. As president of the local ministerial association, I was invited to be a participant. At first, I attended to be polite, but soon found the experience very enriching. The group consisted of an ecumenical mix that included ministers from Episcopal, Catholic, Methodist, Baptist, and Pentecostal traditions. One might wonder how such a group could meet without theological debate, but as we met each week and focused on our gospel study, we discovered we had more about which we agreed than disagreed. In this diversity, each person contributed from his ecclesiastical tradition and was eager to learn about the traditions of others. While I represented the Pentecostal tradition, I received valuable insight into other traditions, especially regarding worship. In discussions with ministerial colleagues, especially the Catholic and Anglican liturgical traditions, I discovered Pentecostal worship could be enriched by developing a deeper understanding and broader appreciation of the sacraments and applying insights from these diverse traditions.

The Pentecostal Movement was not birthed in a vacuum. Pentecostalism is one of the latest in a series of movements by which the Holy Spirit works to renew the church. The Pentecostal church is the beneficiary of the "cloud of witnesses" throughout the history of the Christian church. Pentecostal spirituality is informed by Martin Luther, John Calvin, James Arminius, John Wesley, Phoebe Palmer, A.B. Simpson, and many other Protestant Christians. To the surprise of some Pentecostals, our spirituality has also benefited from the Roman Catholic and Orthodox traditions. This book seeks to give voice to this "cloud of witnesses." Throughout the book, I have sought to allow the voices to speak for themselves. You will find quotations from the early fathers, Protestant reformers, pioneer Pentecostals, and Catholic and Orthodox theologians. Each voice speaks from the conviction that Jesus is Lord.

This book seeks to demonstrate that sacramental worship is essential to Pentecostal spirituality. I should make a few comments about the title—*Pentecostal Sacraments*. First, I have chosen the word *sacraments* over ordinances. As you will discover in the text of the book, many Pentecostals have used the term as well. The thesis of this book is that sacramental worship is more than symbolic. *Sacrament* suggests the mystery and reality of a divine encounter. Second, sacraments are *Pentecostal*. Of course, I am aware that the sacraments belong to all Christians. So, by speaking of *Pentecostal* sacraments, I do not mean to imply an elitist or sectarian meaning. Describing sacraments as *Pentecostal* seeks to express the divine encounter in a fully Trinitarian spirituality. That is, God the Father salvifically embracing humanity with God's two hands—the Son and the Spirit. In this book, Pentecostal spirituality is presented as a Christo-Pneumatic encounter. So, when I employ the term *Pentecostal* sacraments, I am suggesting that sacraments are *Pentecostal* for all Christians.

The first chapter is written devotionally as an introduction to the material. For Pentecostals, the altar is most often the place of encounter. It is also the place of spiritual formation. I provide biblical examples of encountering God at the altar. Chapter 2 is a review of Pentecostal spirituality and provides a theological background and method for the following chapters. If sacraments are to be properly understood, they must be understood within the mosaic of the Christian (and Pentecostal) theological tradition. Chapter 3 is the pivotal chapter as it presents the basis for a Pentecostal sacramental theology. I am hopeful that this material will offer Pentecostals a way to understand sacraments that is biblical, in continuity with the historic church, and faithful to Pentecostal spirituality. The remaining chapters discuss four Pentecostal sacraments: water baptism, the Lord's Supper, footwashing, and "the anointed touch." Although the grace of God may be encountered through other sacramental acts (marriage, child dedication, and ordination), the four sacraments that are discussed in this book are universally salvific. In other words, all believers—single or married, child or adult, lay or clergy—encounter God's salvific grace in water baptism, the Lord's Supper, footwashing, and the anointed touch. I discuss the sacraments as they are presented in the New Testament, their development in the early church, and their significance in the Pentecostal movement. Also, I offer helpful suggestions as to how pastors can make sacraments a meaningful part of Pentecostal worship. My intent is to present a spirituality that strengthens and enriches the Pentecostal encounter.

The last two years have been a season of great joy for me. I have read hundreds of articles and sermons written by Pentecostal pioneers. Often, I felt as if I had discovered a treasure. The early Pentecostals preached and wrote with a palpable passion. Their devotion to Holy Scripture was without measure. Also, and this was surprising to me, they had wide knowledge of the early fathers. As I read the writings of the Pentecostal pioneers, I was enriched and refreshed.

As this volume goes to print, I must express my appreciation to Dr. James Bowers. He gave me the opportunity to publish the earlier work in the *Pentecostal Leadership Series*. Dr. Bowers was eager to assist with this volume as well. Also, Dr. Steve Land has offered many encouraging words. Dr. Randy Turpin has been a friend and an excellent editor for this project. Nellie Keasling should be recognized for her very fine work as copy editor. My wife, Sharon, has read every word, multiple times, and has been a constant source of encouragement. R. Ariel Vázquez is to be credited for the captivating cover design.

Finally, I wish to dedicate this book to all the faithful teachers of the church whom the Spirit has anointed to feed milk and meat to believers so that we may grow in the faith, from spiritual babes to "the measure of the stature which belongs to the fullness of Christ" (Ephesians 4:13).

—**Daniel Tomberlin**
Bainbridge, Georgia
Pentecost 2010

CHAPTER 1

Encountering God At The Altar

Pentecostal altar services are as a tempest with a crash of trees uprooted, rocks loosened and rushing down declivities, frightened birds and beasts fleeing before it and crying out; its confusion and tumult as if God did rend the mountains and come down. It's a combination of tempest, fire and earthquake, then the still small voice of the unknown tongue that witnesses that another has been baptized for duty and called to service, to thanksgiving and to adoration. Glory! Glory! Glory!! [*sic*]

—A Baptist Preacher[1]

In my spiritual journey, there are sacred places where I encountered God—the Baptist church where I was saved, and the altar where I was baptized in the Spirit. My wife and I met God at an altar and affirmed our marriage vows to God and to each other. A few years later, we dedicated our sons at the altar. Over and over again, I have found myself at a sacred place—an altar to meet with God.

As a child raised in a Pentecostal church, there were many times that we gathered around the altar to "pray through" to salvation, sanctification, and baptism in the Holy Spirit. I have vivid memories of the shouts of joy and the cries of lament coming from the praying saints at the altar. On occasion, I would hear someone scream—a scream that would cause my skin to crawl—and I knew that one

---

[1] *The Evening Light and Church of God Evangel* (July 1, 1910) 3.

1

of the sisters had been touched by God. These altar calls were not just demonstrations of emotionalism, they were sober and life transforming. We didn't really have church unless we had a good altar call.

The Evangelical altar call has not always been a part of Christian worship. For centuries, most people became Christian through infant baptism. During the Great Awakening of the eighteenth century, sinners were called to the "mourner's bench" to cry out for forgiveness. Since then, the altar call has been a fixture in most Evangelical worship services. However, in the last few decades, the altar has lost significance in the worship of Pentecostal churches. The altar is no longer the center of our worship. We have moved from having altar services in which believers participate in prayer for each other to the stage where seekers are prayed for by a charismatic leader. In these services, most believers are mere spectators. We often lament the condition of our churches. We know something essential is missing; we have the latest audio and video materials; we are singing the latest in contemporary worship songs; we are celebrating; we are worshipping louder and longer; and we are leaving our churches entertained and even encouraged, but not transformed. Pentecostal churches must be places of prayer where believers participate in prayer at the altar.

Throughout the Old Testament, altars were built as a sacred place where God was encountered. The ancients did not think that God's presence was limited to these sacred places. The prophets of Israel affirmed that God is omnipresent. "Holy, Holy, Holy, is the Lord of hosts, the whole earth is full of His glory" (Isaiah 6:3). Altars were places where God was encountered. God does not need altars, but humans do. Humans need a sacred place to meet God, because humans are creatures of time and space.

When God made the covenant with Israel and gave the Ten Commandments, God commanded that an altar be erected (Exodus 20:22-25). The altar was to be a sacred place—a place where God's name was recorded and the people could encounter God and receive a blessing from God. Many such places are mentioned in the Old Testament. Many of these places have the name of God, *El* or *Yah*, as prefix or suffix to the name of the place. These sacred places give us a space and time where God is encountered.

In giving instructions for the building of the altar, God commanded that the altar be constructed from simple materials—earth or uncut stones. The altar was not to become an idol. The altar was to be a *place* of worship, not an *object* of worship. When the altar, or the church building, becomes an object of worship, God is not glorified. Our sacred places are sacred because of the presence of God. Our altar may be the family coffee table, or bedside. We can build an altar around a hospital bed as we gather to pray for the sick. The point is that an altar is constructed primarily of two things—space and time. If we are to encounter God at a sacred place, then we must set a time and place for that meeting.

The altar is a place of sacrifice. The people were to bring their offerings and give them to God. The blood of the sacrifices was sprinkled upon the altar and the blood atoned for the sins of the people. The cross upon which Jesus Christ was crucified was an altar. Upon that altar the Son of God was nailed and offered as a sacrifice for the sins of the world. The blood of the Savior was poured out upon the cross and was sprinkled over the face of the earth. Humans are called to come to the cross, to be sprinkled by the blood of Jesus Christ for our salvation and sanctification. As we come to the altar, we are called to present ourselves to God as "a living and holy sacrifice, acceptable to God" (Romans 12:1). Here, at the altar, we deny ourselves. Our lives are no longer to be governed by sinful desires, but by the Spirit of God. At the altar we die. Paul wrote, "I have been crucified with Christ; and it is no longer I who live, but Christ lives in me; and the life which I now live in the flesh I live by faith in the Son of God, who loved me and gave Himself for me" (Galatians 2:20). This is why the altar is a struggle for many, because they know that at the altar they die to self so that Christ may live in them.

The Altar of Yahweh Yireh

> The Lord appeared to Abram and said, "To your descen-
> dants I will give this land." So he built an altar there to the
> Lord who had appeared to him. Then he proceeded from
> there to the mountain on the east of Bethel, and pitched his
> tent, with Bethel on the west and Ai on the east; and there
> he built an altar to the Lord and called upon the name of the
> Lord (Genesis 12:7-8).

Abraham was on a journey, moving from one place to another.
Abraham was a person who responded in faith to the call of God.
Everywhere he went, Abraham built altars. Each of these altars
defined his spiritual journey. These were the sacred places where
God met with Abraham and places where Abraham called on God.

The altar was a memorial where Abraham celebrated his
covenant relationship with God. The covenant relationship was
mutual. Abraham and his descendents would live in obedience to
God, and God would bless Abraham by making him the spiritual
father of many nations. In Genesis 12, God made a fivefold promise
to Abraham. Five times God said, "I will . . ."

- I will show you a land.
- I will make you a great nation.
- I will make your name great.
- I will bless those who bless you.
- I will curse those who curse you.

Every time Abraham approached an altar, he was reminded of
God's promises. The altar became a testimony to the faithfulness of
God. Worship at the altar meant that Abraham continued to look
for the fulfillment of God's promises.

Most Pentecostals were saved at an altar. The gospel was
proclaimed, the Spirit convicted and called, and the sinner
responded by *going forward* to the altar. That sacred place where the
sinner kneels to confess sin and accept Jesus as Lord is a memorial
to God's saving grace. Just as Abraham returned again and again
to the altar, so the obedient believer should return to the altar. It is

the place where we call upon the Lord, always *going forward* in our spiritual development. The altar call provides the time and space for us to meet with God once again, to call upon God that we might renew our commitment, to be sanctified, or to pray through to the baptism in the Holy Spirit. Pentecostal worship has always been about *movement*. We pray that the Spirit will *move* among us. We come to church expecting to be *moved* by the Spirit. At some point in the service, we are invited to *move* from our seats to pray at the altar. *Every Sermon Should Challenge the hearer*

The altar is the place where Abraham "called on the name of the Lord." A few years ago my wife's family gathered around a hospital bed to be with her one hundred-year-old grandmother as she was dying. When Mama Bill exhaled her last breath, the family began to weep. At the same time, sounds of joy and laughter were heard in the next room. As my wife's family mourned the death of a precious family matriarch, the family in the next room was rejoicing over a new baby. Life and death, as well as joy and sorrow, represent our spiritual journey. One family would make the journey to church to remember and mourn a life lost; the other family would make the journey to church to celebrate a new life. The altar is a place of joy and sorrow.

We will call upon the name of the Lord in our times of joy.

> Oh give thanks to the Lord, call upon His name; make known His deeds among the peoples. Sing to Him, sing praises to Him; speak of all His wonders. Glory in His holy name; let the heart of those who seek the Lord be glad (Psalm 105:1-3).

When a sinner repents at the altar, the angels of heaven rejoice. The saints rejoice when a seeker is baptized in the Holy Spirit, or when someone testifies to being healed. As a young man and woman come to the altar to give themselves to each other in marriage, their families weep with tears of rejoicing. At the altar, we celebrate the passages of life.

Also, we will call upon the name of the Lord in our times of distress.

I call upon the Lord, who is worthy to be praised, and I am saved from my enemies. The cords of death encompassed me, and the torrents of ungodliness terrified me. The cords of Sheol surrounded me; the snares of death confronted me. In my distress I called upon the Lord, and cried to my God for help; He heard my voice out of His temple, and my cry for help before Him came into His ears (Psalm 18:3-6).

Pentecostal spirituality has suffered the loss of lament in prayer. We have been told (erroneously) that our victory in Christ means that we will not suffer hardship. If we do encounter distress, by faith we should make a positive confession and put a smile on our faces. But that is not the testimony of the Scriptures. In the Scriptures, when faithful people were distressed, they tore their clothes, put ash on their heads, and cried out to God. These prayers of lament are not faithless acts; they are cries of faith. In their distress, they did not turn their faces from God, but toward God. They insisted that God turn His face toward them. This is passionate, meaningful prayer.

The altar was a place where Abraham's faith was sorely tested. "Then they came to the place of which God had told him; and Abraham built the altar there and arranged the wood, and bound his son Isaac and laid him on the altar, on top of the wood (Genesis 22:9). God had asked Abraham to offer his only son, Isaac, as a sacrifice. The altar always costs us something. Remember, at the altar we die. Isaac had been Abraham's greatest joy. The name Isaac means "laughter." Abraham laughed when the angel announced that he and Sarah would have a son. We can only imagine the joy and laughter that Isaac brought to his aged parents. Isaac represented the whole of Abraham's relationship with God. Isaac was the fulfillment of God's promise. The death of Isaac meant the death of God's promise. Living the life of faith is always a struggle. Faith sometimes requires great risk. It requires that the believer trust in the faithfulness of God, even in the most difficult times. As Abraham approached the altar with a heavy heart, he spoke words of faith: "God will provide for Himself the lamb . . ." (Genesis 22:8).

The altar is the place of God's provision. As Abraham raised the knife over Isaac, he heard the voice of the angel: "Do not stretch out your hand against the lad" (Genesis 22:12). As he looked up, he saw a ram caught in the thicket by its horns. He offered the ram as a sacrifice upon the altar that had been built for Isaac. As the flames of the sacrificial fire consumed the ram and the smoke of the fire danced toward heaven, we can imagine the sounds of joy and laughter as Abraham and Isaac worshiped God. Abraham named the altar "*Yahweh Yireh*," that is, God provides. At *Yahweh Yireh*, Abraham experienced the depths of despair. He brought to the altar his greatest treasure—his son. In his act of faithfulness, he discovered the faithfulness of God. Abraham's place as the father of faith was firmly established only after he offered Isaac. The angel of the Lord said, " . . . because you have done this thing and have not withheld your son . . . I will greatly bless you" (Genesis 22:16-17). The altar of *Yahweh Yireh* is a memorial to God's commitment to bless the nations of the earth. Here at *Yahweh Yireh*, despair gives way to hope.

The Altar of Witness

The sons of Reuben and the sons of Gad called the altar Witness; "For," they said, "it is a witness between us that the Lord is God" (Joshua 22:34).

After the partial conquest of Canaan, Joshua began to assign territories of inheritance to the tribes of Reuben, Gad, and Manasseh. The people of these tribes were faithful to the covenant of Moses; they were obedient to the commands of Joshua; and they maintained the solidarity of the community. Because of their faithfulness, they now entered into the rest of the Lord. The territory of Reuben, Gad, and Manasseh was on the east side of the Jordan River. The territories of the other tribes were on the west side of the Jordan. The Jordan formed a natural boundary that separated the tribes of Israel. After settling on the east side of the Jordan River, these three tribes built "a large altar" by the Jordan (Joshua 22:10). When the other tribes of Israel saw the altar that Reuben, Gad, and Manasseh had erected, they took offense.

> When the sons of Israel heard of it, the whole congregation
> of the sons of Israel gathered themselves at Shiloh to go up
> against them in war. . . . They came to the sons of Reuben
> and to the sons of Gad and to the half-tribe of Manasseh,
> to the land of Gilead, and they spoke with them saying,
> "Thus says the whole congregation of the Lord, 'What is this
> unfaithful act which you have committed against the God
> of Israel, turning away from following the Lord this day, by
> building yourselves an altar, to rebel against the Lord this
> day?'" (Joshua 22:12, 15-16).

The tribes of Israel had a reason to be concerned. The people of Israel had a tendency towards idolatry. Their recent history during the wilderness journey was one of rebellion and judgment. The most recent incident was still fresh in the minds of the people. At Shittim the people worshiped at the altar of Baal of Peor. This act was so offensive to God that the leaders of Israel were executed and God sent a plague that killed twenty-four thousand people (Numbers 25:1-9). The tribes of Israel were suspicious of the meaning of the altar that had been built by Reuben, Gad, and Manasseh. It could have signified a return to idolatrous practices. If this was the case, the whole nation would suffer because of the sins of a few.

However, the altar at the Jordan River was not a monument to idolatry. The altar was constructed as a memorial to remind the future generations of Reuben, Gad, and Manasseh that they belonged to the tribes on the west side of the river. They shared a common redemptive heritage, a common covenant, and a common future with their cousins to the west. The altar was named Witness. Its purpose was to be a symbol of the unity of the covenant community.

The altar of Witness signifies the unity of humanity. All too often we tend to focus on the things that separate us. Culture, race, language, and national borders all serve to define our identity. It is easy for us to embrace those things with which we are familiar. I once watched a television program about the making of *The Planet of the Apes* (the original 1968 version). In that movie there were three groups of apes: chimpanzees, orangutans, and gorillas. The actors' costumes and makeup were bulky and required several hours of preparation, so the actors wore the costumes throughout the day. During the lunch breaks the actors began to form groups based upon the costume they were wearing—chimps ate with chimps, orangutans ate with orangutans, and gorillas ate with gorillas. It seems that we have difficulty getting beyond the surface in relationships with others.

When I was a child, we often sang, "Jesus loves the little children, all the children of the world. Red and yellow, black and white, all are precious in His sight, Jesus loves the little children of the world."[2] Even as a child I knew that we didn't believe the words we were singing. All I had to do was listen to the words of my parents, or any of the adults at church, and I knew we didn't love everybody. If a black family would have walked into our church, they would have been met with an unloving reception. I remember the Sunday school lessons where we were taught that being black was a result of the "curse of Ham." As a teenager, I was firmly rebuked by my pastor because I had invited a young black man to church. All would have been well, except he responded to the altar call to get saved. In doing so, everyone in the church became aware of his presence. Forty years later, much has changed in the church. But many are still struggling with issues of race. This is especially true when we begin talking about immigration; or the first black president of the United States. The altar of Witness is a constant reminder that God is Creator and Father of all (Acts 17:22-31; Galatians 3:28).

The altar of Witness signifies the unity of the Christian church. The apostle Paul warned that we should be careful to avoid religious quarrels and divisions: "Now I exhort you, brethren, by the name of our Lord Jesus Christ, that you all agree and that there be no divisions among you, but that you be made complete in the same mind and in the same judgment" (1 Corinthians 1:10). But like the people of Israel and their tendencies toward idolatry, the Christian church has demonstrated tendencies toward division and conflict. We have often sought to justify our schisms, but the church's divisions and conflict represent a failure to be faithful to the call of Christ. Christ is not

---

[2] C. Herbert Woolston (1856-1927).

divided; he is the union of human and divine being. All Christians are baptized into Christ. The church is the body of Christ, and as such, the church should seek to manifest His ontological unity. "There is one body and one Spirit, just as also you were called in one hope of your calling; one Lord, one faith, one baptism, one God and Father of all who is over all and through all and in all" (Ephesians 4:4-6).

The Jordan River separated the twelve tribes. But the altar called Witness was a monument to their shared redemptive heritage and their unity as a community in covenant with God. Christians are called to be a witness of Christ to the world. Jesus said, "By this all men will know that you are My disciples, if you have love for one another" (John 13:35). Paul said that love represents "a still more excellent way" (1 Corinthians 12:31). James said that to "love your neighbor as yourself" is to fulfill the "royal law" (James 2:8). The altar must be a witness to Christian love. At the altar, we share the bread and cup of Holy Communion. This is a communion of love. It represents God's love for the world, Christ's love for his church, and our love for God and each other. At the altar, we wash the feet of our brothers and sisters in a demonstration of Christian love, service, and forgiveness.

Irenaeus, a second-century bishop, prophetically warned of the coming schisms that would divide the church:

> He shall also judge those who give rise to schisms, who are destitute of the love of God, and who look to their own special advantage rather than to the unity of the Church; and who for trifling reasons, or any kind of reason which occurs to them, cut in pieces and divide the great and glorious body of Christ, and so far as in them lies, [positively] destroy it,—men who prate of peace while they give rise to war, and do in truth strain out a gnat, but swallow a camel. For no reformation of so great importance can be effected by them, as will compensate for the mischief arising from their schism.[3]

---

[3] Alexander Roberts, James Donaldson and A. Cleveland Coxe, *The Ante-Nicene Fathers, Vol. I*, (Oak Harbor, WA: Logos Research Systems, 1997), 508.

Several centuries later we have become so accustomed to the various walls of division that we no longer view them as a detriment to the cause of Christ. Even so, Christians must come together and build the altar of Witness, a place where we can affirm our common faith in Jesus Christ. As we seek to build the unity of the church, we must also strive to maintain the truth of the gospel. The church cannot be the body of Christ if it is not faithful to His word.

The altar of Witness signifies the unity of the family. It is here that a man and woman will confess the vows of marriage. Their covenant love will be declared here. The altar serves as a witness to their union. After they have been blessed with a child, they will return as father and mother to dedicate their child to God. Their marriage and the dedication of their child takes place at the altar of Witness, in the presence of God and the assembled communion of the faithful. The altar witnesses to the union of the marriage, and the unity of their family. The altar is a witness of the past covenants and commitments they have made together. As they journey through life together, and face the many tribulations that will come, the altar is a witness to their shared lives in Christ. It is the sacred place they were joined together by God. This altar becomes a witness to the words of Christ: "So they are no longer two, but one flesh. What therefore God has joined together, let no man separate" (Matthew 19:6).

We should be mindful of the sacramental grace of the altar of Witness as a place of blessing. That which the church blesses becomes canon, that is, the measure by which righteousness (rightness) is judged. One of the major social issues before our society is homosexual marriage. Some churches have embraced this concept, thereby blessing and canonizing these relationships. Also, some churches have adopted rites that celebrate divorce. Again, let me say that what the church blesses becomes the norm. The altar of Witness must not become a place that blesses and canonizes covenants, relationships, and behavior that is contrary to the Holy Scriptures.

Aaron's two sons, Nadab and Abihu, offered "strange fire . . . which [God] had not commanded" (Leviticus 10:1; Numbers 3:4; 26:61). The result was disastrous: "And fire came out from the presence of the Lord and consumed them, and they died before the Lord" (Leviticus 10:2). Through Moses, the Lord proclaimed, "By those who come near Me I will be treated as holy, and before all the people I will be honored" (Leviticus 10:3). God must be honored at the altar of Witness. If we come to the altar without due respect for the holiness of God; or if we bring that which is profane to the altar; we cannot expect the blessings of God. Rather, we will incur God's judgment (Malachi 1:6-13). At the altar, sin can be forgiven and the sinner cleansed. But ongoing sinful behavior cannot be blessed or condoned at the altar.

The Altar of Yahweh Shalom

> When Gideon saw that he was the angel of the Lord, he said, "Alas, O Lord God! For now I have seen the angel of the Lord face to face." The Lord said to him, "Peace to you, do not fear; you shall not die." Then Gideon built an altar there to the Lord and named it The Lord is Peace (Judges 6:22-24).

The Hebrew word for "peace" is *shalom* and it means to be complete, to be sound, and it refers to the general welfare of a person's life, or the life of a community. When the people of Israel inherited the land of promise, they were to enter into rest. They were to live in obedience to the covenant with God and their lives in Canaan were to be blessed with *shalom*. However, failure to live in obedience to God's covenant meant that the covenantal blessings would be removed from the people and the land (Deuteronomy 11:26-28). By the time of the Judges, the people of Israel were often falling into apostasy and the *shalom* of the covenant was broken. The "land of milk and honey" had become a land filled with enemy marauders.

When we first meet Gideon, the people of Israel have been delivered into the hands of the Midianites. Gideon is reduced to threshing wheat while hiding in a cave. The narrative says, "So Israel was brought very low because of Midian, and the sons of Israel cried to the Lord" (Judges 6:6). For some reason, we have a difficult time understanding that our sinful actions have dire consequences. Sinfulness is very often a result of arrogance toward God. Arrogance means that we have exalted ourselves above the need for God or the need to be submissive to God. Arrogance is often demonstrated in self-righteousness, which means that we set our own standards of righteousness. The problem is that God is a jealous God (Exodus 20:5). God will not be ignored. God's answer to human arrogance is humiliation. "A man's pride will bring him low" (Proverbs 29:23). The sinfulness of the covenant community has brought Israel "very low."

Israel's humiliation is unbearable, so they have "cried to the Lord" (Judges 6:6). The bitter fruit of sinfulness is demonstrated in many tears. Many people cry out or complain in their distress, but Israel has assembled together and cried out *to the Lord*. Tearful laments to God are often the first step in the restoration of *shalom*. Hearts that have been hardened by sin must be broken. "The Lord is near to the brokenhearted and saves those who are crushed in spirit" (Psalm 34:18). This was an intensely painful spiritual process. God had injured the hearts of the people so that they might be healed. Sinfulness brought the people to a new level of humility. This type of humiliation is redemptive.

God responded to the cries of the people by *sending*. First, God sent a prophet. The message of the prophet was, "Remember." Judges records:

> The Lord sent a prophet to the sons of Israel, and he said to them, "Thus says the Lord, the God of Israel, 'It was I who brought you up from Egypt and brought you out from the house of slavery. I delivered you from the hands of the Egyptians and from the hands of all your oppressors, and dispossessed them before you and gave you their land'" (Judges 6:8-9).

The nation needed to remember their redemptive heritage. They need to remember that the only reason they were in Canaan was because God delivered their ancestors. The prophet also rebuked the nation: "I am the Lord your God. . . . But you have not obeyed Me" (Judges 6:10). The people needed to be mindful that the absence of *shalom* in the land of promise was due to a lack of obedience.

After the prophet, God sent "the angel of the Lord" (Judges 6:11). The prophet was sent to the nation. The angel of the Lord was sent to search out Gideon. The message from the angel of the Lord was, "The Lord is with you" (Judges 6:12). Gideon's reply was somewhat sarcastic and hopeless: "If the Lord is with us, why then has all this happened to us?" (Judges 6:13). The truth is that Israel suffered under the hands of the Midianites because the Lord sent them. From Gideon's perspective, God had forsaken Israel. Even so, the presence of the angel of the Lord signified that God had heard the cries of the people and was now present to deliver.

The angel of the Lord was sent to Gideon at Ophrah so that Gideon could be sent as Israel's deliverer. "The Lord looked at him and said, 'Go in this your strength and deliver Israel from the hand of Midian. Have I not sent you?'" (Judges 6:14). Gideon was overwhelmed by the divine call. He had no experience with the presence of God. The divine call seemed to Gideon to border on absurdity. But even in his doubt, he sought for faith. He offered a sacrifice which the angel of the Lord consumed with fire and then immediately disappeared. Suddenly, Gideon realized that his guest was the angel of the Lord and cried out, "Alas, O Lord God! For now I have seen the angel of the Lord face to face" (Judges 6:22). The Lord responded with three declarations: "Peace to you; do not fear; you shall not die" (Judges 6:23). The Lord's words offered peace, encouragement, and life. The presence of God brought *shalom* back to the nation.

The name "Gideon" actually means "to hew down" or "to break off." This is most likely a prophetic name given to Jerubbaal by the angel of the Lord. It looks forward to the day when he will tear down the altars of Baal that his clan had erected. But Gideon was also an altar builder. At Ophrah he built an altar and called it *Yahweh Shalom*, that is, the Lord is Peace. The altar at *Yahweh Shalom* signified the return of the people to God and God's return to the people. There were struggles ahead. The Midianites were still in the land, but God had returned. The land would once again be a place of *shalom.*

Many of us have made sinful decisions that have wrecked our lives. A decision to be sexually promiscuous has led to an unplanned pregnancy, or even worse, a sexually transmitted disease that threatens life. A decision to commit adultery has destroyed someone's marriage and family. A failure in integrity has cost someone a good-paying job. Failure to properly manage finances has left a family facing bankruptcy. Addiction to alcohol, or other chemical substances, has left someone utterly incapable of dealing with the issues of life. These sinful decisions rob us of *shalom,* the peace of God. In the midst of our distress, we cry out to God. We stumble into a church service carrying the burdens of sinfulness. As the Spirit begins to search our heart, we weep. The Spirit calls. As we approach the altar to cry out to God, we are overwhelmed by God's grace. Our prayer of repentance leaves us deeply cleansed. We discover that as we turn our faces to God in repentance, God's presence restores *shalom* to our lives. There are many struggles of life ahead, but we have returned to God. The altar is *Yahweh Shalom.*

The Altar of Yahweh Elohim

> "Now let them give us two oxen; and let them choose one ox for themselves and cut it up, and place it on the wood, but put no fire under it; and I will prepare the other ox and lay it on the wood, and I will not put a fire under it. Then you call on the name of your god, and I will call on the name of the Lord, and the God who answers by fire, He is God." And all the people said, "That is a good idea."
>
> Then the fire of the Lord fell and consumed the burnt offering and the wood and the stones and the dust, and licked up the water that was in the trench. When all the people saw it, they fell on their faces; and they said, "The Lord, He is God; the Lord, He is God" (1 Kings 18:23-24, 38-39).

The name "Elijah" means "Yahweh is my God." Elijah prophesied in Israel during a time of dark apostasy. During the days of King Omri, many Israelites began to turn away from their ancestral God and turn to the god of the Canaanites, Baal. With the ascension of Ahab to the throne, the apostasy of Israel became complete. Ahab's wife, Jezebel, was an enthusiastic patron of the Baal cult. Under her direction, the prophets of Yahweh were relentlessly persecuted. The prophets of Baal were welcomed at the royal court. Altars to Baal were constructed throughout the land.

Baal is the Canaanite storm god. He is chiefly responsible for the rains and fertility. It would not be an exaggeration to suggest that he represented the prosperity of the people. The seasonal rains were the essential lifeline for the agrarian culture of the Ancient Near East. The rains of Baal enriched the land and caused the crops and orchards to bear their fruit. Maybe we can understand the significance of Baal if we make a contemporary comparison. Baal is the god of energy and economic prosperity. The Baal cult has become the economic engine that drives life in Israel.

Suddenly, a prophet appeared whose name was "My God is Yahweh." Elijah's very name was a prophetic challenge to the Baal cult, and to the political fortunes of Ahab and Jezebel. To simply speak the name "Elijah" was to speak against Baal. Elijah's first prophetic words were directed at the heart of the Baal cult. "By the life of Yahweh, God of Israel, whom I serve, there will be neither dew nor rain these coming years unless I give the word" (1 Kings 17:1, *NJB*). With these words, Elijah killed Baal. The great storm god was unable to produce a single drop of dew. The great rivers were reduced to a trickle, and the streams were dry. The land was barren, and there was a great famine. Throughout the land, the people approached the altars of Baal. They offered sacrifices and cried out, but Baal was silent. There was still no rain.

Elijah boldly provoked a confrontation with the prophets of Baal. Two oxen would be offered: one on the altar of Baal, the other on the altar of Yahweh. Elijah then boldly proclaimed, "The god who answers by fire, He is God" (1 Kings 18:24). Certainly the great storm god, Baal, could muster a bolt of lightning for the sake of his reputation. Also at stake were the reputations of Ahab and Jezebel.

The prophets of Baal offered an ox upon their altar. They prayed for hours, but the storm god could not answer with even a distant thunder. Baal's prophets danced around their altar, they shouted, and ceremoniously offered their own blood to attract the attention of Baal. All day long they sought to hear, but Baal never answered. By the end of the day, no one was even paying attention. It was obvious that the great storm god was impotent.

As the sun began to set, Elijah prepared to offer his sacrifice. Elijah issued an altar call.

> Elijah said to all the people, "Come near to me." So all the people came near to him. And he repaired the altar of the Lord which had been torn down (1 Kings 18:30).

As the people of Israel watched, Elijah repaired the altar of Yahweh. For the first time in a generation, the descendants of Abraham approached the altar of Yahweh. Before Yahweh could be heard, before the fire would fall, the altar had to be repaired. After the altar was repaired, the sacrifice was prepared. Then Elijah offered a simple prayer:

> "Yahweh, God of Abraham, Isaac and Israel," he said, "let them know today that you are God in Israel, and that I am your servant, that I have done all these things at your command. Answer me, Yahweh, answer me, so that this people may know that you, Yahweh, are God and are winning back their hearts" (1 Kings 18:36-37, *NJB*).

The purpose of this entire episode is that God wanted Israel back. Yahweh wanted to be heard. Yahweh wanted to be heard by the prophets of Baal, and by Ahab and Jezebel. But the heart of God was for the people of God—the sons and daughters of Abraham. Suddenly, "Yahweh's fire fell!" All day long the assembled multitude waited to see who would prove to be God. Now there was no doubt. With one voice the people cried out, "Yahweh is God . . . Yahweh is God!" (1 Kings 18:39, *NJB*). The meaning of "Elijah"—Yahweh is my God—had now become the confession of Israel.

Shortly thereafter, "the sky grew dark with cloud and storm, and rain fell in torrents (1 Kings 18:45, *NJB*). The drought had lasted three years. Baal was proved to be an impotent fraud. Yahweh answered with fire and rain. With the fire, the faith of the nation was restored. With the rain, the life of the land was cleansed and restored. But none of this could have happened until Elijah repaired the altar of Yahweh Elohim—Yahweh is God.

Pentecostals have often interpreted the story of Elijah by which the fire of God signifies the pathos of the movement. Pentecostals often speak of God's presence in terms of fire and rain. Pentecostals understood the outpouring of the Holy Spirit to be the "latter rain," that is, the restoration of apostolic Pentecost upon the last-days church. The earliest Pentecostals often spoke of the "baptism of the Holy Ghost and fire." Pentecostals were often heard to testify of "Fire! Fire! Holy Fire!!!" [*sic*][4] Fiery manifestations were often reported in Pentecostal services. A.J. Tomlinson wrote:

> At one time as I stepped out to make an altar call, as I lifted my hands, a kind of blue mist was seen by a number of truthful witnesses as it settled down on the congregation, and not a few fell, and either crawled or were carried into the altar. A few times while the words were spoken, the Holy Ghost fell on all that heard the Word. Streaks of fire have been seen as they darted just above the heads of the people in the congregation, like zigzag lightning, and yet not so quick but that it was easily seen by scores of people.[5]

Speaking of the Elijah story and Pentecostal fire, Tomlinson wrote:

> Little groups will be formed to pray for the power and gifts of the Spirit. Individuals will be lost to this world, with their faces buried in their hands as they lay prostrate on the ground before God. Listen at them as they pray, with tears streaming down from their' eyes and their voices trembling with emotion and the power of God. "Lord, I must have the

---

[4] G.F. Taylor, *The Pentecostal Holiness Advocate*, May 22, 1930, 8.
[5] A.J. Tomlinson, *The Last Great Conflict*, (Cleveland, TN: Press of Walter E. Rodgers, 1913), 215.

power as it was given the Apostles or I can go no further. I am not able to preach another sermon or conduct another meeting in the common way, I must have some special help from Thee." Then a fresh flow of tears, and only a groan will be uttered at intervals as they tarry. Night will come on, but unnoticed by the earnest seeker. No desire for food. No care for prominence. No desire for leadership. No greed for money. No care for this world and its pleasures or business interests. They are only thirsting after God. They want Him.[6]

Generations later it seems that some Pentecostals have lost the initial ethos of the movement. For many, the Pentecostal Movement is no longer driven by the fire of the Holy Spirit. The initial Pentecostal ethos of "love not the world" has been co-opted by a different, world-friendly, gospel. It has been suggested that the single issue that unites Pentecostals is the prosperity gospel.[7] Some Pentecostals no longer emphasize the salvific encounters of being "saved, sanctified, and baptized in the Holy Spirit." Instead, popular Pentecostalism is being driven by "kingdom economics." For these Pentecostals, the goal of salvation is to be healthy, wealthy, and successful.

Jesus said, "No one can serve two masters; for either he will hate the one and love the other, or he will be devoted to one and despise the other. You cannot serve God and wealth" (Matthew 6:24). During the days of Elijah, the temptation of Israel was to worship at the altar of Baal. It seems that the temptation of our day is to worship at the altar of prosperity. During the days of Elijah, God withheld the rains for three years. Before the rains returned, the altar of Yahweh was repaired, the fire fell, and the people confessed, "Yahweh is God." Could it be that God will challenge the false prophets of our day? Could we face an economic collapse so that once again the people of God will forsake the false god and meet at the altar of Yahweh Elohim? Could it be that we must hear again the call of the early Pentecostal prophets?

---

[6] Tomlinson, *The Last Great Conflict,* 110-111.
[7] Ted Olsen, "What Really Unites Pentecostals?" *Christianity Today* (December 2006), 18-19.

Oh, for a million men who would fear nothing but God, filled with such holy zeal and Godly courage, that we could all together burst forth under the power of this mighty baptismal fire and rush to every quarter of the globe like mad men, declaring the gospel of the Son of God, until every tribe, kindred, tongue and people could hear, and thus end this Last Great Conflict![8]

The Altar of Reconciliation

Therefore if you are presenting your offering at the altar, and there remember that your brother has something against you, leave your offering there before the altar and go; first be reconciled to your brother, and then come and present your offering (Matthew 5:23-24).

Jesus speaks these words in the context of murder. In this discourse He reaches into the hearts of His hearers and tells them that when anger is left unchecked, the result is murder. But He goes even further. Jesus tells us that angry words endanger the soul. He said, "But I say to you that everyone who is angry with his brother shall be guilty before the court; and whoever says to his brother, 'You good-for-nothing,' shall be guilty before the supreme court; and whoever says, 'You fool,' shall be guilty enough to go into the fiery hell" (Matthew 5:22). Anger disrupts *shalom* in human community. When a husband and wife allow their hurts to be expressed in words of anger, *shalom* in the home is disrupted. When the saints of a church allow their quarrels and strife to develop into an angry confrontation, then *shalom* in the fellowship is disrupted and the unity of the body of Christ suffers. When these conflicts arise, we often resort to words of anger: "You empty-headed fool!" Or, if we are especially angry, we utter the unthinkable: "Go to h---!" However, when we speak these harsh words of anger we are not assigning our enemy to hell, but we are judging ourselves.

All too often anger and strife find expression at the place of worship. In Genesis 4, we read how Cain and Abel approached an altar to bring their sacrificial gifts. As they worshiped, Cain became

---

[8] Tomlinson, *The Last Great Conflict*, 219.

overwhelmed with envy toward his brother. Cain's envy gave way to anger, and anger moved Cain to murder his brother, Abel. Sadly, we find this situation all too common in our churches. Anger motivates us to injure those we love. The divorce rate in our churches is the same as the unchurched. Domestic violence and sexual abuse exist, even among Christian families. Many of us have been to the altar and repented of our sins, but we find that we still are not well. We suffer from unresolved anger. The problem is that although we have repented, we have not been reconciled and *shalom* in our community has not been restored.

We often go to church, sing our praises to God, give our tithes and offerings, and pray in the altar. But as we are walking out of the sanctuary, we see the face of a person with whom we are in conflict. So, we leave through a different exit. Or, if the conflict is very heated, we decide to go to another church. At least there we will not have to face our enemy. We have been told that our sins are a private matter, between one person and God, and all we need to do is repent and everything will be better. But that is not what Jesus said. Jesus insisted that reconciliation with our "enemy" must occur *before* we come to the altar to worship. We cannot leave our conflict and anger unresolved if we are to offer worship that is acceptable to God.

Christians have been reconciled to God and called to form the covenant community—the church. Paul said, "Now all these things are from God, who reconciled us to Himself through Christ, and gave us the ministry of reconciliation" (2 Corinthians 5:18). Christians are to be ambassadors of Christ, ministers of reconciliation. However, we cannot effectively fulfill the mission until first we resolve our own issues at home, and in the church. Jesus urges us to "Make friends quickly with your opponent" (Matthew 5:25). In other words, we must learn to resolve our conflicts before they escalate into anger. If we are to resolve our conflicts, we must admit that the source of our anger is most often selfishness. We get angry because we have been injured in some way. Anger is often an expression of self-preservation. Here we come to the heart of the matter. Jesus Christ reconciled the world to God through self-sacrifice. He offered Himself upon the altar of sacrifice (the cross) for the reconciliation of humanity. In other words, Jesus surrendered His will to the will of the Father. The first step in reconciliation is the surrender of self. We must be willing to suffer offense. Jesus said, " . . . Whoever slaps you on your right cheek, turn the other to him also" (Matthew 5:39). As ministers of reconciliation, we must be willing to suffer for the sake of righteousness. "Blessed are you when people insult you and persecute you, and falsely say all kinds of evil against you because of Me" (Matthew 5:11).

Reconciliation often requires confrontation. In order to be reconciled, we must face our antagonist. We find an example of reconciliation in the life of Joseph. Joseph was given a dream by God, a dream that spoke of his future leadership over his family. This dream stirred envy, fear, and even hatred in his older brothers. They conspired against him, sought to kill him, and in the end sold him into slavery. They thought they were forever rid of the troublesome dreamer. But God had a sovereign plan. Years later, Joseph and his brothers were again face to face. But now Joseph was prime minister of Egypt and he had the power to repay their evil deeds. They were frightened to the point of speechlessness. But Joseph had no plans for vengeance. Instead, he demonstrated a remarkable act of mercy. From Joseph, we learn that reconciliation is an act in which the offended offers forgiveness to the offender. There is no place for the selfishness of victimization.

Reconciliation requires a passionate love. From the moment Joseph saw his estranged brothers, he was overwhelmed by his love for them. Reconciliation requires a selfless sacrifice. It is a sacrifice of justice in favor of mercy. The offended must choose to forego justice and offer forgiveness. If we choose the path of anger, we will avoid this type of confrontation. We will push away from those who have injured us. But Joseph called to his brothers, "Please come closer to me" (Genesis 45:4). Reconciliation means that we will offer a loving embrace to those who have injured us.

In seeking reconciliation, we must consider that we might be the offender. In this case, we cannot offer forgiveness, but we must be willing to ask for forgiveness and make things right. John the Baptist makes it clear that repentance requires more than confession of sin. We must also be willing to "bear fruits in keeping with repentance" (Luke 3:8). Zacchaeus was a tax gatherer who had become rich by exploiting the citizens of Jericho. But when he met Jesus, he responded by giving half of his wealth to the poor and offering fourfold restitution to those whom he had defrauded (Luke 19:1-10). One can only imagine the goodwill generated in the community by his actions. Zacchaeus made peace with God and with the citizens of Jericho. *Shalom* in the community was restored.

Each time we approach the altar to meet with God we are faced with an opportunity to carefully examine ourselves. We must sincerely seek to maintain *shalom* in our family, our church, and in the greater human community. As we bow before God at the altar, we express humility. But we must remember that before we bow before God in humility we may need to seek out an enemy, or someone we have injured, and bow in humility before them. The altar becomes a witness to the ministry of reconciliation.

The Heavenly Altar

> Then one of the seraphim flew to me with a burning coal in his hand, which he had taken from the altar with tongs. He touched my mouth with it and said, "Behold, this has touched your lips; and your iniquity is taken away and your sin is forgiven" (Isaiah 6:6-7).

In the year King Uzziah died, 742 B.C., Isaiah entered the holy of holies in the Jerusalem Temple to worship. As he worshiped, he was lifted into the Holy of Holies in the Temple of the New Jerusalem. As he was lifted into the divine presence, Isaiah was overwhelmed by the glory and holiness of God. In the divine presence Isaiah has two responses: (1) a sense of dread, and, (2) conviction for his and the nation's sinfulness. Throughout the Scriptures, a sense of dread, or fear, is common to those who encounter God. Adam and Eve sought to avoid their daily encounter with God because of their sinfulness (Genesis 3:8). The people of Israel feared to hear the voice of the Lord lest they be consumed by the fire of God's glory (Deuteronomy 5:22-27). The divine *ousia* (essence or substance) so transcends that of the creature that to encounter God is to experience fear and dread. The apostle Paul wrote that God "dwells in unapproachable light, whom no man has seen or can see" (1 Timothy 6:16). When Isaiah describes what he saw in the heavenly Holy of Holies, he describes the throne and robe of God, but could not explain the essence of God's self. The Psalmist declared that God covers God's self with light as a garment (Psalm 104:2). This implies that the essence of God is brighter and more glorious than even the brightest of the created lights. God's essence is so bright that the light with which God is clothed must be covered by a "thick darkness" (Exodus 20:21; Deuteronomy 4:11; 5:22). Job asked, "Will not His majesty terrify you, and the dread of Him fall on you?" (Job 13:11). Divine presence inspires awe, fear, and dread among the righteous and sinner alike. This is exactly what we encounter as we read the book of Acts. Luke repeatedly tells us that the presence of the Holy Spirit provoked believers and sinners to experience the fear of the Lord (Acts 2:43; 5:5, 11; 9:31). Fear of the divine presence inspires the righteous to self-examination and confession of sinfulness. But the sinner seeks only to hide from God (Revelation 6:16).

This brings us to Isaiah's second response to the divine presence—the conviction of sinfulness. He cried out, "Woe is me, for I am ruined! Because I am a man of unclean lips, and I live among a people of unclean lips; for my eyes have seen the King, the Lord of hosts" (Isaiah 6:5). In the presence of divine holiness, the sinfulness of the creature is exposed. We tend to resist this exposure, for we do not wish to see ourselves as we truly are, nor do we wish for others to see us as we truly are. Just as Adam and Eve tried to cover their exposure by leaves, we prefer to cover our sins in garments of self-righteousness. But the leaves could not cover the sinfulness of the first humans, nor can our garments of self-righteousness cover our own sinfulness. Our efforts in covering our sinfulness lead to destruction and death. When the apostle Peter confronted Ananias and Sapphira with their sinfulness, they responded by trying to cover themselves with lies. If they had confessed and made restitution, then certainly they would have been forgiven. But instead, their efforts to cover their sinfulness ended in their deaths (Acts 5:1-

11). The exposure of our sinfulness is necessary to salvation. The only way our sins can be covered is by the blood of the Lamb. The Hebrew word for atonement is *kippur*, which literally means "to cover." In the Old Testament, the altar was covered by the blood of the sacrifice. Likewise, in the new covenant the penitent believer is sprinkled with the blood of Jesus Christ (1 Peter 1:2).

Isaiah's confession of sinfulness brings him before the altar. At the altar, he is anointed on the lips with a fiery coal. The fire of the altar burned perpetually (Leviticus 6:12-13). Fire is often used as a metaphor of the wrath of God. Isaiah proclaimed, "By the fury of the Lord of hosts the land is burned up, and the people are like fuel for the fire" (Isaiah 9:19). In Ezekiel, God speaks of the "fire of my wrath" (Ezekiel 21:31; 22:21, 31). But the fire also is a symbol of the sanctifying presence of God. Isaiah was sanctified at the altar. His sins were purged, he was set apart as a prophet, and he was sent to a sinful people. The fire of the altar serves as a twofold sign: (1) of God's wrath, and (2) of atonement provided. After Korah's rebellion against Moses, God's wrath burned against the people. Moses ordered Aaron: "Take your censer and put in it fire from the altar, and lay incense on it; then bring it quickly to the congregation and make atonement for them, for wrath has gone forth from the Lord, the plague has begun!" (Numbers 16:46). Again, the fire seems to suggest the wrath of God and also the wrath of God appeased through atonement. Isaiah's anointing with the fiery coal at the altar of God was an expression of God's wrath towards the sinfulness of the nation, but also of God's intent to provide salvation for the nation. This is why Isaiah is sent from the altar. He has been anointed by the fiery coal from the altar so that he may speak words of judgment and salvation to the nation.

Isaiah's encounter at the heavenly altar is not unique. The apostle John was "in the Spirit on the Lord's Day" and was lifted into the holy place (Revelation 1:10; 4:1-2). The apostle Paul testifies to a similar encounter.

> I know a man in Christ who fourteen years ago—whether in the body I do not know, or out of the body I do not know, God knows—such a man was caught up to the third heaven.

And I know how such a man—whether in the body or apart
from the body I do not know, God knows—was caught up
into Paradise and heard inexpressible words, which a man is
not permitted to speak (2 Corinthians 12:2-4).

It may be that his ecstatic experience is reflected in the letter to
the church at Ephesus. In the opening doxology, Paul writes that
God has "blessed us with every spiritual blessing in the heavenly
places in Christ" (Ephesians 1:3). The "spiritual blessing" is the
working of the Holy Spirit. Through the Holy Spirit, believers are
lifted into the "heavenly places." God has "raised us up with Him,
and seated us with Him in the heavenly places in Christ Jesus"
(Ephesians 2:6). In Christ and the Spirit, believers enjoy the benefits
and status of heavenly citizens even in this present age. Christian
life and worship is experienced simultaneously on the Earth and
in the heavenly places. Because Christians are "in Christ," believers
are present with Him where He is—seated at the right hand of the
Father, that is, in the heavenly places.

Worship at Pentecostal altars is often ecstatic, that is, the
worshiper is often lifted into "heavenly places." Pentecostals often
refer to this encounter as "the glory of God coming down." One
early Pentecostal believer testified, "There is a heavenly atmosphere
there. The altar is filled with seekers, people are slain under the
power of God, and rising in a life baptized with the Holy Ghost."[9] To
speak of Spirit "falling" or the glory "coming down" reflects biblical
language.[10] The experiences of salvation, sanctification, and Spirit
baptism are ecstatic because they are "in the Spirit." The presence
of the Holy Spirit brings the believer into fellowship with the Holy
Trinity. A foretaste of heaven is experienced at the altar.

But there is more going on than Spirit "falling" or the "glory
coming down." Because these experiences are ecstatic, the worshiper
is being lifted up. The Spirit "falls down" so that worshipers may be
"lifted up" into heavenly places. This is the movement of worship.
Worship begins at designated times and spaces. As worshipers

---

[9] *The Apostolic Faith* (October 1906), 1.
[10] Ezekiel 11:5; Acts 10:44; 11:15.

come together in singing, prayer, giving, sharing the Word, and sacraments, the Spirit is encountered and worshipers enter "into His gates." The presence of the Spirit makes worship transcend the designated time and space so that "worship in Spirit and truth" becomes an otherworldly encounter. The legend of the conversion of Russia tells us that Prince Vladimir sent delegates throughout the world to investigate the great religions. When his delegates returned from their visit to Hagia Sophia in Constantinople, they exclaimed, "We did not know whether we were in earth or heaven!" Pentecostal worshipers can testify to similar sentiments. At the altar where the Spirit is present, worshipers enter the heavenly places.

"Your Spiritual Service of Worship"

"I urge you, brethren, by the mercies of God, to present your bodies a living and holy sacrifice, acceptable to God, which is your spiritual service of worship" (Romans 12:1).

Paul was very familiar with the Old Testament practices of offering animal sacrifices, which were burned upon the altar. As Paul penned these words, he may have been reflecting upon the Elijah story—of fire falling from heaven. Here, he offers a new perspective on the practice of worship. No longer are we to offer an animal as a substitution, but God has called all believers to present themselves as living sacrifices. As living sacrifices we burn with the fire of the Holy Spirit. As living, fiery sacrifices, we present ourselves to God for service, and this is the highest form of worship. Worship is not to be limited to formal rites and confessions, or to anointed sermons, dynamic songs, and long prayer lines. Paul has not defined worship as "a spiritual worship service," but as a life given in spiritual service.

Spiritual service begins with a transformation of human *being* (Romans 12:2). When Paul speaks of transformation, he uses the same Greek word used in Matthew and Mark regarding the transfiguration of Jesus. He also used this word in writing to the church at Corinth: "But we all, with unveiled face, beholding as in a mirror the glory of the Lord, are being transformed into the same image from glory to glory, just as from the Lord, the Spirit" (2 Corinthians 3:18). Paul is speaking of nothing less than the complete transformation of human *being* whereby corrupt and sinful human nature is transformed by the Spirit so that human *being* may reflect the glorious image of Christ.

For Paul, this transformation of *being* begins in the renewing of the mind. Paul wrote that the human mind has been given over to a "depraved mind." The depraved human mind does not acknowledge God and is governed by unrighteousness, wickedness, greed, and evil (Romans 1:28-29). However, a mind renewed by the Holy Spirit enables one to "prove what the will of God is, that which is good and acceptable and perfect" (Romans 12:2). The mind is renewed and the will of God is discovered as the believer commits to the study of the Word of God.

The renewed mind is characterized by humility. Paul wrote that a transformed person is "not to think more highly of himself than he ought to think" (Romans 12:3). Humility is expressed as the "mind of Christ" (Philippians 2:5). This is especially important for those who seek to be filled with the Holy Spirit, exercise spiritual gifts, and offer leadership in the church. Too often, the temptation is to become arrogant or jealous (1 Corinthians 13:4). However, the Christian life is not defined by one's exalted status, but by one's humble service.

The renewed mind is characterized by sound judgment. The Greek word Paul used here is used by Mark and Luke to describe the transformation of the demonized man in the country of the Gerasenes. After Jesus had cast out the demons, the man was in his "right mind" (Mark 5:15; Luke 8:35). Paul also used this word in the sense of being "sensible" (Titus 2:6). The corrupted mind of humanity follows after the passions of the flesh, which is an expression of self-idolatry (Romans 1:24-25). However, those who have been renewed and transformed by the Holy Spirit demonstrate sound judgment in that they do not offer their lives in self-serving, idolatrous practices, but as a living sacrifice to God. Sound judgment is reflected in right worship.

The renewed mind is characterized by faith, that is, we have turned from our idolatrous passions and we now acknowledge God and worship Him. This speaks to a relationship, which has been initiated by God, and to which we correctly respond. Paul's emphasis here is not that some are given more faith than others, but that faith is the common grace by which all believers are transformed. Whether one is a Pharisee or fisherman, Centurion or slave, Bishop or deacon, all must come to God by faith.

Our "spiritual service of worship" is offered to God in the context of the Christian community. All too often we think of the church as a building, or a location. However, Paul has spoken of the church as the body of Christ, that is, a living organism. We have come to God through a common faith in Jesus Christ. It is our common faith in Christ that provides for the unity of the church. But Paul presses the metaphor to speak of the diversity of the church. We are one body in Christ, we share a common faith, but we are individuals who are diverse. The diversity within the body is not a weakness, but it is essential to the very nature of the body. The diversity of the body extends to race, social and cultural background, and gender. Paul has written, "There is neither Jew nor Greek, there is neither slave nor free man, there is neither male nor female; for you are all one in Christ Jesus" (Galatians 3:28). At the altar, human *being*, as expressed individually and communally, is transformed to reflect the glory of God.

Spiritual worship is expressed in the sacraments. As a sinner is convicted by the power of the Holy Spirit and responds to the call to salvation, he moves to the altar and presents himself as a living sacrifice. As living sacrifices, new converts present themselves for water baptism. Believers are nourished at the Table of the Lord and regularly present themselves at the Table as living sacrifices. From time to time, believers need to be refreshed, so they return to the altar, presenting themselves as living sacrifices to be refreshed as their feet are washed. Each act of "spiritual worship" requires the presentation of one's "body" as a "living sacrifice." Properly expressed, sacramental devotion is spiritual worship.

CHAPTER 2

Pentecostal Spirituality: The Spirit of Grace

Pentecostalism is a Spirit-*movement*; therefore, Pentecostals favor worship in which the Spirit *moves*. For Pentecostals, worship means experiencing the Holy Spirit in the fellowship of the church. While anointed singing and preaching are highly valued, they are not the goals of worship; they are a means to the desired end—an encounter with God at the altar. It is at the altar that souls are "gloriously saved," converts are sanctified, the sick are healed, and seekers are baptized in the Holy Spirit. Whether these altar calls are noisy and dynamic, or somber and tearful, those who witness and participate in this spiritual worship walk away from the altar deeply moved and inwardly transformed. Pentecostal worship is not simply enthusiasm, neither is it entertainment—it is an evangelistic encounter with God's holy presence.

John C. Jernigan was converted in 1921, and in 1944 he was elected as the fifth general overseer of the Church of God. In his autobiography, *From the Gambling Den to the Pulpit,* Jernigan recalled his conversion:

> A mighty spirit of prayer moved upon the people and that inspiration took hold of me. I poured out my very soul before God. . . . I felt that burden on my heart begin to rise and it continued to get lighter and lighter until I said, "Lord,

I know you have saved me now." I arose to my feet praising
God for what He had done for me.

Later that same evening, after the worship service had moved from
the parsonage to the church building, Jernigan was sanctified and
baptized in the Holy Spirit. He recounts:

> At the close of the sermon, I went with many others to
> the altar for prayer and deeper consecration. As I prayed,
> yielding my entire life to Him, I felt the cleansing tide as
> it swept over my soul. . . . With great joy I arose from the
> altar, and was immediately slain by the power of the Spirit.
> There, completely lost in His love, I had the most wonderful
> experience of my life. Unbelievable though it may seem, I
> saw the presence of God. It appeared around me as a mist
> mingled with fire. After arising to my feet, I momentarily
> lost control of my vocal organs, and spoke in a beautiful
> new language. . . . The entire building seemed to be filled
> with the presence of God.

Jernigan's testimony is an excellent example of the traditional
threefold work of grace that defines Pentecostal conversion—saved,
sanctified (Jernigan's "cleansing tide"), and baptism in the Holy
Spirit. His testimony is representative of many believers who have
encountered the Holy Spirit in Pentecostal churches. However, it
would be a mistake to assume that the whole of Jernigan's conversion
experience occurred in one evening. Writing of his "early religious
impressions," Jernigan recollected that as a nine-year-old boy, he
attended a revival conducted by "a sanctified Methodist preacher."
This meeting had a lifelong impact upon him. He wrote, "Such
singing and preaching, unctionized by the power of God, moved me
to be a lover of holiness all the days of my life." Jernigan recalls many
such occurrences throughout his life—times when the Holy Spirit
was calling him to salvation. Long before the day of his conversion,
Jernigan had encountered the Spirit in the worship of God's people.
Later, he acknowledged Jesus as Lord and Savior as he encountered
the Holy Spirit in the worship of the church. It was in the context
of the worshiping church that he was sanctified and baptized in the

Holy Spirit. His call to salvation was a call to life in the church. As he lived in fellowship with the church, he continued to be informed and transformed by the interaction of the Spirit and the Word. The testimony of John Jernigan is of great significance in understanding the heart of Pentecostal worship.[11] To perpetuate worship true to Pentecostal spirituality, the church must continue to affirm the significance of encountering God at the altar. So, what was the message that brought Jernigan to the altar?

The full Gospel

A.J. Tomlinson, first general overseer of the Church of God, once listed the tenets of the Pentecostal "full gospel" as being "repentance, sanctification, the Holy Ghost, the church, water baptism, the Lord's supper, feet washing, *and everything else*" (emphasis mine). Early Pentecostals were adamant that the "whole counsel of God" must be preached if the power of God was to be manifested. Tomlinson insisted:

> God honors his word and he wants us to tell it all. If a part of it is left off it is not the full gospel. We may preach tithes and offerings but if we leave off healing it will not be full. May preach everything else besides feet washing it is not full [sic]. It is the gospel of the kingdom, which includes the whole of the teachings of Jesus, that must be preached in all the world for a witness.[12]

Many Pentecostal scholars have suggested that the "full gospel" is the fivefold proclamation:

- Jesus Christ is our Savior.
- Jesus Christ is our Sanctifier.
- Jesus Christ is our Spirit Baptizer.
- Jesus Christ is our Healer.
- Jesus Christ is our coming King.

---

[11] John C. Jernigan, *From the Gambling Den to the Pulpit.* Revised edition, 1939.

[12] A.J. Tomlinson, "Warriors for Jesus," *Church of God Evangel* (July 13, 1918), 1.

If we are to take seriously the proclamation of the earliest Pen-tecostals, we should also consider "the Bible" and "the church" as prominent theological themes.

Pentecostal spirituality is expressed as a Christo-Pneumatic ecclesiology—encountering Christ and the Spirit in the church. This is a faithful expression of God the Father's redemptive call to humanity and the "double sending" of the Son and the Spirit. Irenaeus, a second-century bishop, said that the Son and the Spirit are the two hands of God the Father at work in creation and redemption.[13] The "full gospel" is that God sent the "only begotten Son" *and* the Holy Spirit to redeem those in bondage to sin.[14] The death, resurrection, and ascension of Jesus prepared the way for the redeemed to receive the fullness of the Holy Spirit. Easter anticipates Pentecost. The redeemed are born by the Spirit, matured in the Spirit, and glorified through the Spirit.[15] Through Jesus Christ and the Holy Spirit, God the Father offers a salvific embrace to fallen humanity.

This Christ-centered proclamation is empowered through the Holy Spirit. The goal of salvation is to be in Christ and filled with Spirit. This is reflected in the common testimony of many early Pentecostals: "Praise God, I'm saved, sanctified, and full of the sweet Holy Ghost!" Pentecostal theology is the reclamation of true Trinitarian theology in the church. For some Catholics, the Holy Spirit has often been lost in discussions of church organization and liturgy; or identified with Marian devotion. Often, Protestant theology is more or less binitarian (Father and Son) as one can see by looking at many Protestant systematic theology texts. In many cases, there will be no chapters dedicated primarily to the person of the Holy Spirit. For Protestants, the Holy Spirit has often been lost in discussions about salvation.[16] It has been the advent of the modern

---

[13] *The Ante-Nicene Fathers, Vol. I,* 487.

[14] John 3:16; 14:26; 15:26; 16:7; Galatians 4:4-6.

[15] Acts 2:32-33, 38; Romans 8:2; Ephesians 3:19.

[16] Discussing the Evangelical means of salvation, N.T. Wright has written, "But there is something missing – or rather some*one* missing. Where is the Holy Spirit?" *Justification: God's Plan and Paul's Vision* (Downers Grove: Intervarsity Press, 2009), 10. Also, Wright has noted the tendency to ignore the Holy Spirit's role in worship. He said, ". . . it appears strange that those who have written about the Holy Spirit in the New Testament have not usually given much attention

Pentecostal Movement that has moved the church to embrace once again a theology that is fully Trinitarian.

Jesus Christ Is Our Savior

For Pentecostals, salvation is a crisis of conversion that deeply penetrates and transforms the repentant sinner. Conversion involves an inner struggle between spirit and flesh. Due to the fallen nature of humanity, there exists an enmity in humans towards their Creator. Even so, the image of God within humanity cries out for reconciliation. Humans are intuitively religious creatures. Human life is lived with this inner tension. This is a spiritual struggle in which humans innately seek for the divine, but are wholly incapable of overcoming the enmity toward God that is caused by the corruption of sin. Humanity's search for the divine is little more than groping in darkness. In the midst of this spiritual darkness, Jesus Christ, who is the Word made flesh, is the light and life of humanity. The Incarnation is God reaching toward fallen humanity in love, breaking through human enmity, and reconciling repentant humans to God's self.

Conversion begins with conviction. This is the work of the Holy Spirit. Jesus said that when the Holy Spirit comes the Spirit "will *convict the world* concerning sin and righteousness and judgment" (John 16:8). Paul proclaimed, "Our gospel did not come to you in word only, but also in power and in the Holy Spirit and *with full conviction*" (1 Thessalonians. 1:5). There are two Greek words used in these texts that are translated as *conviction*. In John 16:8, the word is *eléncho* which means "to expose, to reprove." The presence of the Holy Spirit is a divine light that shines upon the darkness of the human heart and exposes the truth regarding the human condition. Conviction suggests the need for correction, that is, repentance and conversion. In 1 Thessalonians 1:5, Paul uses the Greek word *plerophoría,* which means "full assurance." In this case, it seems that Paul was suggesting

---

to worship, and those who have written about worship in the New Testament have not usually given much attention to the Holy Spirit." See: "Worship and the Spirit in the New Testament" (2008). Internet: www.ntwrightpage.com/Wright_Yale_Worship_Spirit.htm.

that conviction has a dual purpose. First, the preacher of the gospel can proclaim the message with full assurance of the truth of the message. This conviction is seen in Paul's statement to Timothy: "It is a trustworthy statement, deserving full acceptance, that Christ Jesus came into the world to save sinners" (1 Timothy 1:15). Second, the hearer of the gospel can be assured of Jesus Christ's power to save. "So faith comes from hearing, and hearing by the word of Christ" (Romans 10:17). The acts of preaching the gospel and of hearing the gospel are powerful and gracious works of the Holy Spirit. Conviction is an essential part of salvific grace. The Spirit proclaims the gospel and wrestles with the heart of the hearer, convincing the hearer of one's own sinfulness and need of salvation. John Wesley spoke of conviction as the "divine *elegchos*," the very essence of saving faith. It is the Spirit's stirring of the slumbering soul, awakening the sinner to repentance. Wesley wrote:

> If to this lively conviction of thy inward and outward sins, of thy utter guiltiness and helplessness, there be added suit-able affections,—sorrow of heart, for having despised thy own mercies,—remorse, and self-condemnation, having thy mouth stopped,—shame to lift up thine eyes to heav-en,—fear of the wrath of God abiding on thee, of his curse hanging over thy head, and of the fiery indignation ready to devour those who forget God, and obey not our Lord Jesus Christ,—earnest desire to escape from that indignation, to cease from evil, and learn to do well;—then I say unto thee, in the name of the Lord, "Thou art not far from the kingdom of God." One step more and thou shalt enter in. Thou dost "repent." Now, "believe the gospel."[17]

Regarding conviction in early Pentecostal spirituality, A.J. Tom-linson wrote:

> Conviction for sin is the first work of God's Spirit upon the heart. . . . it is the will of God that conviction should not only be real, but deep and pungent—that the soul should have a deep and awful sense of danger and need together

---

[17] John Wesley, *Sermons on Several Occasions*, (Grand Rapids: Christian Classics Ethereal Library) 35, 48, 61, 63.

with strong movings of the Spirit to repentance, and the God-ordained means for bringing this about are the faithful teaching and preaching of the Word and the power of the Holy Ghost.[18]

Conversion is more than intellectual assent, or the recitation of a simple sinner's prayer. Conviction is most often expressed as lament. After Peter preached to the assembled crowds on the Day of Pentecost, the hearers were "pierced to the heart" (Acts 2:37). The Greek word *katanusso* suggests that being "pierced to the heart" is a violent act that is very painful. The pain of conviction is expressed in "godly sorrow." Paul wrote:

> I now rejoice, not that you were made sorrowful, but that you were made *sorrowful to the point of repentance*; for you were made sorrowful according to the will of God, so that you might not suffer loss in anything through us. For the sorrow that is according to the will of God produces a repentance without regret, leading to salvation, but the sorrow of the world produces death (2 Corinthians 7:9-10, emphasis mine).

In the Spirit's convicting work, the heart of the sinner is injured. The hardness of the sinful heart must be broken. The purpose of conviction is not to bring the sinner to despair and guilt, but to move the sinner beyond guilt and despair to the joy of salvation. However, the spiritual path that leads from despair to joy is often a trail of tears. The heart-broken sinner often expresses the suffering of conviction through tears and mourning. Repentant sinners must "pray through." Evangelist J.W. Buckalew reported:

> We are having one of the best meetings I ever saw. Over one hundred have received the baptism with the Holy Ghost. Two thousand people stand around the tent until midnight *listening at the cries of souls praying through to God* (emphasis mine).[19]

---

[18] A.J. Tomlinson, "Warriors for Jesus," *Church of God Evangel* (July 13, 1918) 1.
[19] J.W. Buckalew, *The Evening Light and Church of God Evangel* (October 15, 1910), 7.

This prayerful expression of godly sorrow is not limited to Pentecostals. The writings of the postapostolic church, like those of Tertullian and Cyprian (second and third centuries), frequently mention the prayerful groanings associated with repentance. Similar expressions occurred among the repenting sinners during the eighteenth century revivals of Wesley, Whitfield, and Edwards, as well as the nineteenth century Awakening at Cane Ridge, Kentucky, and the subsequent camp meetings of the Holiness Movement. The mournful sounds and gestures of a sinner "praying through" are the first utterances of the Spirit in the penitent seeking new birth.

> And not only this, but also we ourselves, having the first fruits of the Spirit, even we ourselves groan within ourselves, waiting eagerly for our adoption as sons, the redemption of our body . . . . In the same way the Spirit also helps our weakness; for we do not know how to pray as we should, but the Spirit Himself intercedes for us with groanings too deep for words (Romans 8:23, 26).

The phrase "groan within ourselves" does not imply inaudible groans, but that through the Holy Spirit these groans come from deep within the soul. This Spirit-inspired utterance has been referred to as the "primal speech" of humanity—the language of the heart.[20] It is much like the groans and cries of a small child who has not yet learned to speak. When a child is hungry or in distress the child groans or cries out for attention. An attentive parent hears and understands the nuances of these inarticulate sounds and responds accordingly. But these inarticulate sounds are not limited to small children. We too encounter situations that are beyond articulate verbal expression. I have witnessed this on several occasions, especially in times of sorrow.

A few years ago, early one morning, I received a telephone call from my brother, Tim. In a trembling voice he said, "Danny, I need you." I asked, "What's wrong?" He replied, "I think Danielle is dead." Danielle was his eighteen-year-old daughter. She had recently

---

[20] Harvey Cox, *Fire From Heaven* (New York: Addison-Wesley Publishing Company, 1994) 82.

married and was pregnant. She, with her husband, had been in an automobile crash. After a few seconds, Tim said, "I've got to go, the doctor is coming." I anxiously waited for his call back. After a few minutes, the phone rang and I answered. Tim cried out, "Danny, my baby is dead." I immediately left for the three-hour drive to Tim's home. The night was very dark—no moon and no stars. It seemed as if the whole world had been overcome by the dense, dark night. I arrived at Tim's home at dusk. About the same time, our father also arrived. Dad and I looked into each other's eyes, tearfully shaking our heads. We walked into Tim's home together. As we came into the living room, Tim walked out of his bedroom. We never spoke. We couldn't. We didn't have the words, or even the power of speech. We were all overcome by deep sorrow. The three of us embraced and wept bitterly. For several minutes, the only sounds that could be heard were three grown men bitterly weeping and moaning. We were lamenting, because we had been tragically separated from a loved one. This is the language of the heart.

The lament of the Spirit comes because we have been separated from God by sin. These groans and utterances transcend all human language. When sinful humans encounter the holiness of God, the only proper expression is that of sorrow. These sorrowful expressions are given words in the prayers of lament in the Old Testament, which are rather noisy expressions of despair.

> And they will make their voice heard over you and will cry bitterly. They will cast dust on their heads, they will wallow in ashes. Also they will make themselves bald for you and gird themselves with sackcloth; and they will weep for you in bitterness of soul with bitter mourning (Ezekiel 27:30-31).

> Gird yourselves with sackcloth and lament, O priests; Wail, O ministers of the altar! (Joel 1:13).

> Because of this I must lament and wail, I must go barefoot and naked; I must make a lament like the jackals and a mourning like the ostriches (Micah 1:8).

In the midst of these despairing laments, we also hear cries of hope.

> For His anger is but for a moment, His favor is for a lifetime; Weeping may last for the night, but a shout of joy comes in the morning (Psalm 30:5).

> You have turned for me my mourning into dancing; You have loosed my sackcloth and girded me with gladness (Psalm 30:11).

> Make me to hear joy and gladness, let the bones which You have broken rejoice (Psalm 51:8)

> My soul weeps because of grief; strengthen me according to Your word (Psalm 119:28).

These groanings, inspired by the Spirit, which come from within the soul of the penitent are not simply negative expressions of the pain and guilt of sin. They are also positive expressions—the joyful and hopeful anticipation of new life in Christ. The tears shed at the altar of salvation are therapeutic—they cleanse and heal the soul. The cries of lament become shouts of joy.

Jesus Christ Is Our Sanctifier

Pentecostal lament does not end with the initial experience of salvation. The Pentecostal way of salvation is expressed in a life of prayer, seeking after God. Once the penitent person has been saved, the new believer must press on and pray through to sanctification. Paul wrote, "You were washed, but *you were sanctified*, but you were justified *in the name of the Lord Jesus Christ* and in the Spirit of our God" (1 Corinthians 6:11). When the believer experiences initial conversion, it is the *beginning* of new life in Christ. The believer's sins are forgiven and washed away, and the righteousness of Christ is imputed. However, the believer continues to live in this present corrupt age, and in the weakness of sinful flesh. Frank Peretti has described sin as . . .

> the monster we love to deny. It can stalk us, bite a slice out of our lives, return again and bite again, and even as we bleed and hobble, we prefer to believe nothing has happened. That

makes sin the perfect monster, a man-eater that blinds and numbs its victims, convincing them that nothing is wrong and there is no need to flee, and then consumes them at its leisure.[21]

The "lust of the flesh and the lust of the eyes and the boastful pride of life" exist deep in the soul of fallen human nature (1 John 2:16). The sinful desires of the love of money and power, as well as unholy expressions of sexuality are monsters of temptation that stalk and endanger the believer. The believer discovers that the principle of sin, the "old man," remains and can be a formidable foe in the pursuit of holiness. Also, self-righteousness, which is often expressed in legalism, is of great danger to the believer. This is especially insidious because the self-righteous person covers sin under religious vestments and spiritual gifts (Matthew 7:21-23; 23:13-26). Self-righteousness is nothing less than self-justification and self-deception. There is the appearance of righteousness, but the heart is dark and corrupt. The danger for the believer is that if sin is not recognized and holiness is not pursued, then faith may be lost. Apostasy, which is falling from grace, is a very real danger.[22] Sanctification is the believer's protection against apostasy.

Experiencing God's grace is more than being forgiven and cleansed of our sinfulness. The reception of God's grace is to be anointed, or empowered by the Holy Spirit unto sanctification. To be sanctified means to be made holy; to be set apart from sin and unto God. For Pentecostals, salvation is more than a juridical declaration of pardon from sin. Sanctification means that believers may share in God's holiness. Believers are sanctified through the Spirit, the blood of Jesus Christ, and the Word of God.[23] As high priest, Christ has offered His own blood and offers prayers of intercession on behalf of His church. Sanctification is the work of God directed towards the whole human person—spirit, soul, and body. Sanctification is the work of God, but it requires human cooperation. Sanctification

---

[21] Frank Peretti, *The Oath*. (Nashville: WestBow Press, 1995), ix.
[22] Matthew 13:20-21; Galatians 5:4; Hebrews 12:14-17; 2 Peter 3:17.
[23] John 17:17; 1 Thessalonians 5:23; 1 Peter 1:2.

is the *pursuit* of holiness. Holiness is pursued through the spiritual disciplines of prayer, fasting, the study of the Scriptures, and worship in the church. The spiritual disciplines transform the inner person. Holiness is pursued as the believer presents the body to God as an instrument of righteousness, as "a living sacrifice" (Romans 6:13; 12:1). This often means that the believer must practice self-denial rather than self gratification. It also means that sanctification is expressed in proper care and behavior of the believer's body—resisting the passions of the flesh. The Christian must "abstain from sexual immorality" and be careful to avoid "works of the flesh" such as drunkenness and the abuse of chemical substances. Proper care of the body also means dress and adornment that reflects modesty and godliness, rather than vanity and sensuality.[24]

Sanctification is expressed in love. It is more than the believer's personal pursuit of holiness. Sanctification must be expressed as love in human community. Jesus said, "A new commandment I give to you, that you love one another; as I have loved you, that you also love one another. By this all men will know that you are My disciples, if you have love for one another" (John 13:34-35). Christian love must be understood as self-giving service to others. That means giving preference to the needs of others, rather than to one's own needs and desires. Christian love extends beyond the Christian community. In the Sermon on the Mount, Jesus said, "Love your enemies and pray for those who persecute you, so that you may be sons of your Father who is in heaven; for He causes His sun to rise on the evil and the good, and sends rain on the righteous and the unrighteous" (Matthew 5:44-45).

Sanctification is not only the pursuit of holiness; it is also the pursuit of "peace with all people" (Hebrews 12:14). This means that the sanctified believer will often have to "turn the other cheek" (Matthew 5:38-42). It also means that the sanctified believer must confront evil for the sake of justice, and in doing so, be willing to suffer for the sake of righteousness.[25]

---

[24] Galatians 5:19-21; 1 Thessalonians 4:1-8; 1 Timothy 2:8-10; 1 Peter 3:3-4.
[25] Luke 4:18-19; John 15:20; 2 Timothy 3:12.

Some Pentecostals have presented sanctification as a salvific grace that is received in a singular crisis experience. After this experience of "entire sanctification," the believer is made perfect. Perfection is not defined as sinlessness, but as victory over sin. The perfected believer remains subject to temptation, but is empowered to choose against sin. However, sanctification might best be understood as growth in grace through the spiritual disciplines *and* a series of crisis experiences in which the believer is strengthened by the Spirit in the struggle against sin. In either case, the struggle with sin and the victory over sin is the primary issue in sanctification.

My earliest memories of Pentecostal worship are the sounds of the saints praying in the altar. The cacophony of voices sounded otherworldly, as if they originated from heaven. The passion of prayer was tangible. No one had to tell the children to "be still and behave." We intuitively knew that we were in the divine presence— something very special was happening. Sinners were passionately "praying through," seeking peace with God. Others were "tarrying" at the altar seeking to be sanctified and/or baptized in the Holy Spirit. Mothers and fathers were in the altars crying out to God for the salvation of their children. Through the years, I have noticed that these sounds have been muted in most Pentecostal churches. We have traded the sounds of lament for the sounds of celebration. But I wonder if we have misplaced something that is essential to Pentecostal spirituality. Have we forgotten that before we can celebrate we must lament? Pentecostal prayer—lament and "praying through"—has an eschatological expectation. The early Pentecostals fervently believed they were living in the last days. They believed in the imminent return of Jesus Christ. They also believed in the reality of hell. They prayed with passion, they groaned with the Spirit, because they wanted to be ready for the coming of the Lord. They cried out to God for the salvation of lost souls, because they could not bear to lose a loved one to the eternal torments of hell.

Pentecostals must not forfeit the pathos of eschatological expectation. Pentecostals must passionately proclaim the coming of the Lord. The healing of humanity, as well as the cosmos, is the goal of the Incarnation and Pentecost. Our Pentecostal patriarchs and matriarchs "loved not this present age" and understood the tribulations of this life as signs of an eschatological redemption that is "drawing near" (Luke 21:28). Pentecostals must not forsake the pursuit of holiness. The flames of hell are real. Pentecostals must not become intoxicated with the wine of this present age. Instead, they must allow the Spirit to affirm the ache in their souls for the kingdom of God. Pentecostal fervor is expressed in the ache of the soul that cries out for the coming kingdom of God. We must "pray through."

Jesus Christ Is Our Spirit-Baptizer

Sanctification is preparation for Spirit baptism. The purpose and goal of sanctification is to be filled with the Holy Spirit. This is wonderfully expressed in the words of an early Pentecostal believer:

> It is so blessed to be sanctified, cleansed, crucified, nailed to the cross of Christ. Old things have passed away, the old man is crucified, slain, and Jesus Christ is enthroned in the heart and crowned within. He sits upon the throne of our hearts reigning as a king, swaying His scepter of righteousness and true holiness, and keeping the heart clean and pure from sin. Then you are just ready to receive the baptism of the Holy Ghost and fire.[26]

Peter preached, "Repent, and each of you be baptized in the name of Jesus Christ for the forgiveness of your sins; and you will receive the gift of the Holy Spirit" (Acts 2:38). As high priest, Jesus bestows the gift of the Holy Spirit upon His church. Pentecostals affirm that the Holy Spirit is active in salvation and sanctification. To be "born again" is to be born of the Spirit. Believers receive the "Spirit of adoption" at initial conversion. It is the witness of the Spirit that assures the believer of salvation. The Spirit is the pledge, the "down payment," that assures the consummation of human salvation. For Pentecostals, the Spirit as *pledge* is the point. In salvation and sanctification, the believer encounters the Spirit as *pledge,* but God desires that believers be *filled* with the Holy Spirit. Spirit baptism is eschatological in that it anticipates the return of the Lord, and positions the believer firmly

---

[26] *The Apostolic Faith* (December 1906), 1.

in the "already, but not yet" of the kingdom of God. Jesus told His disciples that they would receive the "promise of My Father" and be "clothed with power from on high" (Luke 24:49). On the Day of Pentecost, "they were all filled with the Holy Spirit and began to speak with other tongues, as Spirit was giving them utterance" (Acts 2:4). The filling of the Holy Spirit subsequent to the new birth is repeated throughout the book of Acts. The Jerusalem Pentecost event is not confined to a single day or location, but is ongoing. The Spirit was poured out at Caesarea, Ephesus, Corinth, and in many other places throughout the ages where the gospel is preached. Peter proclaimed, "For the promise is for you and your children and for all who are far off, as many as the Lord our God will call to Himself" (Acts 2:39). God is pouring out the Holy Spirit upon all flesh (Joel 2:28; Acts 2:14-21). The gift of the Spirit transcends any one Christian church and all human ethnic groups and cultures. The Spirit will be poured out until "the earth will be filled with the knowledge of the glory of the Lord, as the waters cover the sea" (Habakkuk 2:14).

The Holy Spirit baptism is usually associated with the mission of the church (Luke 24:46-49; Acts 1:8). The Holy Spirit transformed a fearful and uncertain group of disciples into a missionary fellowship that would boldly carry the gospel of Christ throughout the world. They would face tribulations and persecution, and some would be martyred. But they pushed forward, empowered by the Holy Spirit. The same Spirit that filled and empowered the Christians of the first century continues to fill and empower Christians of the twenty-first century. The mission of the church cannot be fulfilled without men and women who are filled with the Holy Spirit.

Spirit baptism is more than empowerment for mission. It should be understood as the goal of salvation. Too often Protestants, some Pentecostals included, have spoken of the Spirit as the agency, or means, of appropriating the benefits of Christ's redemptive work. Salvation is often spoken of in terms of *receiving Christ*. While it is true that the Spirit is the agent through whom believers enjoy the redemptive work of Christ, the Spirit is more. Christ died that we might *be filled with the Spirit*. The Spirit is the agent through whom believers receive

Christ, and Christ is the agent through whom believers receive the Spirit. Spirit baptism anticipates the believer's glorification. The end of salvation is the glorification of humanity. "Beloved, now we are children of God, and it has not appeared as yet what we will be. We know that when He appears, we will be like Him, because we will see Him just as He is" (1 John 3:2). Through the Spirit, the Son assumed human nature. Likewise, through the salvific work of the Holy Spirit, redeemed humans will be glorified with Christ.

Most Pentecostals affirm that tongues speech, as the initial evidence of the baptism in the Holy Spirit, is normative. Spirit-inspired speech—tongues and prophecy—are associated with Spirit baptism in the book of Acts. While it is true that the church experienced a decline in tongues and prophecy after the third century, it is not true that these spiritual gifts ceased. There is evidence of tongues and prophecy being experienced by Christians through the centuries, most often associated with renewal movements. For Pentecostals, the issue is one of biblical norm. The Spirit is not limited to the first century, but is being poured out throughout the generations until the return of Jesus Christ. If the first Christians spoke in tongues as the Spirit gave the utterance, then twenty-first century Christians should encounter the same Spirit with accompanying gifts.

Speaking with tongues as the initial evidence of Spirit baptism signifies the healing of the universal human community. In Genesis 11, God confused the tongues of humanity as an act of judgment against human arrogance and rebellion. Human unity without the headship of God is nothing less than idolatry. The confusion of tongues is an ongoing sign of the judgment at Babel. But at the Jerusalem Pentecost, and subsequent Pentecost events, the presence of the Spirit upon all flesh is evidenced through diverse tongues which give praise to God. In the outpouring of the Spirit at Pentecost, the redeemed human community is united with God. The gift of tongues is the language of the Spirit which transcends the brokenness of human community and the alienation of humans from communion with the Holy Trinity. Through inspiration of the Spirit, the gift of tongues becomes the language of worship by which humans offer praise and prayer to God.

Jesus Christ Is Our Healer

For Pentecostals, salvation is more than the "saving of the soul." Believers are healed because of the shed blood of Jesus Christ. The apostle Peter wrote that Jesus "bore our sins in His body on the cross, so that we might die to sin and live to righteousness; for by His wounds you were healed (1 Peter 2:24). Many Pentecostals have interpreted this verse to associate salvation with healing. In other words, healing is provided in the Atonement. The salvation of humanity is not simply the salvation of the soul, but of body, soul, and spirit. Divine healing is the sanctification of the body. Some early Pentecostals held so firmly to this tenet of the faith that they often refused medical treatment for themselves and members of their families.

A common affirmation among Pentecostal believers is that "Jesus Christ is the same yesterday, today, and forever" (Hebrews 13:8). This means that through the Holy Spirit the various miraculous gifts associated with the ministry of Jesus are continued in the church throughout the ages. Offering an explanation for the healing of a lame man, Peter said, "It is the name of Jesus which has strengthened this man whom you see and know; and the faith which comes through Him has given him this perfect health in the presence of you all" (Acts 3:16). Luke wrote to Theophilus "about all that Jesus *began* to do and teach (Acts 1:1)." He then wrote his history of the apostolic church, the "Acts of the Apostles," in which he related many miracles preformed by apostles, deacons, and prophets of the early church. These miracles were done "in the name of Jesus Christ" (Acts 3:6; 4:10; 16:18). If healings and miracles were associated with the apostolic church, then Pentecostals insist they must be associated with the Spirit-filled church. The church is the continuation of the ministry of Christ through the Spirit. Testimonies of healings and other miracles have been common to Pentecostal worship services since the beginning of the Movement.

Believers are healed because of the presence of the Holy Spirit. Jesus told His disciples, "He who believes in Me, the works that I do, he will do also; and greater works than these he will do, because I go to My Father" (John 14:12). Because Jesus is the Spirit baptizer, the Spirit is present in the church. With the Spirit comes many spiritual gifts. Among these spiritual gifts are gifts of "healings" and "miracles."[27] Throughout the book of Acts, healings and miracles are associated with the gift of the Spirit. Immediately after the Jerusalem Pentecost, Luke tells of a "notable miracle" in which a forty-year-old man, who had been lame since birth, was healed (Acts 3:1ff). This miracle brought much notoriety and persecution to the church. During the persecution, the apostles offered a prayer which revealed their understanding of the significance of healing. They prayed, "Now, Lord, look on their threats, and grant to Your servants that with all boldness they may speak Your word, *by stretching out Your hand to heal, and that signs and wonders may be done through the name of Your holy Servant Jesus*" (Acts 4:29-30). If the healing miracle had been performed in the name of Moses, there would have been no controversy among the Jewish leaders. The controversy was that the miracle had been performed in the name of Jesus. This healing was a sign that this same Jesus, who was crucified in Jerusalem just a few weeks before, was alive and continuing his ministry. Healing is a sign of the resurrection of Jesus Christ and of the present and coming kingdom of God. Healing is a sign of the life-giving Spirit and anticipates the resurrection from the dead.

Believers are healed because of the faith of a praying church. James wrote, "Is anyone among you sick? Let him call for the elders of the church, and let them pray over him, anointing him with oil in the name of the Lord" (James 5:14). The suffering and healing of believers is done in the context of the Christian community. No one should suffer alone, and no one is healed alone. Praying for the healing of the sick and suffering has always been a significant part of Pentecostal worship. However, not all will be healed in this present age. Those who are healed will eventually die. This leads us to the climax in the Pentecostal "full gospel."

---

[27] Romans 12:3-21; 1 Corinthians 12:9-10; 1 Corinthians 12-14; Ephesians 4:7-16.

Jesus Christ Is Our Soon Coming King!

Pentecostals have always understood the outpouring of the Holy Spirit as an eschatological event. The prophet Joel spoke of the advent of the Holy Spirit as a sign of the imminence of the Day of Yahweh (Joel 2:28ff). On the Day of Pentecost, the apostle Peter echoed the words of Joel, interpreting the Pentecost event as a sign of the arrival of the kingdom of God in the person of Jesus Christ (Acts 2). Early Pentecostals were preoccupied, almost to obsession, with the return of Christ. Central to this eschatological self-consciousness among the early Pentecostal preachers are the words of Matthew 24:14: "And this gospel of the kingdom shall be preached in the whole world as a testimony to all the nations, and then the end will come." C.W. Downey proclaimed, "This gospel of the Kingdom shall be preached in all the world . . . . We believe under God this is the great message for these days . . . we are on the threshold of the greatest event in the history of the world, viz: The imminent appearing of Jesus Christ."[28] Elizabeth Baker wrote, "God meant a witness should be given to all the people of the earth, that Jesus Christ has come and is coming again, as the King of the earth, and He himself cannot come until this is preached."[29] It was this eschatological self-consciousness that motivated early Pentecostals to world mission. William Faupel states, "Despite the apparent concern for the souls of humanity, the early adherents did not understand their task to be converting the world to Christ. Their *real* concern was to engage in activity which would hasten the return of Christ."[30]

Baptism in the Holy Spirit with the evidence of speaking in other tongues was understood as empowerment for eschatological mission. Many early Pentecostals believed glossolalia to be actual, living, human languages—missionary tongues—a gift of the Holy Spirit to the church for the express purpose of the worldwide proclamation of the gospel of the kingdom. E.A. Sexton wrote, "If Jesus tarries

---

[28] C.W. Downey, "The Gospel of the Kingdom," *The Word and Witness* (20 March 1914), 2.

[29] Elizabeth V. Baker, "The Gospel and the Kingdom." *Trust* (Feb. 1914), 3.

[30] William D. Faupel, *The Everlasting Gospel* (Sheffield: Sheffield Academic Press, 1996), 21.

until we have to learn all languages of the world in colleges, He will not come soon . . . . The gift of languages of the world by the Holy Spirit is of more importance."[31] Although the gift of "missionary tongues" did not materialize as expected, the eschatological fervor of Pentecostalism continued unabated.

This sense of eschatological mission was very dramatic. In relating his call to ministry, A.J. Tomlinson spoke of a visionary experience in which he saw "the Church of God of the last days." He exhorted his followers to "Remember we are now in the last great conflict. Now is the time to press the battle and wage a strong warfare against the devil and all his allurements and devices." Tomlinson often spoke of the Church of God as "the evening light." He believed in the "Church of God of the last days" to which the faithful of all denominations would gather "in order to prepare the world for the second coming of Christ and the end of the age."[32] For Tomlinson and the early Pentecostal preachers, the baptism of the Holy Spirit with the evidence of tongues speech was a means to an end, that is, the empowerment for eschatological mission which would be consummated in the return of Jesus Christ.

Early Pentecostals maintained the conviction that the twentieth-century outpouring of the Holy Spirit was an eschatological event signifying the imminent, even immediate return of Jesus Christ. There were many signs that seemed to point to Christ's imminent return. The great earthquake in San Francisco on April 18, 1906, occurred just four days after W.J. Seymour opened the Azusa Street Mission. For many Pentecostal preachers, this was more than a coincidence, it was one of the signs of the times. Azusa preacher Frank Bartleman wrote a tract in which he attributed the San Francisco earthquake to "the voice of God to the people on the Pacific Coast."[33] The earthquake, along with the advent of World War

---

[31] E.A. Sexton, "College vs. Gifts of the Spirit," *The Bridegroom's Messenger* (October 1, 1907) 1.

[32] A.J. Tomlinson, *The Evening Light and Church of God Evangel* (March 1, 1910), 1.

[33] Frank Bartleman, *Azusa Street.* (South Plainfield, NJ: Bridge Publishing Inc., 1980), 53.

I, the communist revolution in Russia, the flu pandemic of 1918, and the Great Depression all contributed to the rise of fundamentalist dispensationalism. Again and again, the Pentecostal preachers cried out, "Jesus is coming soon!"

Throughout the twentieth century, Pentecostal eschatology deteriorated into eschatological speculation. Anyone who has been involved in Evangelical and Pentecostal circles since the last three decades of the twentieth century will remember the series of popular books authored by Hal Lindsey: *The Late Great Planet Earth* (1970), *There's a New World Coming* (1973), *The 1980's: Countdown to Armageddon* (1980), and others. Lindsey's books are representative of the eschatology embraced by many Pentecostals. The problem with this type of eschatological speculation is that somewhere along the way Pentecostal eschatology was no longer integrated with the mission of the church. Further, there are some very real dangers involved in this type of speculation, not the least of which is to link the authority of sacred Scripture to an interpretive scheme that can only lead to speculation and dubious conclusions. After years of interpretation and reinterpretation, the dispensational scheme has begun to lose credibility. The end result is that the church has no credible eschatological hope or mission.

Pentecostals must seek to reclaim the integration of eschatological hope and mission. Ray H. Hughes has proclaimed:

> There is no greater motivation for evangelism than the belief in the imminent return of our Lord. . . Our outreach of evangelism is proportionate to our vision of His soon coming . . . . Any man who allows the return of our Lord to possess him and to grip him cannot live without a burden for the lost . . . . When there is a waning interest in our Lord's return, there is a corresponding lack of interest in evangelism . . . . For this reason, the church should renew and recapture the vision of His return. It must again be fresh on our minds. It must dominate again our lives. It must influence everything we do, because it is our hope, it is our comfort, and it is our future.[34]

---

[34] Ray H. Hughes, "Until Men Are Ready for His Soon Coming" *Church of God Evangel* (22 Oct 1973), 15-17.

As the Pentecostal community moves into its second century, there needs to be serious consideration given to how eschatological hope and mission will guide the church. Our present situation is not unlike that of the first-century church, who preached of the imminent return of Jesus (Revelation 22:7, 12, 20), only to be forced to consider the possibility that His coming might be delayed (2 Peter 3:8-13). After a century of proclaiming that the return of Jesus Christ is soon—imminent—the Pentecostal church must develop and articulate an eschatology that is not held captive to speculation which must be reinterpreted decade after decade. The Pentecostal Movement was birthed in the midst of an eschatological event, the coming of the Spirit, which nurtured an eschatological hope. Eschatological event and hope gave Pentecostals the sense of being an eschatological people with a mission—tarrying until He comes. The challenge is to go into a new century as a Movement without losing any of these essential elements. Pentecostals must understand that the imminence of Christ's return does not necessarily imply immediacy. To believe in the imminence of Christ's return is an expression of the eschatological pathos of the Holy Spirit. The Holy Spirit keeps the anticipation of the Kingdom alive in our souls. The Spirit groans and we groan, in anticipation of the coming Kingdom. The Spirit makes us restless—it seems we can't wait. This restless anticipation is our motivation for mission. In this context, imminence may be understood in terms of the *suddenness* of Christ's return. It has been two thousand years since the Jerusalem Pentecost event. Christians have been anticipating the great "Day of the Lord" for centuries. It will come, and when it comes, it will be sudden.[35]

The last words of Jesus in the Scriptures are: "Behold, I am coming quickly, and My reward is with Me, to render to every man according to what he has done" (Revelation 22:12). Redemption is eschatological, that is, redemption is completed at the end of the age. Everything that the believer enjoys in Christ in this present age is a foretaste of the glory that shall be revealed. There are various theological themes prominent within the contemporary Pentecostal

---

[35] Mark 13:35-37; Luke 21:34-36; 1 Thessalonians 5:2.

and Charismatic Movements. It seems that many Pentecostals are no longer yearning for the coming kingdom of God, but are at home in this present age as long as they can be healthy and rich. However, the heart of the gospel is that Jesus came that death might be defeated. "For the wages of sin is death, but the free gift of God is eternal life in Christ Jesus our Lord" (Romans 6:23). Death is no respecter of persons. The healthy and sick, rich and poor will die. It is the promise of the resurrection of the dead that is the hope of the Christian. "If we have hoped in Christ in this life only, we are of all men most to be pitied" (1 Corinthians 15:19). The suffering and death associated with this present age will be destroyed with the revelation of the new heavens and new earth (Revelation 21:1-4).

The Church of the Bible

"Thank God, I'm saved, sanctified, baptized in the Holy Ghost, and a member of the great Church of God!"

Pentecostal theology is expressed in testimony. Many Pentecostals affirmed the threefold grace of redemption—saved, sanctified, and Spirit baptized. Some Pentecostals also joyously testified to being a member of the "Church of God of the last days." From their earliest days, Pentecostals have been committed to the study of Scripture. It was in the study of God's Word they found validation for the Holy Spirit's outpouring they were experiencing. For many early Pentecostals, it was this single-minded devotion to Scripture that assured a latter-day restoration of the New Testament church. Therefore, the Spirit-renewed church would be *the church of the Bible*.[36] As the church *of the Bible*, the Spirit-renewed church should reflect the life, doctrine, and polity of the apostolic church. Pentecostals justified their faith and practice by the Bible. Speaking in tongues was the initial evidence of the baptism in the Holy Spirit because it was "the Bible evidence." Converts were to receive water baptism; believers were to partake of the Lord's Supper and wash the saints' feet; church members were to practice tithing; the sick

---

[36] Tomlinson, *The Last Great Conflict*, 26, 144, 146, 155f.

were to be prayed for and receive divine healing—all because "it's in the Bible." Sam C. Perry declared:

> As true followers of the Lord Jesus Christ, we desire in all things to conform to the teaching set forth in the Holy Scriptures.
>
> The Word of God, our guide, the Christian's only standard, sets forth the doctrines to be held, the experiences to be possessed, the life to be lived, and the service to be rendered to God and our fellow man.[37]

As the church *of the Bible*, the church should be devoted to the study of the Scriptures, and its theology should be free of all "man-made creeds." Early Pentecostals sought to study the Scriptures free from preconceived theological traditions. Traditions and creeds of the historic churches were considered a hindrance to the move of the Holy Spirit. Pentecostals trusted that the Holy Spirit would give illumination and guide the sincere student of the Word. This Pentecostal way of doing theology would not survive the Movement's early controversies, which were many. Prominent early controversies included fanatical views of Spirit baptism; various understandings of sanctification; tongues speech as the initial evidence of Spirit baptism; and the "Jesus Only" doctrine—a variation on an old heresy regarding the person of Jesus Christ. By the time the Movement was about fifty years old, many of its churches had written their own official creeds, which often were little more than a Pentecostal reworking of earlier Catholic and Protestant creeds. The Movement which strongly protested the creeds and traditions of the historic churches developed its own theological traditions.

For Pentecostals, searching the Scriptures is an encounter with the Holy Spirit. One early Pentecostal proclaimed, "This Bible becomes a new book to those baptized with the Holy Ghost."[38] Theology is not simply an intellectual pursuit, but a life lived in obedience to God. Pentecostal theology is not simply a study of God's past revelation;

---

[37] Sam C. Perry, "The Church," *The Church of God Evangel* (September 15, 1912), 6.
[38] *The Apostolic* Faith (January 1907), 3.

it is also reflection upon God's ongoing revelation. The reality of the eternal Spirit brings together past and present. French Arrington has written:

> When the modern reader's experience of the Holy Spirit reenacts the apostolic experience of the Spirit, the Spirit serves as the common context in which the reader and author can meet to bridge the historical and cultural gulf between them. The Bible is then a book for the believer. The commonality of the experiences of the modern reader and the ancient author lies in their shared faith in Jesus Christ and their walk with the Paraclete whom he promised.[39]

Pentecostal theology is more than a creedal confession; it is worship expressed in preaching, singing, and testimony. It is verbally expressed and audibly experienced. Spirit-inspired preaching is prophetic. It is a holy conversation in which the Spirit, through the preacher, speaks to the church. Those assembled to hear the Word respond with shouts of affirmation, tears of repentance, and testimonies to the work of God in their lives.

Pentecostals remain committed to the authority of the Bible as the Word of God. In working through the Movement's controversies, Pentecostals developed their way of reading, studying, and proclaiming the Bible—a Pentecostal hermeneutic. The Bible is the authoritative written revelation of God. The priority of the Scriptures within the community of faith is assumed. The Spirit guides the study and proclamation of the Bible. The proper place of this interaction between Spirit and Word is the church. This way of theology cannot be sustained by the lone scholar, or by the academic community, because it demands the participation of the entire faith community. The church is a community of interpreters and no single bishop, teacher, or theologian is an authority unto oneself. The preaching and teaching of one is subject to the discernment of the community of the faithful.[40]

---

[39] *Dictionary of Pentecostal and Charismatic Movements.* s.v. "Hermeneutics."
[40] 1 Corinthians 14:29, 32; 1 Thessalonians 5:19-22; 2 Peter 1:20-21; 1 John 4:1.

The community of interpreters may be understood as the "great cloud of witnesses" which surrounds us (Hebrews 12:1). These witnesses include the historic fathers and doctors of the church to whom we must appeal for the sake of orthodoxy and continuity that is the great tradition of the church. These witnesses also include the present community with whom we worship and study the Scriptures together. These witnesses include the generations of the faithful who will succeed the present generation. It will be the "cloud of witnesses" of future generations who will pass final judgment upon the proclamation of the present community of interpreters. We find an example of this in the early Christological controversies. Following the Council of Nicea in 361, the Arians convinced Constantine, and many of the bishops, to reconsider their position. It was not until 381 at the Council of Constantinople that the work of the Council of Nicea was affirmed as orthodox and authoritative. At the Council of Chalcedon in 451, the work of the councils of Nicea and Constantinople were reaffirmed and expanded. Between 361 and 451, there were many rival councils that sought to undermine the work of the Nicene bishops. In the tradition of the church, it has been succeeding generations who have affirmed the work of the faithful of generations past. Of course, the final witness who will judge the church's faithfulness in "rightly dividing the word of truth" will be Christ himself (2 Timothy 2:15; 4:1).

Many Pentecostals may object, "But we don't appeal to the tradition of the church as authoritative." Early Pentecostals viewed church tradition as contributing to the demise of the *charismata* (they were correct to some degree). However, when theological error threatened the Movement, they often appealed to theological tradition and established their own theological traditions. For many Pentecostals, their official creeds have become *canon*—the standard of the faith. However, Ray Hughes has written that creeds and statements of faith are not the ultimate authority in the church, but should be viewed as "an amplification of 'Thus saith the Lord' to communicate the word of God and the purpose of the church."[41]

---

[41] Ray H. Hughes, *Church of God Distinctives*. (Cleveland, TN: Pathway Press, 1968), 106-107.

In other words, for Pentecostals, the traditions of the church are interpretive and do not enjoy canonical status.

So then, how do we resolve the tension between the authority of the Scripture and the value of tradition? Jesus rebuked the Pharisees because their traditions were more authoritative than Scripture: "You have made the commandment of God of no effect by your tradition" (Matthew 15:6). Peter warned that human redemption does not depend upon "aimless conduct received by tradition from your fathers, but with the precious blood of Christ" (1 Peter 1:18-19). Paul warned, "Beware lest anyone cheat you through philosophy and empty deceit, according to the tradition of men, according to the basic principles of the world, and not according to Christ" (Colossians 2:8). However, the tradition of the church can be helpful in the study and interpretation of the sacred text and the proclamation of the gospel. Tradition must be a faithful reflection of the inspired Word of God. Paul encouraged the church to "stand fast and hold the traditions which you were taught."[42]

Maybe Pentecostals can come to appreciate *tradition* if it is understood as *testimony*. Testimony is the way Pentecostals reflect upon their encounter with the Word and Spirit in worship. Testimony is the story of faith. Pentecostals do not view testimony as authoritative, but as informative and inspirational. The ultimate authority is the Word of God. Testimony is the narrative that explains the various encounters along the *way of salvation*. For Pentecostals, testimony of divine encounter shapes theological reflection. The Pentecostal "full gospel" is shaped by Pentecostal testimony. Pentecostal theology is not simply a creed to be confessed, but it is a reflection of the testimony of those who have encountered God at the altar. So, when Pentecostals appeal to the church fathers, or the writings of the men and women of faith throughout the centuries, they are not appealing to a *tradition* with binding authority, but to the *testimony* of the faithful. Because of Protestant propaganda and anti-Catholic prejudice, some Pentecostals are suspicious of the early church fathers. However, because Pentecostals view themselves as

---

[42] 2 Thessalonians 2:15; also 1 Corinthians 11:2; 2 Thessalonians 3:6.

a restoration of the early church, the testimony of the early church fathers can be an important source for Pentecostal theological reflection. Many early Pentecostals often referred to the writings of the church fathers to support their Pentecostal proclamation.

When believers gather together as the church to study the Word, the Spirit is present as teacher. This way of Pentecostal theology is a seamless interaction—*perichoresis*—involving the Spirit, the Word, and the church.[43] The Spirit proceeds from God, the church is born of God, and the Scriptures are the Word of God. The Spirit inspires the Word and forms and inhabits the church. The Word is the canon and expression of the Spirit and church. The Word guides the church in discerning the Spirit. The church is the incarnation of the Spirit and the Word. The Spirit and the Word perfect the church so that she may be presented to Christ without blemish. This Pentecostal hermeneutic can be described as *Spirit and Word in/over the church*. Pentecostals are very careful to maintain the authority of the Spirit and the Word over the church as the interpretive community.

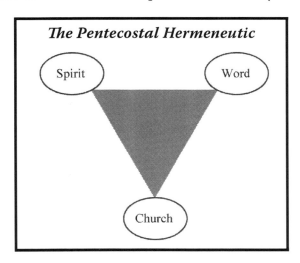

The Pentecostal Hermeneutic

Spirit

Word

Church

---

[43] *Perichoresis* is a Greek term used by later Church fathers to speak of the mutual indwelling of the Trinity whereby "one is as invariably in the other two as they are in the one." The term was also used in speaking of the unity of the two natures of Christ. Christ is fully human and fully divine in one person. The human and divine natures are not confused, but they interpenetrate. I employ the term here to suggest a similar relationship involving the Spirit, the Word, and the Church.

The Government of Christ

Some early Pentecostals developed a profound and rich ecclesiology. Like most early Pentecostals, the founding leaders of the Church of God believed the outpouring of the Holy Spirit to be the restoration of *the church* of the Bible. Many adherents praised God that they were part of the "grand *old* Church of God" (emphasis mine). They did not date the origin of their Movement to the Christian Union (1886); the Shearer Schoolhouse Revival (1896); nor to the date of the "first General Assembly" (1906). They testified that the Church of God is "the real Bible church" and as such had its origins in the Day of Pentecost. Peter moderated the "first church business conference" (Acts 1:15-26); and James moderated the first general assembly (Acts 15). The true church fell into obscurity throughout the "Dark Ages," but its influence is seen in the development of the great doctrines of reformation and restoration. Martin Luther's doctrine of justification, John Wesley's doctrine of sanctification, A.B. Simpson's doctrine of divine healing, and W.J. Seymour's doctrine of Spirit baptism proceed from the true Church of God. A.J. Tomlinson declared, "The Church of God is to the gospel . . . as the trunk or body of the tree is to the branches, leaves, and fruit." Through the activity of the Holy Spirit, the church is the government of Christ in this present age. The government of the church is theocratic; not legislative, and therefore "there should be no voting or majority ruling in the churches" because "the Bible settles all questions pertaining to church government." Proper church government will reflect "apostolic order" and "uniform interpretation" so that all will be of "one mind in teaching and practice." The government of the church is *executive* and *judicial*. The church is to rightly *judge* the Scriptures and faithfully *execute* the mission of Christ. The church is the visible and literal presence of God's government on the earth. All true believers would eventually "see the light" and join the Church of God. The rule of the church, through the power of the Spirit, in this present age anticipates the rule of the righteous in Christ's millennial kingdom. The terms "church" and "government" were often synonymous.[44]

---

[44] A.J. Tomlinson, *The Last Great Conflict*, 26, 144, 146, 155f; R.G. Spurling, "The Church," *The Evening Light and Church of God Evangel* (March 15, 1910) 4; *The*

For these early Pentecostals, a revelation of "the real Bible church" was essential to their spirituality. J.L. Thornhill wrote, "The church is the necessary indispensable pillar and ground of the truth;" and, that membership in "the Bible church" was part of the "divine order" in the Pentecostal *way of salvation*.[45] The church of the New Testament was to reflect proper ecclesiastical order, unity of fellowship and mission, a common confession, and the power of the Spirit.

The adherents of the early Church of God developed a "catholic" ecclesiology from their reading of the Bible. This is rather amazing in that they were adamantly anti-Roman Catholic. Their criticism of the Roman Catholic Church was based on the extra-biblical traditions of the Post-Nicene church that, in their view, led to the demise of the spiritual gifts. With this in mind, it should be noted that these early Pentecostals were also anti-Protestant. Any tradition— Catholic or Protestant—that did not reflect the ecclesiology of the New Testament was not faithful to the Church of God. These early Pentecostals did not view themselves as Catholics or Protestants. They were "the real Bible Church"—the restoration of the apostolic church.

As we reflect on this early Pentecostal ecclesiology, we should be careful not to reject it as naïve or unsophisticated. This early

Evening Light and Church of God Evangel (September 15, 1910) 1; A.J. Tomlinson, "Christ, Our Law-Giver and King," *The Evening Light and Church of God Evangel* (November 1, 1910) 2; Sam C. Perry, "The Church," *The Church of God Evangel* (September 15, 1912) 6; Mrs. E.S. Hubbell, "Efficiency," *The Church of God Evangel* (June 13, 1914) 6; J.B. Ellis, "The Church Literal or Invisible," *The Church of God Evangel* (June 10, 1916) 3; A.J. Tomlinson, "The Government of God," *Church of God Evangel* (June 14, 1919) 1; E.B. Culpepper, "The Church of God—Is Visible or Invisible, Which?" *Church of God Evangel* (July 5, 1919) 1; Jesse P. Hughes, "Is the Church of God Losing Her Power?" *The Church of God Evangel*, (January 17, 1920) 4; Mattie Buckalew, "The Church of God—A Visible Organization," *Church of God Evangel* (July 17, 1920) 1; John C. Jernigan, "The Church of God from a Bible Standpoint," *The Church of God Evangel* (May 27, 1922) 4; Thomas J. Richardson, "Theocratic Government," *The Church of God Evangel* (July 7, 1923) 4. Dale M. Coulter, "The Development of Ecclesiology in the Church of God," *Pneuma 29.1* (2007), 59-85.
[45] J.L. Thornhill, "The Church of God—The Pillar and Ground of the Truth," *The Church of God Evangel* (April 28, 1923) 1.

Pentecostal ecclesiology is echoed in the theology of Jürgen Moltmann, who has written:

> Christ's 'church government' belongs within the framework of his rule over the world. All the gifts and powers of his liberating Spirit in the church are directed towards the world freed from the 'elemental spirits.' . . . The church is the earthly form of Christ's lordship."[46]

Contemporary Pentecostal theologians should build upon this early Pentecostal understanding of the church and develop a mature Pentecostal ecclesiology that takes seriously the biblical vision of our early leaders—a visible church that reflects the New Testament catholicity of "one Lord, one faith, one baptism" (Ephesians 4:5).

A Charismatic Fellowship

For Pentecostals, the church is a charismatic communion and its mission is to proclaim the message of the coming kingdom of God. Spirit baptism is the event by which the church is defined. Tomlinson wrote:

> There are none so hungry for the demonstration of God's great power as those who are nearest to it. From many quarters comes the cry, from Spirit-filled souls, for the manifestations of God's power as was shown in the time of the Apostles . . . . The gifts are for the church and they will make their appearance in their fullness and glory as soon as she is freed from the power and dictations of man. [47]

Through Christ and the Spirit, God has given the *charismata*—spiritual gifts—to guide the church in its worship and mission. The mission of the church is to preach the gospel throughout the world, so that the coming kingdom of God can be hastened. The spiritual gifts are given to the church so that lordship of Christ may be exercised in this present age. The gifts of leadership and administration guide the church. The teaching and preaching gifts inform and transform the church. Gifts of miracles and healings demonstrate that the

---

[46] Jürgen Moltmann, *The Church in the Power of the Spirit* (San Francisco: Harper Collins Publishers, 1991), 293-294.
[47] Tomlinson, *The Last Great Conflict*, 150f.

power of the coming Kingdom is within the church in this present age. The gift of exorcism demonstrates that the powers that seek to govern this age are limited and ultimately defeated. The gift of prophecy provokes sinners to repent and acknowledge the lordship of Jesus Christ. The gifts of tongues and interpretation of tongues serve as a sign of the universal nature of God's kingdom. The gift of martyrdom reminds us that we do not fear the powers of this world, but trust in Him who is the resurrection and the life. The gifts of mercy, giving, and voluntary poverty demonstrate the economics of God's kingdom in which the treasures of this age are of value only when governed by principles of compassion and generosity. Empowered by the Holy Spirit, the church is God's "government in exile," awaiting the coming of the King in power and glory.

Pentecostals encounter the Spirit and the spiritual gifts in the context of the church's worship and mission. A mature Pentecostal spirituality understands that one's encounter with the Spirit is informed by the Word in a Spirit-filled church. Ray Hughes has offered wise counsel:

> While we are living in the Age of the Spirit, we must not forget that we are also living in the Age of the Church. In times of great spiritual outpourings there is a danger in emphasizing experience to the exclusion of basic truths. . . . It is harmful to go beyond the teachings of the Scripture . . . . *It is at this point that the Church serves as a guardian of our experience* . . . . (emphasis mine)[48]

Pentecostal spirituality recognizes the value of discerning elders and bishops who guide the church carefully through seasons of revival, as well as seasons of spiritual drought. Throughout the history of the church there has been an ongoing tension between the "institutional church" and the "charismatic church." The institutional church has often emphasized the work of Spirit in the established hierarchical leadership. The charismatic church has often demonstrated a glaring lack of respect for hierarchical leadership in

---

[48] Ray Hughes, "The Church and Your Pentecostal Experience," *Church of God Evangel* (May 12, 1975), 10.

favor of leaders whose spiritual authority is demonstrated in their spiritual manifestations.

The second and third century conflict between the Montanist and the catholic bishops serves as an unfortunate example. Contrary to popular belief, the primary issue in this conflict was not the *charismata* among the Montanists. Montanism was not immediately viewed as a threat by the church. In about 177, Irenaeus delivered letters to Pope Electherius in Rome which informed him about Montanus and his teaching. Irenaeus was no friend of the Montanists, but he affirmed the *charismata*.[49] It seems that his primary objection to the movement was that women were prophesying.[50] Pope Electherius apparently did not view the movement as a threat, because he took no action against the Montanists, but instead negotiated "for the peace of the churches."[51]

Tertullian declared that the teachings of the Montanist churches expressed continuity with the apostles. He wrote, "We are in communion with the apostolic churches because our doctrine in no way differs from theirs; this is a sign of truth."[52] Tertullian offered an apology of Montanism in which he argued that the contention between the Montanists and the Catholic bishops was not a matter of orthodox doctrine, but a matter of discipline. He wrote, "It is these which raise controversy with the Paraclete; it is on this account that the New Prophecies are rejected: not that Montanus and Priscilla and Maximilla preach another God, nor that they disjoin Jesus Christ (from God), nor that they overturn any particular rule of faith or hope, but that they plainly teach more frequent fasting than marrying."[53]

The primary issue of conflict was the proper authority of the bishop. The Catholic Church held that the bishop's authority existed in proper ordination and apostolic succession. This meant that all spiritual authority was primarily located in the office of the bishop.

---

[49] *The Ante-Nicene Fathers, Vol.I*, 409, 531.
[50] *The Ante-Nicene Fathers, Vol.I*, 429.
[51] Philip Schaff, *The Nicene and Post-Nicene Fathers, Second Series, Vol. I.* (Oak Harbor, WA: Logos Research Systems, 1997), 218.
[52] *The Ante-Nicene Fathers, Vol. III*, 252.
[53] *The Ante-Nicene Fathers, Vol. IV*, 102.

Tertullian insisted that the true qualification and appointment to the office of bishop is direct endowment by the Holy Spirit, rather than outward ordination and apostolic succession. Also, he and his fellow Montanists accused the Catholic bishops of a lack of moral integrity. The Catholic bishops resisted the rigorous moral disciplines of the Montanists. The Montanists seemed intent upon enforcing their extra-biblical disciplines upon the church. Apparently, the diversity of the spiritual gifts combined with the threat of charismatic leaders with questionable teachings fueled a conflict within the church that the bishops were unwilling to accept. In retrospect, the heart of the conflict was probably due to Montanists excesses and the Catholic bishops striving after power. By A.D. 200, Pope Zephyrinus hesitantly condemned Montanism. The movement was so controversial that a series of councils were called (the first since the Jerusalem Council) to deal with the matter and eventually the Montanists were excommunicated. The demonstration of the *charismata* became suspect and began to decline.

As we reflect upon this ancient controversy and its implications for the contemporary church, we should listen to the voices of the past. Irenaeus wrote:

> True knowledge is that which consist in the doctrine of the apostles... the distinctive manifestation of the body of Christ according to the successions of the bishops... *and above all, it consists in the preeminent gift of love* which is more precious than knowledge, more glorious than prophecy, and which excels all the other gifts of God (emphasis mine). [54]

Irenaeus insists that the bishops of the church must reflect Christ's love for His church. Any church authority that does not exemplify the "preeminent gift of love" is not authentically Christian. This love is properly expressed in selfless service to the people of God in which the spiritual gifts are encouraged and nurtured. Concerning the proper authority of the bishop, Tertullian wrote that laity, deacons, and presbyters should respect the authority of the bishop. While

---

[54] *The Ante-Nicene Fathers, Vol. I*, 508.

he acknowledges certain functions (particularly baptism) could be administered by all, he said:

> But how much more the rule of reverence and modesty incumbent on laymen, seeing that these powers belong to their superiors—lest they assume to themselves the specific function of the bishop! Emulation of the episcopal office is the mother of schisms. The most holy apostle has said that "all things are lawful, but not all are expedient.[55]

Tertullian insisted that the office of the bishop must be respected. Somewhere in the controversy, mutual love and respect was lost and the Christian communion suffered. The Catholic bishops would not tolerate the challenges that Montanism represented, so Montanism was condemned. Robin Fox offers an ironic observation: "Five generations after Pentecost, Christian leaders were exorcising fellow Christians, mouthpieces of the Holy Spirit."[56]

The Holy Spirit continuously works in the church so that the church may be renewed throughout the generations. Irenaeus said, "Our faith, which, having been received from the church, we do preserve, and which always, *by the Spirit of God, renewing its youth*, as if it were some precious deposit in an excellent vessel, *causes the vessel itself containing it to renew its youth* also."[57] The Holy Spirit preserves the faith of the church, and the Spirit renews the faith of the church. Renewal movements within the church are to be anticipated as the continuing ministry of the Holy Spirit. But all renewal

---

[55] *The Ante-Nicene Fathers, Vol. III*, 677. Most Tertullian scholars make a distinction between his pre-Montanists writings (which are considered orthodox) and his Montanists writings. Tertullian would not have appreciated this distinction. In fact, it is interesting that some Protestants saw Tertullian as a proto-Protestant who rejected apostolic succession and the Catholic priesthood. The nineteenth-century church historian, Philip Schaff, wrote, "Montanism was not a departure from the faith, but a morbid overstraining of the practical morality and discipline of the early church . . . an excessive supernaturalism and Puritanism against Gnostic rationalism and Catholic laxity" (*History of the Christian Church*, 2:10:110, Logos Research Systems, 1997). With the advent of modern Pentecostalism, Tertullian suffered from a Protestant reappraisal in which his "heterodoxy" was frequently used to scandalize Pentecostals.

[56] Robin Lane Fox, *Pagans and Christians*. (New York: Alfred A. Knopf, Inc., 1989), 408.

[57] *The Ante-Nicene Fathers, Vol. I*, 458.

movements must be discerned as being faithful to the teachings of the Holy Scriptures. The desire for renewal should never comprise discernment in the church. Proper discernment is the guardian of spiritual renewal.

The conflict between the institutional church and the charismatic church should be viewed as a necessary tension, which like two magnets correctly positioned, will draw the two together as one body in Christ. However, if the two magnets are otherwise positioned, the effect is separation. If the institutional church and the charismatic church will correctly position themselves with the disposition of "a more excellent way," then tradition and *charismata* will enhance and compliment each other. The institutional church will be saved from "holding to a form of godliness, although they have denied its power" (2 Timothy 3:5). The institutional church needs "times of refreshing . . . from the presence of the Lord" (Acts 3:19). The charismatic church needs the great tradition of the institutional church for the sake of unity and continuity with the church catholic. The great tradition will protect the charismatic church from excess and heresy so it may "stand firm and hold to the traditions which you were taught" by the apostles (2 Thessalonians 2:15; 3:6). After all, we must come to realize that the institutional church and the charismatic church are one church in Christ.

A Prophetic Community

The church is a prophetic community in which the saving acts of God are revealed to all humanity. God has spoken through the Son and continues to speak through the Holy Spirit.[58] The prophetic nature of the church can be experienced during worship. The apostle Paul wrote, "But if all prophesy, and an unbeliever or an ungifted man enters, *he is convicted by all, he is called to account by all; the secrets of his heart are disclosed; and so he will fall on his face and worship God, declaring that God is certainly among you*" (1 Corinthians 14:24-25, emphasis mine). As worshipers sing, hear the preached word, and celebrate the sacraments, the Holy Spirit

---

[58] John 1:1-18; Acts 2:4, 11; 4:31; 6:10; 18:25; 19:6; 21:11; Hebrews 1:1-4; 2 Peter 1:21.

is present, actively searching the hearts of those gathered together. Unbelievers may be profoundly affected by the prophetic Spirit. The Spirit can be grieved or quenched, but one cannot escape the Spirit's searching. The Spirit opens the sinful heart to judgment and the sinner encounters divine grace. Overwhelmed by the Spirit of grace, the repentant sinner worships God in humility and testifies to the saving power of God. The church is a redemptive community through which fallen humanity may receive the transforming grace and power of God.

Due to human rebellion at Babel, human society is broken, confused, and oppressed (Genesis 11:1-9). Humans struggle among themselves creating greater and exceedingly painful divisions. However, John envisioned a redeemed community "which no one could count, from every nation and all tribes and peoples and tongues, standing before the throne and before the Lamb" worshiping God (Revelation 7:9). This community is foreseen in the Jerusalem Pentecost event where the judgment of Babel is corrected. The confused languages of Babel are transformed by the Holy Spirit into ecstatic languages of worship. Pentecost fulfills the reconciling mission of Christ and anticipates the glorification of redeemed humanity. The Azusa Street outpouring reflected the prophetic character of a Spirit-formed community. Harvey Cox wrote the following about the prophetic nature of the 1906 Azusa event:

> God was doing a great new thing. History was reaching its climatic moment and there were signs and wonders to prove it. The New Jerusalem was coming. Now the rich and the proud would get their just deserts. The destitute, the overlooked, and the forgotten would come into their own. Even more central for Seymour, in a segregated America, God was assembling a new and racially inclusive people to glorify his name and save a Jim Crow nation lost in sin. In retrospect the interracial character of the growing congregation on Azusa Street was indeed a kind of miracle. It was, after all, 1906, a time of growing, not diminishing, racial separation everywhere else. But many visitors reported that in the Azusa Street revival blacks and whites and Asians and Mexicans sang and prayed together . . .

> black and white deacons, and both black and white women
> . . . were exhorters and healers . . . . For Seymour . . . [Los
> Angeles] was not an earthly city at all. Nor was it the new
> Rome. It was the heavenly Jerusalem. [59]

Pentecostal worship is prophetic because it anticipates a redeemed human community where violence and oppression cease. Pentecostals envision a community where "there will no longer be any death; there will no longer be any mourning, or crying, or pain" (Revelation 21:4).

As a prophetic community, the church is essentially an eschatological community. The church exists in this present age as a sojourning community seeking the kingdom of God (Hebrews 11:8-10, 13-16). The church is a *waiting* community. Often this waiting is expressed in the lament "How long, O Lord?" How long will the righteous suffer at the hands of the wicked? How long must we live in this corrupt age? How long will God be patient with injustice? This lament expresses the church's certain hope that God will act to install His's righteous reign. The church's journey is a tearful pilgrimage of faith and hope. The hope of the church is the hope of the world as well. Paul wrote, "For the anxious longing of the creation waits eagerly for the revealing of the sons of God" (Romans 8:19). The waiting of the church and creation is expressed as the groans and labor of birth pangs. As a prophetic and eschatological community, the church is the "sacrament of the world's future."[60] As the church sojourns in this present age, Spirit leads the way. Irenaeus wrote that "While the Church is scattered throughout all the world, and the 'pillar and ground' of the Church is the Gospel and the spirit of life . . . breathing out immortality on every side, and vivifying men afresh."[61] The church has the "firstfruits of the Spirit" (Romans 8:23). The word "firstfruits" signifies the Spirit's ministry in sealing and guaranteeing the redemptive work of God. Also, it implies a greater harvest in the future. As the church makes its pilgrimage in

---

[59] Harvey Cox, *Fire From Heaven*, 58-59.
[60] Carl E. Braaten, *Mother Church: Ecclesiology and Ecumenism* (Minneapolis: Fortress Press, 1998), 60.
[61] *The Ante-Nicene Fathers, Vol. I*, 428.

this world, she sows the seeds of grace. The presence of the Spirit in and with the church signifies that the church is the hope of the world. In other words, what the Spirit has begun in the church, the Spirit will complete in creation.

The Spirit of Grace

The church is a Trinitarian fellowship—God in fellowship with redeemed humanity. Tertullian, the third-century charismatic theologian, wrote:

> Since both the witness of faith and the guarantee of salvation have the safeguard of the three Persons, the reference to the Church is of necessity added. *Where the three, the Father, the Son, and the Holy Spirit, are, there too is the Church, which is the body of the three Persons* (emphasis mine).[62]

In Christ, the nations of the world form a new human community that exists in fellowship with God the Father, God the Son, and God the Holy Spirit. The church is the "body of Christ" filled, empowered, and indwelt by the Holy Spirit.[63] The church is the special dwelling place of God's Spirit on earth. Irenaeus, a second-century bishop of Lyons, proclaimed, "For where the Church is, there is the Spirit of God; and where the Spirit of God is, there is the Church and all grace; but the Spirit is truth."[64] Irenaeus claims an essential unity, a dynamic fellowship, between the church and the Spirit because of the power and demonstration of the Spirit within the church.

> Wherefore, also, those who are in truth His disciples, receiving grace from Him, do in His name perform [miracles], so as to promote the welfare of other men, according to the gift which each one has received from Him. For some do certainly and truly drive out devils, so that those who have thus been cleansed from evil spirits frequently both believe [in Christ], and join themselves to the Church. Others have foreknowledge of things to come: they see visions, and utter prophetic expressions. Others still, heal the sick by lay-

---

[62] *The Ante-Nicene Fathers, Vol. III,* 672.
[63] 1 Corinthians 1:9; 12:13; 2 Corinthians 13:14; Galatians 3:28; Philippians 2:1; Colossians 3:11; 1 John 1:3.
[64] *The Ante-Nicene Fathers, Vol. I,* 458.

ing their hands upon them, and they are made whole. Yea, moreover, as I have said, the dead even have been raised up, and remained among us for many years. And what shall I more say? It is not possible to name the number of the gifts which the Church, [scattered] throughout the whole world, has received from God, in the name of Jesus Christ . . . which she exerts day by day for the benefit of the Gentiles . . . . For as she has received freely from God, freely also does she minister [to others].[65]

In *The Apostolic Tradition,* attributed to Hippolytus (third century), the church is referred to as the "the place where the Holy Spirit abounds." This statement is made in the context of the teaching and preaching of Holy Scripture. Hippolytus says that hearing the word "strengthens the soul." The use of the Greek word *parakalein* (strengthens) suggests that Hippolytus was speaking of the spiritual gift of prophecy abounding in the church.[66] In response to this Pneumatic ecclesiology, some early Pentecostal leaders would have shouted, "The Church of God, the Church of God! . . . Hallelujah, Hallelujah! Glory, Glory!"[67] Pentecostal theologian Simon Chan has built upon this ancient pneumatology, offering a compelling vision of the relationship between the Spirit and the church. He has written:

> . . . not only is the church Spirit-filled, but the church is also the special place where the Spirit is present on earth. We do not deny that the Spirit is present in creation and in the historical process, but the Spirit is present in the church in a way that he is not present in the world. In other words, it is not only true to say that the Spirit constitutes the church giving the church its unique identity as a Spirit-filled body, but it is also true that the church thus constituted gives to the Spirit his distinctive character as the church-located and church-shaped Spirit.[68]

---

[65] *The Ante-Nicene Fathers, Vol. I,* 409.
[66] Hippolytus, *On The Apostolic Tradition,* 35.2 & 41.3. Translation by Alistair Stewart-Sykes. (New York: St. Vladimir's Seminary Press, 2001), 156, 164.
[67] Tomlinson, *The Last Great Conflict,* 159.
[68] Simon Chan, *Pentecostal Theology and the Christian Spiritual Tradition* (Sheffield: Sheffield Academic Press, 2000), 110-11.

The church is a Trinitarian fellowship in which the Spirit is encountered and grace is received. The Holy Spirit is the "Spirit of grace" (Zechariah 12:10; Hebrews 10:29). Grace is more than God's affection toward humanity, and it is more than the efficacy of redemption. Divine grace in its fullest sense is to encounter the Spirit. The Holy Spirit effected the Incarnation in the womb of Mary. The union of God the Son with human nature means that, in Christ, human nature exists in intra-Trinitarian fellowship. Likewise, the Spirit of grace makes it possible for humans to be "in Christ" and reconciled to God. In Christ and through the Spirit, redeemed humanity lives in fellowship with the Holy Trinity.

We can see the relationship between the Spirit and grace by examining four related Greek words.

- chara - joy
- charis - grace
- charismata – spiritual gifts
- eucharistéō – blessing, thanksgiving

The Spirit endows the church with *charismata*, that is, various spiritual gifts. The *charismata* flow from the *charis* (grace) of the Spirit. The spiritual gifts are gifts of grace in that they are freely given by the Spirit so that believers may "grow in the grace and knowledge of our Lord and Savior, Jesus Christ" (2 Peter 3:18). The spiritual gifts signify the Spirit in action. It was because of "great grace" that the apostles were empowered to witness to the resurrection of Jesus through miracles (Acts 4:33). Because Stephen was "full of grace and power" he preformed "great wonders and signs among the people" (Acts 6:8).

Related to *charismata* are the worshipful acts of thanksgiving and blessing—*eucharistéō*. Both terms have as their root the word *charis.* Jesus and Paul use *eucharistéō* in reference to the prayer of blessing, or thanksgiving, at the celebration of the Lord's Supper.[69] Therefore, the Lord's Supper is often referred to as the Eucharist. Paul associates *eucharistéō* with "praying in the Spirit" (1 Corinthians

---

[69] Matthew 26:26-27; Mark 14:22-23; Luke 22:17, 19; 1 Corinthians 11:24.

14:16-17). The root of each of these Greek terms, *charis, charismata,* and *eucharistéō* is the word *chara,* that is, joy. The Spirit graces (*charis*) the church with spiritual gifts (*charismata*). The church worships and prays in the Spirit (*eucharistéō*). The life and worship of the church expresses the grace (*charis*) and joy (*chara*) of the Spirit. Samaria became a city of "great joy" because of the works of the Spirit in the ministry of Philip (Acts 8:6-8). Even in the face of great persecution, Spirit-filled disciples of Christ experienced the joy of the Holy Spirit.[70] While imprisoned, the apostle Paul wrote to the church at Philippi: "Rejoice in the Lord always; again I will say, rejoice!" (Philippians 4:4). In this present age, believers are graced with the heavenly fruit of the Spirit—love, joy, and peace (Galatians 5:22). Worship is a joyful and ecstatic experience, because as believers worship, the Spirit of grace is encountered.

---

[70] Acts 13:50-52; 1 Thessalonians 1:6; 1 Peter 1:6; 4:13.

CHAPTER 3

SACRAMENTAL
WORSHIP:
THE SPIRIT
IN SACRAMENTS

The Holy Spirit descended in clouds of glory, wave after wave of glory broke upon me. Tidal waves of resurrection life and glory surged through every organ of my body, so that I was constrained to cry aloud for everything within me shouted "Glory" and could not be silenced.

—M. J. D.[71]

We had an all day service. . . . In the baptismal service, twelve followed the Lord in water baptism. In the afternoon we had the Lord's Supper and feet washing with the usual results—shouting and other demonstrations of the Spirit.

—Mrs. B. L. Shepherd[72]

Pentecostalism is an *embodied spirituality.* Spirit baptism means that human being—flesh and blood, soul and spirit—is immersed in the Holy Spirit. Further, Spirit baptism means that the Holy Spirit dwells within human being. Believers are filled with the Spirit, and the Spirit is enfleshed in human being. Just as Jesus Christ is "God *with* us," the Holy Spirit is "God *in* us." Salvation, understood in terms of being "saved, sanctified, and baptized

---

[71] "A Wonderful Baptism in England." *The Apostolic Faith* (October 1907), 2.
[72] *Church of God Evangel* (July 7, 1917), 3.

in the Holy Ghost," effects an ontological change in human nature that anticipates glorification. Believers are *in* Christ and *shall be like Christ* (1 John 3:2). Spirit baptism means that the Holy Spirit and matter (human body) are joined and that by this joining (infilling), the essential *"being-ness"* of humanity is transformed. Redeemed humans are partakers of the divine nature. Pentecostal preachers often encourage their listeners to live holy lives because "your bodies are a temple of the Holy Ghost!" The Spirit-baptized believer is empowered to be a witness to the full gospel of Jesus Christ in this present age.

Baptism in the Holy Spirit is a sacramental encounter. It is often assumed that Pentecostal spirituality is essentially anti-sacramental. It is true that early Pentecostals were anti-liturgical, favoring spontaneous worship over the formal worship of traditional churches. However, it is a mistake to assume that Pentecostalism is anti-sacramental. The embodied spirituality of Pentecostalism, expressed in the doctrine of the baptism in the Holy Spirit, suggests that Pentecostalism is essentially sacramental. Pentecostal worship is experiential in a variety of ways. Worshipers sing, shout, clap, and dance. They speak in tongues as the Spirit "gives the utterance" and hear tongues speech. In prayer, a worshiper may be anointed with oil and prayed for with the "laying on of hands." Pentecostal worship is ecstatic and somatic: that is, "out of the body" or S/spiritual, and "of the body."

One of the earliest Pentecostal statements of faith may be found in *The Apostolic Faith*, the official organ of W.J. Seymour's Apostolic Faith Mission. This statement of faith includes an exposition on the "three ordinances in the church, footwashing, the Lord's Supper and water baptism." Footwashing is "a type of regeneration," and an "expression of humility toward each other in real love." The Lord's Supper has a threefold meaning: (1) the sprinkled blood signifies redemption; (2) "the body of the Lamb eaten for health and healing;" and (3) the Christian Passover, that is, the blood of Jesus Christ "gives us victory over all the powers of the enemy." Water baptism is an essential ordinance (but not salvific) because it is commanded by the Lord. Water baptism identifies the believer with the death, burial, and resurrection of Jesus. Believers are exhorted not to reject "the command of our Lord and Savior, Jesus Christ, or these different ordinances that He has instituted." Early Pentecostals embraced these sacred acts of devotion due to their desire to be faithful and obedient to the Bible. They insisted that they were "seeking to displace dead forms and creeds . . . with living, practical Christianity." Their understanding of "living, practical Christianity" included sacramental worship.[73]

The sacramental essence of Pentecostal spirituality is demonstrated in the worship of early Pentecostal churches. The sacramental practices of water baptism, the Lord's Supper, and the washing of the saints' feet were common occurrences. The sacraments were commonly observed in conjunction with Pentecostal revival meetings. At the conclusion of Pentecostal revivals, converts were invited to join the church and receive water baptism; and, the Lord's Supper and footwashing were observed. Occasionally, healings were reported in conjunction with sacramental worship. W.A. Looney reported from Rising Fawn, Georgia:

> About thirty-three were saved and nearly all of the thirty-three were sanctified and 12 or 15 received the Holy Ghost. I led seventeen down into the water and baptized them while the singing, shouting and talking in tongues were in full force on the creek bank. A large crowd stood and witnessed newborn babies being buried with Christ in baptism. An invalid woman was carried down to the water and baptized. She raised one of her hands and praising the Lord that she had not used for years. Sunday we observed the Lord's Supper and feet washing and one of the sisters reported that the power struck her and she splashed the water nearly out of the pan with her feet and she had not been able to use them for several years before.[74]

For early Pentecostals, baptism in the Holy Spirit brought into their lives a "real presence" they had not experienced in the churches of the Reformation. Spirit baptism made Jesus a present and living person in the lives of believers. A.A. Boddy declared:

---

[73] "The Ordinances Taught by Our Lord." *The Apostolic Faith* (September 1908), 2.
[74] W.A. Looney, *Church of God Evangel* (October 2, 1920), 2.

> . . . so this same Holy Spirit is the power and the only power,
> in which we may live out Christ's life on earth, and ever
> gain the victory over His enemy and ours. He makes the
> indwelling Christ very real to us.[75]

Likewise, Sam Perry proclaimed:

> The religion of our Lord Jesus Christ is not merely a life
> of forms and ceremonies and outward ordinances, but
> a spiritual force within the human soul. It is true that the
> outward ordinances, duties, etc., must be attended to, but
> there is no amount of outward service and show that can be
> of any profit if the inner heart is not touched with Jesus the
> source of all life and power.[76]

Spirit baptism is the dynamic that transformed the Reformed
and/or Wesleyan theology of early Pentecostals into a distinctive
Pentecostal theology. Spirit baptism moved theological confession
into the realm of spiritual encounter. Spirit baptism transformed
Christian worship into a living and dynamic Trinitarian fellowship.
This "real presence" extended to the way Pentecostals experienced
the sacraments. R.E. Stockton wrote:

> Well, some people are afraid of forms and ceremonies
> because the Catholics practice them in place of salvation.
> No! The trouble with the Catholics is they lack the Spirit
> which makes the ceremonies real, while our Church with
> the Holy Ghost to back up all we say or do gets blessed and
> edified greatly in the practice of ordinances.[77]

Pentecostal sacraments are "essential ordinance (s) of righteousness."[78] They are to be observed "literally and *in the Spirit* and
for the purposes set forth in the Scriptures."[79] Early Pentecostals
intuitively knew that there is a "real presence" in the celebration of

---

[75] A.A. Boddy, "The Holy Ghost for Us," *The Weekly Evangel* (September 1,
1917), 1.

[76] Sam C. Perry, "Spiritual Life and Power." *The Church of God Evangel* (February
2, 1913), 3.

[77] R.E. Stockton, "Education and the Church of God." *The Faithful Standard*
(November 1922), 21.

[78] *Book of Doctrines* (Cleveland, TN: Church of God Publishing House, 1922), 58.

[79] *Word and Witness* (June 1915), 1.

the sacraments. This can be seen in the terminology they used. They would often use the words "ordinance" and "sacrament" in the same writings, as if these words were synonymous. In the early published writings of the Church of God, the Lord's Supper was known as "the Sacrament."[80] Also, even as they explained the Lord's Supper as a memorial, or water baptism in terms of an act of obedience, they wrote (and preached) with a deep sacramental devotion. They *knew* there was something more, even if they could not fully articulate their theology.

A Pentecostal Theology of Sacraments

I have had many opportunities to worship with believers throughout the world. During these services, I often found myself somewhat lost because of my inability to understand the languages as they were being sung or spoken. However, when the pastor broke the bread and raised the cup of Holy Communion, I found myself at home, seated at the Lord's Table. This is worship in Spirit and truth in its purest form—God-centered worship grounded in the Holy Scriptures and the long devotional history of the church. Because Pentecostals pursue true spiritual worship, there must be an ongoing theological discussion regarding the proper celebration of sacraments.

Observance of the sacraments is among the oldest features of Christianity. Water baptism and "the breaking of bread" are essential to the message and celebration of the church throughout the Acts of the Apostles. Water baptism cannot be separated from the call to repentance.[81] The "breaking of bread" cannot be separated from the worshiping community (Acts 2:42, 46; 20:7). The practice of the "laying on of hands" or "anointing with oil" for prayer and healing began with Jesus and is continued in the ministry of his disciples (Mark 6:13; 16:18; James 5:14). Whether or not we understand the mystery of how we encounter the grace of God through the sacra-

---

[80] *Book of General Instructions for the Ministry and Membership* (Cleveland, TN: Church of God Publishing House, 1927), 5. Also, the *Discipline of the Pentecostal Holiness Church* (1908) refers to the Lord's Supper" as "a sacrament of our redemption by Christ's death."

[81] Acts 2:38, 41; 8:12, 16, 36-38; 9:18; 10:47; 16:15, 33; 18:8; 19:3-5; 22:16.

ments, we cannot diminish their significance in the life of the early Christian community. To early Christians, participation in the holy sacraments was theology in action. N.T. Wright explains:

> . . . by the middle of the second century baptism and Eucharist, as significantly new forms of religious praxis, had become so much second nature to the Christian church that new questions and theories could be advanced about them. They were not strange actions which some Christians might on odd occasions perform, but ritual acts which were taken for granted, part of that praxis which constituted the early Christian worldview.[82]

The Christian faith is expressed in the sacred acts of Christian worship. As believers assemble together to celebrate the Eucharist, the church witnesses about the redemptive ministry of Jesus Christ to the unbelieving world. When new converts present themselves for water baptism, they publicly confess Jesus as Lord and testify to new life in Christ. When the elders of the church pray for the sick, the power of the resurrected Lord is demonstrated. Unbelievers who witness the sacred acts of Christian worship see and hear the gospel. Jesus told us that the first commandment is "you shall love the Lord your God with all your heart, and with all your soul, and with all your mind, and with all your strength" (Mark 12:30). Worship is the deepest expression of love for God. Worship as an expression of love must engage all human senses, as well as the mind. Sacramental worship offers the opportunity for the worshiper to see, hear, taste, smell, feel, and reflect. As the church worships in Word and sacrament, believers are nourished and the gospel is proclaimed to the world.

Sacraments or Ordinances?

So that we may have a clear understanding of the issue before us, we must define the terms *sacrament, sacramental,* and *ordinance.* The term *sacrament* is defined as "the signs and instruments by which the Holy Spirit spreads the grace of Christ the head throughout the

---

[82] N.T. Wright, *The New Testament and the People of God* (Minneapolis: Fortress Press, 1992), 361.

Church which is his body."[83] In other words, to receive the sacrament is to receive salvific grace. Leo the Great wrote that after Christ ascended to heaven, He now is present with believers through the sacraments. In Roman Catholic theology, the sacraments are the effective agents of God's grace because they are the "sacramental presence" of Christ.[84] The sacraments are a means of grace *ex opera operato*, that is, "by virtue of the act itself."

> Sacraments are "power that comes forth" from the body of Christ, which is ever-living and life-giving. They are actions of the Holy Spirit at work in his Body, the Church. They are "the masterworks of God" in the new and everlasting covenant.[85]

As long as the sacrament is received by a priest in apostolic succession, and grace is not resisted, the sacrament conveys redemptive grace.

In the Roman Catholic tradition, there are seven sacraments: Water Baptism, Confirmation, Eucharist, Penance, Anointing the Sick, Holy Orders, and Matrimony. The sacraments of Christian initiation are Water Baptism, Confirmation, and Eucharist. Water Baptism is the effective cause of the new birth. Confirmation is the act that guarantees the seal of the Holy Spirit. When one partakes of the Eucharist, the real body and blood, soul and divinity, of the Lord are consumed. Penance is a sacrament of reconciliation, which is the means by which the Christian who has fallen into sin may be restored to fellowship with Christ and the church. Penance involves the conviction, confession, and reparation for sin with the prayer of absolution by the priest. The sacrament of Anointing the Sick was at one time known as "extreme unction" and was given as the "last rite" to a person close to death. However, Vatican II redefined this rite so that all who are sick may receive this sacrament. This sacrament offers those who are sick and dying the special gifts of the Holy Spirit that strengthen both body and soul. The sacrament of Holy Orders confers apostolic ministry upon the deacons, priests, and bishops of

---

[83] *Catechism of the Catholic Church, 2nd edition* (Washington, DC: United States Catholic Conference, 1994, 1997), 204.
[84] *The Nicene and Post-Nicene Fathers, Second Series, Vol. XII*, 188.
[85] *Catechism of the Catholic Church*, 289.

the church. The sacrament of Matrimony is a permanent covenant between one man and one woman. The self-denial and self-giving required in the marital relationship is a reflection of the character and grace of the Lord. Therefore, each spouse is a minister of grace to the other.

The term *sacramental* refers to sacred signs of grace obtained through the prayers of the church. Although similar to sacraments, sacramentals are not gifts of grace in the same manner of sacraments. A sacramental act would include the prayer of blessing over a meal, an object, or a person. In sacraments, God's grace is mediated through the waters of baptism, or through the bread and cup of the Eucharist. In sacramentals, God's grace is mediated, not through association with the blessed object, but through the prayers of blessing and intercession of God's people.

During the Reformation, many Protestants rejected the Catholic understanding of sacraments as miracle and mystery through which one may receive God's grace. Protestant reformers favored rationalism over mysticism and many rejected the possibility of miracles. For rational Protestants, the mysterious was thought to be mere superstition. Also, the Protestant reformers sought to deny the authority of the bishops of the Catholic Church, especially in regard to conferring the grace of God. The Catholic sacraments were offered under the auspices of the bishop. It was thought that to receive the grace of God one must be in the bishop's good graces, that is, in proper fellowship with the bishop. In effect, the bishop held in his hand the keys of salvation. The most radical Protestants insisted that human salvation is through Christ and the mediation of the church and its ministers are incidental. Many Protestants rejected the term *sacrament* in favor of the term *ordinance*. An ordinance is an act of worship ordained by Christ as a visible sign of redemptive grace. Most Protestants limit the number of ordinances to two: water baptism and the Lord's Supper. The term *ordinance* has been preferred over *sacrament* so as not to assign salvific grace. God's grace is not received through the ordinance, but directly from God through the act of obedience of the believer. In other words, water baptism does not *cause* the new birth, but is a symbol of redemption already appropriated due to the faith of the believer. The bread and cup of the Lord's Supper merely *represent* the body and blood of the Lord; they do not *become* the Lord's body and blood, and there is no "real presence." When the believer is baptized or partakes of the Lord's Supper, it is merely a symbolic act. Ordinances are observed as obedience to the Scriptures. This view of the sacred acts of worship tends to make them incidental, or even unnecessary. If the sacred acts of worship are not understood to be a means of grace, then they are observed rarely, or not at all. It may be that this minimalist view of the sacraments has robbed many Evangelical and Pentecostal churches of a vital source of spiritual life.

SPIRIT IN SACRAMENTS

"The Holy Spirit . . . sheds incorporeal grace on corporeal things."

—Ambrose, *On the Holy Spirit*[86]

Early Pentecostals often used the terms "ordinance" and "sacrament" as synonyms. Even so, some Pentecostals have historically favored the term "ordinance" over "sacrament." Recently, some Pentecostal theologians have begun using the term "sacramental ordinances" to emphasize the charismatic nature of these rites in worship. For example, Kenneth Archer has written that "the concept of 'ordinances' must be re-visioned" because Pentecostals expect to encounter the presence of God in the worship of the church. Archer writes:

These sacraments are means of grace providing opportunities for the Spirit to work redemptively in the faithful participants within the Pentecostal proleptic worship service. The sacramental ordinances evoke remembrance of the past and provoke playful anticipation of a future (promise) that collapses into the present mysterious salvific experiences.[87]

---

[86] *The Nicene and Post-Nicene Fathers Second Series Vol. X*, 101.
[87] Kenneth J. Archer, "Nourishment for our Journey: The Pentecostal *Via Salutis* and Sacramental Ordinances," *Journal of Pentecostal Theology 13:1* (October 2004), 95. Also, John Christopher Thomas, "Pentecostal Theology in the Twenty-First Century," *Pneuma: The Journal for Pentecostal Studies* 20:1 (Spring 1998), 3-19.

This suggests the willingness of some Pentecostals to reconsider how the Spirit of grace may be encountered through the sacraments. The term "sacramental ordinances" implies that the Spirit is encountered as the worshiping community participates in the sacred acts of worship. It is "sacramental" in that the worshiping community observes the "ordinances" in a prayerful way. In this understanding, it is in the act of prayer united with the acts of observance that forms a "sacramental ordinance."

For our purposes *sacrament* is defined as "a sacred act of worship blessed by Christ the High Priest through which the worshiper encounters the Spirit of grace." Sacraments are the priestly gifts of Christ to His church. Sacraments are sacred dramas in which all the faithful are actors in redemptive history. Sacraments nurture and edify believers. Sacraments are significant acts of devotion and discipleship through which believers are sanctified. Proper sacramental worship requires the presence of Christ and the Spirit with the community of believers and a material means—water, bread, the fruit of the vine, oil—through which grace may be received. Understanding sacraments as "means of grace" where worshipers encounter the Holy Spirit should be an easy "leap of faith" for Pentecostals. Pentecostals have believed in the "transfer of divine energy" or a "tangible anointing." Following the example of Scripture, many "anointed handkerchiefs" and other objects have been used to effect healing and otherwise assist in working miracles through the power of the Holy Spirit (Acts 19:11-12). Therefore, if healing can be effected by the Holy Spirit through the means of an anointed handkerchief, could not the consecrated "bread and wine" of Holy Communion convey saving grace when received in faith by the worshiper?

The Pentecostal belief in the "transfer of divine energies" finds a historical precedent in the teaching of Gregory Palamas. Palamas, a fourteenth-century Greek theologian, suggested that God's divine essence is unknowable. But God's uncreated divine energies, which permeate all things, could be communicated to humans and encountered as saving grace. According to Gregory, the radiant light proceeding from the transfigured Christ is an example of the "uncreated divine energies" of God. He wrote, "This mysterious light, inaccessible, immaterial, uncreated, deifying, eternal, this radiance of the Divine Nature, this glory of the divinity, this beauty of the heavenly kingdom, is at once accessible to sense perception and yet transcends it."[88] Pentecostals describe this as the "Shekinah" of God.

> O that men and women would tarry for the baptism with the Holy Ghost and fire upon their souls, that the glory may be seen upon them just as it was upon the disciples on the day of Pentecost in the fiery emblem of tongues. The tongues of fire represented the great Shekinah glory. So today the Shekinah glory rests day and night upon those who are baptized with the Holy Ghost, while He abides in their souls.[89]

Gregory insisted that the divine energies are in God and proceed from God, but are distinct from the unknowable divine essence of God. The divine energies are accessible to sanctified human sense perception through the power of the Holy Spirit.

Many Protestant and Catholic theologians take issue with Palamas' doctrine of "divine energies." Catherine Mowry LaCugna has suggested that Palamas' doctrine is the "defeat of the doctrine of the Trinity." She has written, "By locating the divine persons in the inaccessible, imparticipable divine essence, Gregory in effect has removed the Trinity from our salvation."[90] The difference in Orthodox and Catholic thought is the distinction between *ousia* and *energy*. *Ousia* is the DNA of God, the "stuff" of which God is made. *Energy* is the power, or presence, that flows from the divine *ousia*. The distinction between the *ousia* and *energy* of God has great bearing upon Pentecostal thought as it relates to the doctrine of the baptism in the Holy Spirit. This question must be posed: "Are believers baptized in the *ousia* of Spirit, of the *energy* of Spirit, or both?" In fairness to Palamas and the Orthodox tradition of divine energies, it should be noted that for Palamas the divine energies are of the *ousia* of the Holy

[88] Gregory Palamas, *The Triads*, translated by Nicholas Gendle (New York: Paulist Press, 1983), 80.
[89] W.J. Seymour, *The Apostolic Faith* (May 1908), 3.
[90] Catherine Mowry LaCugna, *God for Us* (San Francisco: HarperCollins, 1991), 197-198.

Trinity. *Energy* does not exist apart from the *ousia*. In the Orthodox tradition, the distinction is between that which is knowable and that which is unknowable. For Catholics, that which has been touched by the *ousia* of the Spirit permanently shares in God's holiness. Hence, the consecrated bread and wine of the Eucharist are ontologically transformed—transubstantiated—into the full humanity and divinity of Christ. Likewise, the remains of saints become holy relics with special powers. Most Pentecostals would reject this. But most Pentecostals can accept that the Spirit *moves* and *rests* upon physical objects such as the bread and cup of Holy Communion, the waters of baptism, or an anointed handkerchief. A Pentecostal sacramental theology implies that the Spirit *moves* upon the sacramental elements which become a "means of grace" in the context of the worshiping church as Trinitarian fellowship.

Pentecostals have long affirmed that God can effect miraculous healing through the sacramental acts of "anointing with oil" and the "laying on of hands." Because Pentecostals affirm the power of God and the authority of the Holy Scriptures, miracles such as Christ's turning water into wine and the multiplication of loaves and fishes are believed without criticism. It is simply a matter of faith. Is it not also a matter of faith that through the words of Christ and the power of the Holy Spirit, the elements of holy sacraments can be permeated by God's divine energies? Therefore, due to the animating presence of the Spirit, baptismal waters are sanctified, and all who enter by faith are cleansed. In like manner, the Holy Spirit effects the consecration of the "bread and wine" so that by partaking of this simple meal, believers partake of the body and blood of the Savior. Sacraments are charismatic by nature.[91] Sacraments are spiritual graces and those who participate in faith encounter the "real presence" of Christ through the Holy Spirit. As we approach the altar to participate in sacramental

---

[91] Oskar Skarsaune wrote, "The charismatic understanding of the ministries of the ordained clergy therefore corresponds to the dominant role accorded to the Spirit in the Eucharist as well as in baptism. Without the Spirit, baptism and Eucharist would be empty rites, conferring nothing on those partaking. Where there is no Spirit, there cannot be any real sacraments." *In the Shadow of the Temple: Jewish Influences on Early Christianity* (Downers Grove, IL: InterVarsity Press, 2002), 346.

worship, we do so "in the Spirit." The Holy Spirit makes us aware of heavenly realities, and we experience heavenly mysteries.

Once I was talking with a friend regarding the charismatic nature of the sacraments. In particular, we were discussing how the bread of the Eucharist is the body of Christ. During the conversation, he said, "Well, it just looks like bread to me." I replied, "Well, Jesus appeared to be just a man." That is the nature of the Incarnation. Jesus Christ is the union of God and humanity—He is fully God and fully human. To those who saw him in the flesh, Jesus appeared to be a simple Jewish carpenter. On occasion, at His baptism and transfiguration, those near Him received a glimpse of His divine glory. Even after His resurrection, Jesus still had the appearance of a mere human. His divinity was hidden within His humanity. He will return in glory, but even then He is fully human and fully God. Jesus Christ is the permanent and eternal union of divine and human.

The problem for many people is the tendency to separate the spiritual from the material. That is why many Greeks could not accept the Incarnation. They did not believe it to be possible that matter and spirit could have anything in common. Therefore, Jesus only *appeared* to be human. This was one of the earliest heresies in the church. John proclaimed, "By this you know the Spirit of God: Every spirit that confesses that Jesus Christ has come in the flesh is from God" (1 John 4:2). The relationship between spirit and matter is assumed in the Judeo-Christian worldview. According to the Old Testament, all matter has its source in S/spirit. God is spirit (John 4:24). God, who is spirit, created all matter—the heavens and earth. The Spirit of God moves over creation and is poured out upon all flesh (Genesis 1:2; Joel 2:28). All matter is held together through the power of God (Colossians 1:17). In creation, there is an essential and causal relationship between S/spirit and matter. In the womb of the Virgin, Spirit and flesh became permanently united in the person of Jesus Christ. This is important to the way the Spirit interacts with the various sacramental elements. Eugene Rogers has written:

> Oil, water, bread, wine, the bodies of human beings to be baptized, married, or ordained: in many and various ways the matter of the world becomes the element of a sacrament.

> To think about the Spirit, it will not do to think "spiritually":
> to think about the Spirit you have to think materially.[92]

The Holy Spirit rests "paraphysically" upon creation and material objects.[93] To insist that the Spirit is present in (or upon) the baptismal waters is not extraordinary, but ordinary. To believe that the Spirit makes Christ present in the bread and cup of Holy Communion is not abnormal, but normal. God is present and at home in creation. God makes all things possible. The waters of the baptismal pool, the bread and cup of the Eucharist, and the anointing oil can indeed be sacraments, that is, they are a means through which believers encounter the Spirit of grace. The elements of the sacraments are material substances which the Spirit *touches*. In the observance of the sacraments, believers *touch* the elements and are *touched* by the Spirit. The elements of the sacraments are mediating gifts of grace because of the presence of the Spirit of grace.

The paraphysical aspect of Pentecostal spirituality is evident throughout the Jerusalem Pentecost event (Acts 2). The Holy Spirit descended "from heaven" into this present age, into this physical world. Believers *heard* "a noise like a violent rushing wind;" they *saw* "tongues as of fire." The Divine *Pneuma* (wind/Spirit) "*filled* the whole house;" tongues of fire *rested* upon the believers and they were "*filled* with the Holy Spirit." Believers "began to *speak* with other tongues" and the crowd *heard* "them *speak* . . . in our own language." Peter explained the advent of the Holy Spirit as the gift of Father and Son "which you both *see* and *hear*." Luke tells us that "those who had received his word were *baptized*" and that believers devoted themselves to "the apostles' teaching and to fellowship, to the breaking of bread (*taste, nourishment*) and to prayer." The pathos

---

[92] Eugene F. Rogers, Jr. *After the Spirit: A Constructive Pneumatology from Resources Outside the Modern West*. (Grand Rapids: Eerdmans Publishing Co., 2005), 56, 98-99. Also, Sergius Bulgakov has written, "The action of the Holy Spirit in the world is manifested, first of all, in the sanctification or spiritualization of the cosmic matter. . . . One should not diminish the importance of the fact that, in the sacraments, the church sanctifies matter—bread and wine, water, oil, chrism, as well as the human body." *The Comforter* (Grand Rapids: Eerdmans Publishing Company, 2004), 343.

[93] Ibid.

of the Pentecost event was *"feeling* a sense of awe."* Pentecostal spirituality is not simply *spiritual*; it is *encountering* the Holy Spirit with our human senses as the Spirit moves and interacts in our *physical world*. Pentecostalism is a *physical spirituality*.

Sacraments and the Pentecostal Way of Salvation

Within Pentecostalism there have been two predominant theories of Atonement: (1) the finished work theory, and (2) the Wesleyan *way of salvation*. This debate is centered in the understanding of sanctification. For the proponents of the finished work theory, the believer is sanctified at the moment of conversion. All of the benefits of salvation are experienced in a single event. However, many early Pentecostals favored the theology of John Wesley. For Wesley, human salvation was more than a single confessional event, but an ongoing saving process in which the believer grows in grace.

> All experience, as well as Scripture, show this salvation to be both instantaneous and gradual. It begins at the moment we are justified . . . . It gradually increases . . . till, in another instant, the heart is cleansed from all sin, and filled with pure love to God and man.[94]

Wesley's doctrine of sanctification was a spark that ignited the fire of the Holiness Movement of the nineteenth century and the ongoing Pentecostal Movement. The preachers of the Holiness Movement spoke of sanctification as the "second blessing." Pentecostals testify to three works of grace by proclaiming, "Thank God, I'm saved, sanctified, and baptized with the Holy Ghost!"

The Pentecostal *way of salvation* is best expressed as a series of crisis experiences along *the way*. Salvation is a process of spiritual growth within the community of faith. The *way of salvation* begins with an effectual call of the Holy Spirit to draw a sinner to repentance, regeneration, and union with Christ. The *way of salvation* continues in sanctification and Spirit baptism, and it is

---

[94] John Wesley, *The Works of John Wesley*, *3rd edition, Vol. 6* (Albany, OR: Ages Software, 1997), 540-541.

completed in glorification. The Spirit's effectual call comes through the preached Word. The human response is faith demonstrated by repentance and continuing devotion to God. This occurs in the context of the worshiping church.

Kenneth Archer has suggested how sacraments may be integrated into the proclamation of the Pentecostal fivefold gospel.[95] He identifies God's redemptive work (*way of salvation*), Pentecostal proclamation, and corresponding sacraments as experiences in the worshiping church. Because the sacraments directly correspond to Pentecostal proclamation, the sacraments can rightly be called "full gospel sacraments." Therefore, sacraments are not empty ritual, or mere symbol, but dynamic opportunities through which the worshiper encounters the Spirit of grace in salvation, sanctification, Spirit baptism, and healing.

Archer's Integration of Pentecostal Proclamation and Sacraments		
Fivefold Gospel	**Way of Salvation**	**Sacramental Sign**
Jesus is our Savior	Justification and Regeneration	Water Baptism
Jesus is our Sanctifier	Sanctification	Footwashing
Jesus is our Spirit-Baptizer	Spirit baptism	Tongues Speech
Jesus is our Healer	Healing	Laying on hands and anointing with oil
Jesus is our soon coming King	Glorification	The Lord's Supper

Many Pentecostals affirm that the *way of salvation* occurs in the context of life in the church, but resist attempts to affirm the salvific efficacy of the church. Therefore, the relationship between salvation and church is often neglected. Ecclesiology and soteriology are parallel theological considerations that are never allowed to

---

[95] Archer, "Nourishment for our Journey," 90-95.

intersect. However, if the church is indeed the "body of Christ" and "the fellowship of the Holy Spirit," then Pentecostals must affirm a place for formal initiation into the visible church and participation in the sacraments within the *way of salvation*. The church is not incidental to God's redemptive plan; the church is essential. Many early Pentecostal evangelists understood this. At the end of their revival meetings, they often extended an opportunity for the newly converted to join the church. In the language of the Acts of the Apostles, revival reports often ended with a report of how many souls were "added to the church" (Acts 2:41).

The church is the "body of Christ" which is filled, empowered, and indwelt by the Holy Spirit. As such, the church is an extension and perpetuation of the Incarnation. Therefore, as Jesus Christ is the incarnation of the eternal Son, so the church is the incarnation of the eternal Spirit. As the incarnation of the Holy Spirit, the church is the "temple of the Holy Spirit" (1 Corinthians 3:16; 6:19). The temple of the Holy Spirit is constructed with Jesus Christ as the cornerstone. Spirit-filled apostles and prophets are the foundation stones (Ephesians 2:20). Each redeemed human is an "earthen vessel" which contains heavenly treasure—the glory and Spirit of God (2 Corinthians 4:7). These human vessels, filled with Spirit are the stones with which the temple of the Holy Spirit is erected. Further, each human vessel is presented as "a living and holy sacrifice, acceptable to God" in the "spiritual service of worship" (Romans 12:1). As a living sacrifice, each Spirit-filled believer burns with the fire of the Holy Spirit. As a living, fiery sacrifice, believers present themselves to God for service, and this is the highest form of worship. Just as the temple in Jerusalem was the special dwelling place of Yahweh (2 Chronicles 7:2, 16), so too, the church as the temple of the Holy Spirit is the special dwelling place of God on the earth.

The church is the spiritual mother of all believers. Cyprian, a third-century bishop of Carthage, wrote, "He can no longer have God as his Father, who has not the Church for his mother."[96] The

---

[96] *The Ante-Nicene Fathers, Vol. V,* 423.

metaphor of the church as "mother of the faithful" is a biblical tradition. Jerusalem is proclaimed to be the mother of Israel.

> Be joyful with Jerusalem and rejoice for her, all you who love her; be exceedingly glad with her, all you who mourn over her, that you may nurse and be satisfied with her comforting breasts, that you may suck and be delighted with her bountiful bosom. For thus says the Lord, "Behold, I extend peace to her like a river, and the glory of the nations like an overflowing stream; and you will be nursed, you will be carried on the hip and fondled on the knees. As one whom his mother comforts, so I will comfort you; and you will be comforted in Jerusalem" (Isaiah 66:10-13).

Jerusalem herself is birthed of God. She is the city of God, and as such, she is the source of national nourishment and comfort. The imagery of Jerusalem as the spiritual mother of the nation is common in Jewish literature during the period of the second Temple. The apostles often used words and images of the Old Testament in reference to the church as the new covenant people of God—Jews and Gentiles who have accepted Jesus Christ as Lord. The apostle Paul continues this imagery when speaking of Christian believers: " . . . but the Jerusalem above is free; she is our mother" (Galatians 4:26). Paul insists that those who have faith in Christ are the true children of Abraham.[97] He referred to the church as the "Israel of God" (Galatians 6:16). When reminding certain Hebrew Christians of the redemptive blessings of the new covenant in Christ, the author of Hebrews used the imagery of the heavenly Jerusalem as the "church of the firstborn who are enrolled in heaven" (Hebrews 12:23). Peter used the covenant language of the Old Testament to identify the church as the people of God (1 Peter 2:9-10). James spoke of the church as the "twelve tribes who are dispersed abroad" (James 1:1). One of the most powerful images of the New Jerusalem is found in the Revelation:

---

[97] Romans 9:6; Galatians 3:7, 29; Philippians 3:3.

And I saw the holy city, new Jerusalem, coming down out of heaven from God, made ready as a bride adorned for her husband. And I heard a loud voice from the throne, saying, "Behold, the tabernacle of God is among men, and He will dwell among them, and they shall be His people, and God Himself will be among them, and He will wipe away every tear from their eyes; and there will no longer be any death; there will no longer be any mourning, or crying, or pain; the first things have passed away" (Revelation 21:2-4).

The Jerusalem from above is the bride of the Lamb—the church.[98] The church is united with Christ. To be Christian is to be "in Christ." In Isaiah, God nurtures Jerusalem, and Jerusalem is the mother of the nation. In the new covenant, Christ is the bridegroom and the virgin bride is the church. In both realities, God is the ultimate source of life. The divine life is experienced in the community of God—the New Jerusalem.

Just as an infant receives vital nourishment from the breast of its mother, believers receive spiritual nourishment and nurture for proper Christian formation from the church. Although Pentecostals have emphasized various discipleship models (such as Sunday school) from their earliest days, it is the worship service that has been the primary method in which Pentecostals are taught the truths and practices of the faith. The church in worship has a profound impact on believers. The combined effect of anointed biblical preaching, dramatic personal testimonies, and spiritual singing wields a powerful influence on the spiritual nurture of believers.

The question that must be addressed by Pentecostals is this: "Is participation in the sacramental life of the church essential to salvation?" The answer is that sacraments are essential inasmuch as worship and life in the church are essential to the *way of salvation*. Writing from Pentecostal and Baptist traditions, Miroslav Volf says:

To be sure, the sacraments can be an indispensable condition of ecclesiality only if they are a form of the confession of faith and an expression of faith. This is indeed the case.

---

[98] 2 Corinthians 11:2; Ephesians 5:25-26; Revelation 21:9.

> First, they are a public representation of such confession
> . . . . Second, the mediation of salvific grace through the
> sacraments is bound to the faith of those receiving them
> . . . . Thus does faith precede baptism . . . and the Lord's
> Supper is inconceivable without faith . . . . There is no church
> without sacraments; but there are no sacraments without
> the confession of faith and without faith itself. [99]

Participation in the sacramental life of the church is normative, but may not be absolutely essential to salvation due to God's prevenient grace. In the thought of John Wesley, prevenient grace is "free in all and for all." Its purpose is to prepare the sinner to receive justifying grace. All humans have an innate awareness of the divine and some sense of God's moral law (Romans 1:19-20; 2:14-16). This intuitive awareness of God prepares the human heart for the call to salvation. Thomas Oden has written, "It is rash to assume that there cannot be other extraordinary acts of grace or any other means by which the Spirit can address the conscience and the heart . . . . Those who remain outside the pale of baptism can nonetheless be saved by making use of the graces God gives them preveniently."[100] Like the thief on the cross, many individuals may not have adequate opportunities to receive water baptism or otherwise participate in the sacramental life of the church. However, this is the exception, rather than the rule. Believers who have the opportunity should joyfully participate in the life and sacramental worship of the church. To disregard the sacraments is gross error, even sinful.[101] Some early Pentecostals suggested that failure to receive water baptism after conversion could lead to apostasy.[102] W.G. Anderson offered a compelling defense of sacramental practices in the Church of God, suggesting that those who oppose sacraments are false prophets.

---

[99] Miroslav Volf, *After Our Likeness: The Church as the Image of the Trinity* (Grand Rapids: Eerdmans Publishing Co., 1998), 153-154.
[100] Thomas Oden, *Systematic Theology, Volume 3: Life in the Spirit,* (Peabody, MA: Prince Press, 1998), 328.
[101] Mark 16:16; John 6:53; 13:8, 14; James 4:17.
[102] *Book of General Instructions for the Ministry and Membership,* 4.

> When we hear men willfully ignoring the holy commandments of the Lord and declaring that holy baptism was only intended for Jews, that observing the holy sacrament is not required for the children of God in these days, that washing the saints' feet is only practiced by the weak-minded and fanatics; and thus fleecing the Immaculate Lamb of every visible ordinance that He has left for his true children to remember His example, to follow in His steps and remember His suffering in having his body broken and his blood shed, we are brought face to face with the Scripture—Many false prophets shall arise . . .
>
> Not only are these false teachers cutting out all the sacred ordinances of the Lord Jesus, but they are denying the existence of a literal, visible Church of God in the world.[103]

Anderson presents a very straightforward Pentecostal understanding of church and sacraments. A visible church with visible sacraments is not contrary to Pentecostal spirituality, but essential to it. Christian worship without the Word and sacraments cannot be worship in Spirit and truth.

The salvific efficacy of the church and sacraments must be understood in relation to the economic Trinity, that is, the way God has manifested God's self in the history of redemption. God the Father gave the Son and sent the Spirit as *primary salvific gifts*. Through the Son and the Spirit, humans are redeemed and the church is established. In this economy of salvation, the church and its sacraments are *secondary salvific gifts* which naturally proceed from the Son and the Spirit. The sacramental worship of the church is a means of grace through which sinners experience the blessings of salvation. The salvific efficacy of the church and sacraments is wholly dependent upon the saving acts of the Holy Trinity.

Celebration of the sacraments affirms the church as a Trinitarian fellowship. The effective call of the Holy Spirit is a call to life *together*. The Holy Spirit calls us to eternal life in fellowship with the Holy Trinity—Father, Son, and Spirit. The Spirit calls us that we may

---

[103] W.G. Anderson, "The Fight is On," *Church of God Evangel* (April 20, 1918), 4.

share eternal life in the fellowship of the redeemed. Jesus gave us a basic definition of the church: "For where two or three have gathered together in My name, I am there in their midst" (Matthew 18:20). Jesus' definition of the church serves to challenge two contemporary myths about the church. The first myth is that a proper church must be a megachurch. Jesus says a church can be as small as "two or three." The second myth is that the church consists of "Jesus and me." Jesus and Paul insist that the church properly exists as a plural body where individuals are members of one another (Romans 12:5; Ephesians 4:25). When the church gathers to worship, God is present. The celebration of sacraments requires the gathering of believers as a faith community. When a convert is baptized, it is normally in the presence of the worshiping community. When believers gather together around the Lord's Table, it is a community fellowship meal. When a believer takes up the towel and basin, it is done so that another's feet may be washed. Believers who are suffering call for the elders of the church to pray. The observance of sacraments cannot be properly experienced alone, apart from the worshiping community. James Bowers has written:

> The call to the Spirit-filled life is also fundamentally a call to a covenant community of the Spirit. Participation in the relationships, experiences, and disciplines of the Spirit-filled community—prayer, praise, fellowship, searching the Scriptures, communion, footwashing, witness, and so on—is essential to personal spirituality. Consequently, *communal* experience of the Spirit is the primary context for development of *personal* life in the Spirit.[104]

It is through participation in the worshiping community that the worshiper encounters the Spirit of grace. As the worshiper continues the journey along the *way of salvation* the worshiper's spiritual life is developed.

---

[104] James Bowers, "A Wesleyan-Pentecostal Approach to Christian Formation." *Journal of Pentecostal Theology* 6 (1995), 76.

Sacramental Worship and Spiritual Renewal

The celebration of sacraments has often been at the center of spiritual renewal in the church. This is seen in a negative way in the Protestant Reformation. It was the perceived (and real) abuses of sacraments in the medieval Catholic Church that sowed the seeds of the Reformation. In the process of reforming Christian dogma, the reformers focused on how salvific grace is dispensed and received. Although Luther and Calvin rejected the Catholic doctrine of transubstantiation, they nonetheless held a high view of the sacraments. But sacramental worship suffered in the churches of the radical reformers, being reduced to ordinance and memorial.

Pentecostalism is a renewal movement. Pentecostals may be surprised to discover that sacramental worship was at the heart of many great renewal movements. Here we will discuss two historic renewal movements and their sacramental theology. First, we will consider the sacramental worship of John Wesley.[105] Wesley is considered the grandfather of modern Pentecostalism because of his doctrine of sanctification. Wesley viewed salvation as an ongoing process, stages of growth, which would eventually lead to perfection. Inherent in this sanctifying process were the "means of grace." Wesley understood the "means of grace" to be "outward signs, words, or actions, ordained of God, and appointed for this end, to be the ordinary channels whereby (God) may convey to men, preventing, justifying, or sanctifying grace." The means of grace in Wesleyan spirituality are prayer, study of the Scriptures, and "receiving the Lord's Supper, eating bread and drinking wine in remembrance of Him." The methodical practice of these spiritual disciplines is ordained of God "as the ordinary channels of conveying His grace to the souls of men." The observance of the spiritual disciplines is not seeking salvation by works, because the observances of the spiritual disciplines are acts of faith. Wesley was not concerned

---

[105] John Wesley, *Sermons on Several Occasions.* (Grand Rapids, MI: Christian Classics Ethereal Library). Internet: http://www.ccel.org/ccel/wesley/sermons.html

with proper liturgical form because "external worship is lost labor" unless the worshiper has "a heart devoted to God." He considered faithless forms of worship to be "an utter abomination to the Lord." For Wesley, there is a distinction between liturgical *form* and true sacramental *worship*. He wrote, "Every believer in Christ is deeply convinced that there is no merit but in Him; that there is no merit in any of his own works; not in uttering the prayer, or searching the Scripture, or hearing the word of God, or eating of that bread and drinking of that cup." The spiritual disciplines are sacramental acts of devotion wholly dependent upon the presence of the Spirit of God and the faithful response of the believer. The goal of these sacramental acts is "a heart renewed after the image of God." Wesley insisted the believer has a "duty of constant Communion." The frequency of Communion "will not lessen the true religious reverence, but rather confirm and increase it."

> The grace of God given herein confirms to us the pardon of our sins, by enabling us to leave them. As our bodies are strengthened by bread and wine, so are our souls by these tokens of the body and blood of Christ. This is the food of our souls: This gives strength to perform our duty, and leads us to perfection. If, therefore, we have any regard for the plain command of Christ, if we desire the pardon of our sins, if we wish for the strength to believe, to love and obey God, then we should neglect no opportunity of receiving the Lord's Supper.

Wesley held to a Pneumatic view of the "real presence" in Holy Communion, similar to that of John Calvin. The Holy Spirit is the effective agent in sacramental devotion. The Holy Spirit appropriates Christ's atonement to the faithful. Likewise, the Holy Spirit makes Christ present in the Lord's Supper.

> The cup of blessing which we bless, is it not the communion, or *communication,* of the blood of Christ? The bread which we break, is it not the communion of the body of Christ? (1 Corinthians 10:16). Is not the eating of that bread, and the drinking of that cup, the outward, visible means, whereby God conveys into our souls all that spiritual grace,

that righteousness, and peace, and joy in the Holy Ghost, which were purchased by the body of Christ once broken and the blood of Christ once shed for us? Let all, therefore, who truly desire the grace of God, eat of that bread, and drink of that cup.

The Wesleyan renewal was a renewal of sacramental worship that affected Christian devotion on two continents for generations. The decline of sacramental devotion within the Methodist Movement may be one of the causes of the loss of vitality in Methodist spirituality.

One of the greatest renewal movements in the history of Christianity in North America is remembered as the Cane Ridge (Kentucky) Campmeeting of 1801. The Cane Ridge event was actually known as the Cane Ridge *Communion*, and it was an expression of Presbyterian sacramental worship that had its roots in Scotland and the northern region of Ireland. The Cane Ridge Communion has been called "America's Pentecost."[106] Following the tradition of the Scotch-Irish Presbyterian immigrants, "the Communion" was a regular event in which many congregations came together for several days. The climax of the event was the observance of Holy Communion. The Presbyterians held to Calvin's Pneumatic view of the holy meal, meaning that they believed Christ is spiritually present in the cup and loaf. Hundreds, even thousands, usually attended the Communion. The event included preaching, singing, a day of fasting, the Communion day, and concluded with a day of thanksgiving. The regular Communion was often the stimulus for revival and renewal among attending congregations. The Cane Ridge Communion was scheduled for August 1801. There had been many local revivals preceding the Cane Ridge Communion, and there was much anticipation that the Cane Ridge event would be special. Indeed, it was a spectacular event. Most estimates place the attendance at more than ten thousand people. Remember, this is Kentucky in 1801. People traveled to the event on foot, horseback, and in wagons. Necessities, like food and water were

---

[106] Paul K. Conkin, *Cane Ridge: America's Pentecost* (Madison, WI: The University of Wisconsin Press, 1990).

of short supply. There were no toilet facilities for humans or animals. Most of the attendees camped in tents, or under the open sky. Several prominent ministers preached simultaneously throughout the day in various locations. It was a noisy, even chaotic event that sounded like a roar for miles around. The Cane Ridge Communion is most notably remembered for the spiritual "exercises" that were manifested. A prominent minister who attended the event, James Campbell, described the spiritual pathos of the Communion:

> Sinners dropping down on every hand, shrieking, groaning, crying for mercy, convoluted; professors [of religion] praying, agonizing, fainting, falling down in distress, for sinners, or in raptures of joy! Some singing, some shouting, clapping their hands, hugging and even kissing, laughing; others talking to the distressed, to one another, or to opposers of the work, and all this at once—no spectacle can excite a stronger sensation. And with what is doing, the darkness of the night, the solemnity of the place, and of the occasion, and conscious guilt, all conspire to make terror thrill through every power of the soul, and rouse it to awful attention [sic].[107]

Not everyone who attended the Cane Ridge Communion actually participated in the Sunday Communion service. Only those who had carefully prepared in the prescribed spiritual disciplines and had Communion tokens could be admitted into the Communion service. The Communion services were orderly events but deeply affected the communicants. Even those who were not given to the more dramatic emotional exercises of the event openly wept at the Communion table. Pentecostals may be surprised to learn that the camp meeting tradition associated with the nineteenth century revivals was actually a later development that began with the regular Communion event. Sadly, the Cane Ridge Communion was the last major sacramental event associated with the camp meeting movement. Even as the camp meeting movement developed, church membership and sacramental devotion declined in American Evangelical churches. Spectacular events overshadowed the ecclesial and sacramental devotion of

---

[107] Conkin, *Cane Ridge: America's Pentecost*, 93-94.

American Christians. This continues to be a problem for churches in our day, especially among Pentecostal and Charismatic churches.

The Wesleyan and Presbyterian sacramental piety was instrumental in the spiritual formation of those who participated. Congregations, as well as the individual believers within them, were strengthened. These sacramental events were significant for two reasons. First, spiritual preparation included attention to the Scriptures, prayer, and fasting. These spiritual disciplines prepared one's heart, mind, and body for sacramental worship. Second, the participants held to a high view of the sacraments. Christ was really present. They expected a divine encounter. Pentecostals often look back to these renewal movements as proto-Pentecostal. The "exercises" associated with the Cane Ridge Communion are very familiar to Pentecostals. The Wesleyan way of salvation is similar to that of many Pentecostals.

The anticipation of a divine encounter is central to Pentecostal worship. As we have previously noted, many early Pentecostal churches celebrated the sacraments as the climax of a revival meeting. Those who had been converted during the revival were baptized in water. Also, it was customary that the Lord's Supper and/or footwashing would be observed at the end of the revival. Revival reports published in various Pentecostal periodicals can attest to this practice. Pastor I.H. Marks reported from Ft. Myers, Florida:

> Sunday afternoon four followed Jesus in water baptism and were added to the church. Sunday evening we partook of the Lord's Supper and washed the saints' feet, the Lord met with us, Glory to God! Such leaping, dancing, shouting, and talking in tongues [sic]. We will surely not forget that time soon.[108]

Sister Beatrice Roberson reported from Surrency, Georgia:

> The meeting at the Church of God, four miles south of Surrency, Georgia, began July 24 and closed August 12. Three were saved, sanctified and filled with the Holy Ghost, five added to the Church and two followed the Lord in water baptism. The services were conducted by Brother

---

[108] I.H. Marks, *Church of God Evangel* (October 30, 1915), 2.

J.A. Hipps. Brother Earl Paulk was with us a few nights and preached three soul stirring sermons. It was wonderful how the Lord blessed in giving out the Word. Hot lamp chimneys were handled under the power. The Lord's Supper and feet washing was observed . . ."[109]

G.W. Stanley reported from Dry Fork, Virginia:

There were several saved and ten . . . got sanctified . . . about seven got the Holy Ghost, for which I praise God. There were twenty added to the church. We had a baptizing, and there were twenty-one baptized. . . . We administered the Lord's Supper and washed feet, and while they were at the altar three got sanctified. While we were taking the bread and wine folks were going through to victory. On that same day there were some making threats and that night they were found in the altar crying to God for mercy. I thank God that among the number my oldest boy and girl got saved and sanctified. My little girl was on her knees at the altar sacrament, just as she drank the wine the Lord sanctified her. [110]

These reports are representative of early Pentecostal faith and practice. The full gospel was preached under the inspiration of the Holy Spirit. Sinners were saved, sanctified, and Spirit-baptized. New converts received water baptism and were added to the church. Believers were blessed as they partook of the Lord's Supper and washed the saints' feet. The Spirit's presence was manifested in dancing, shouting, and tongues speech. These are expressions of an embodied Pentecostal spirituality which is charismatic and sacramental. As Pentecostal pastors seek to lead their congregations, it might be that a focus on sacramental devotion will prove to be a meaningful and powerful way to Christian formation and spiritual renewal.

All Christian traditions have understood that worship is an encounter with the Holy Spirit. But they have understood this encounter in various ways. Typically, Christian worship traditions can be

---

[109] Beatrice Roberson, *Church of God Evangel* (August 25, 1923), 2.
[110] G.W. Stanley, "Dry Fork, Virginia." *The Pentecostal Holiness Advocate* (August 1, 1918) 7.

categorized into three groups—liturgical, reformed, and Pentecostal. In liturgical worship traditions, represented by the Roman Catholic, Orthodox, and Anglican churches, the worship emphasis is on the sacraments as a means of saving grace. Regeneration comes through water baptism; the Spirit is conferred by the laying on of hands; and the focus of Sunday worship is the Eucharist, also known as the Lord's Supper. For these believers, worship is defined as "mystery," and the Spirit is encountered in the reception of the various sacraments—water baptism, confirmation, and the Eucharist. Entering the sanctuary of a liturgical church, one will notice immediately that the center of the sanctuary is the altar where the Eucharist is received. These believers attend church to receive the Eucharist.

In reformed worship traditions, represented by various Presbyterian, Baptist, and Free Church groups, the worship emphasis is on the preached Word. The focus of worship is on the pulpit, which may be elevated or located in the center of the sanctuary, representing the centrality of the Holy Scriptures. The Spirit is encountered through the preached Word, and Christian worship is understood as rational or reasonable. These believers attend church to hear a sermon and make a decision.

Pentecostal believers have much in common with the worship traditions of both liturgical and reformed churches. Pentecostal churches observe the sacraments, and they believe and practice the centrality of the preached Word. However, a distinction exists in Pentecostal worship. To liturgical worshipers, the Spirit is present in the sacraments. To reformed worshipers, the Spirit is present in the Word. However, to Pentecostal worshipers, emphasis is on the Holy Spirit who is encountered as a Person, and personally experienced. *The center and focus of Pentecostal worship is the altar.* Pentecostal worship is defined by redemptive experiences. In Pentecostal altars, men and women are saved, sanctified, healed, and baptized in the Spirit. Pentecostals attend church to encounter the Holy Spirit.

Each worship tradition standing alone has shortcomings. Liturgical worship without the Word and the Spirit may lead to dead formalism. Reformed worship without sacraments and the Spirit may

lead to sterile intellectualism. Pentecostal worship without sacraments and the Word may lead to shallow emotionalism. The church
must promote worship that affirms the Word and Sacrament in the
Spirit. Therefore, the challenge for Pentecostals is to develop and
lead worship with a focus on the altar that is a holistic event. In Pentecostal worship, believers encounter the Spirit of grace by participating in God's redemptive events as expressed in the observance
of the sacraments. Pentecostal worshipers are informed and formed
through Spirit-inspired preaching of the Word. This is how Pentecostals are spiritually formed and discipled. Pentecostal worship is
transformative because worshipers encounter the Holy Spirit and
are sanctified and Spirit-baptized.

The church, devoted to Jesus Christ and living in fellowship with
the Holy Spirit, is a means of grace to all who encounter God in
worship. Those who enter the worshiping church encounter the
Spirit of grace. God has endowed the church with ministry gifts,
empowered by the Holy Spirit, for the purpose of proclamation and
spiritual formation.

> And He gave some as apostles, and some as prophets, and
> some as evangelists, and some as pastors and teachers, for
> the equipping of the saints for the work of service, to the
> building up of the body of Christ; until we all attain to the
> unity of the faith, and of the knowledge of the Son of God, to
> a mature man, to the measure of the stature which belongs
> to the fullness of Christ (Ephesians 4:11-13).

As worshiping churches pray in the Spirit and sing spiritual
songs, the redemptive power of the kingdom of God breaks
forth.[111] This is where sinners are convicted and repent, the sick
are healed, and the demonized are delivered as the Spirit imparts
"great power" and "abundant grace" to the church (Acts 4:33; 6:8).
Through the power of the Spirit of grace, the church is a life-giving
community through which saving grace is both dispensed and

---

[111] Acts 1:14; 2:1-4; 2:42-47; 4:24-35; 5:14-16; 8:15; 9:10-19, 26-32; 10:44-47;
11:19-24; 14:1-3; Romans 8:26-27; 1 Corinthians 14:14, 15; Ephesians 5:19; Colossians 3:16; Jude 20.

received. Pentecostal spirituality is expressed in terms of a Christo-Pneumatic ecclesiology—encountering God through Christ *and* the Spirit *in* the church. Jesus Christ is proclaimed as Savior of all and High Priest and Bishop of the church.[112] The church is the body of Christ and the fellowship of the Holy Spirit.[113]

AN ONGOING ALTAR CALL

The celebration of the sacraments is an ongoing altar call. For most Pentecostal churches, the altar call is the central event of the worship service. Sinners are encouraged to come forward to the altar to "pray through" to salvation. Believers are encouraged to come to the altar to pray for sanctification, or to "pray through" to the baptism in the Holy Spirit. During the altar service, those who are sick, or otherwise in need, are encouraged to come to the altar. There the church elders will anoint with oil, lay their hands upon the sick, and pray for healing. The celebration of the sacraments in Pentecostal worship should be understood as an opportunity to invite the saints of God once again to the altar to encounter the Holy Spirit in the celebration of water baptism, the Lord's Supper, footwashing, and the laying on of hands. Each sacrament directly corresponds to the redemptive work of the Holy Trinity. In this regard, *the sacraments are an ongoing altar call in which the believer encounters God through the Holy Spirit.* Just as the Spirit animates Pentecostal worship in inspired preaching, anointed singing, joyful shouts of praise, and dancing, the Spirit also animates the sacraments. When believers experience water baptism, Holy Communion, or footwashing, they encounter Christ's priestly ministry through the Spirit of grace. When the sick call for prayer, holy hands anoint the sick with oil and the Spirit is present. Through the Holy Spirit, worshipers transcend time and space as they share sacramental experiences with Christ and the redeemed community. When believers enter the baptismal water and are baptized into Christ, they share in His personal baptism in the Jordan River. When believers gather at the

---

[112] Ephesians 1:22; 5:23; Colossians 1:18; 2:10; Hebrews 3:1; 1 Peter 2:25; 5:4.
[113] 1 Corinthians 12:27; 2 Corinthians 13:14; Ephesians 1:22-23; 4:12; Philippians 2:1; Colossians 1:18, 24.

Lord's Table to share bread and wine, that is, the body and blood of Jesus, they join with the Lord and all believers of the past who have received bread and wine, and all those in the future who will receive bread and wine. When believers take the towel and basin to wash the feet of another, it is because they have been baptized into Christ and are participants in Christ's reconciling and sanctifying work. Through Christ the High Priest and the Spirit of grace, sacraments are more than mere reenactments or memorials to God's redemptive acts; the baptismal water, the towel and basin, the bread and wine, and the anointing oil become mediatory gifts. In Christ and the Spirit, celebration of the sacraments becomes participation in God's redemptive acts. Worship becomes an expression of ongoing saving faith.

The challenge for Pentecostals is, "How can the celebration of sacraments enrich Pentecostal worship?" This is not a call for the establishment of a formal Pentecostal liturgy, nor is it a suggestion to diminish spontaneity or "Spirit movement" in Pentecostal worship. The Holy Spirit is utterly free. The Spirit cannot be domesticated, manipulated, or institutionalized. The Spirit cannot be confined to an established liturgy. Pentecostals should understand that the freedom of the Spirit means that the Spirit is free to act as an agent of grace in sacraments. The sacraments originate in the Spirit-empowered ministry of Jesus Christ. Sacraments are common to most Christian churches. The intent here is to suggest ways sacraments can be fully appreciated in Pentecostal spirituality. The Spirit's movement in and through the sacraments is the agent of spiritual formation in the worshiping community.

The Evening Light and Church of God Evangel
July 15, 1910

"Fourth of July at Tabernacle"
"The Services Wonderfully Blest of God"

...and then commenced one of the most victorious services I ever witnessed in the taking of the bread and wine and washing of the saints' feet. Scores of people brim full of the love of God engaged in this sacred and wonderful service. To describe it would be impossible. As the bread was broken and mention made of the broken body of Jesus, He seemed to manifest His presence in the midst. As I stood there in the presence of God and before the large audience with the broken bread; a piece in each hand, I seemed to get a broader view of the Christ and wonderful scheme of redemption than ever before. The form of the "Fourth" seemed to be there. The altars were filled as they knelt in companies one after another, all quiet except groans and sobs as the deacons passed the bread and wine, and singing and music while one company would rise and march away and another company take their place at the altar. It took some little time on account of the number. Then the feet washing commenced. The men occupied one side of the tabernacle and the women the other, with the singers and organs between. This service was wonderful. Tears, shouts, praises, embracing, handshaking, talking in tongues, singing, etc. Once the power fell on my daughter at the organ, and she played for several minutes under the power of the Spirit, while my son sang with the Spirit in other tongues, and my other daughter, with some others, were greatly exercised with the manifestations of the Spirit. The meeting went on into the night services without closing. The people began to assemble for the night service the power began to fall again when messages and interpretations were given, and signs and wonders were done by some that are indescribable. No preaching except by the Spirit. Some began to fall into the altar crying for mercy; some fell back in the congregation down between the benches. When there was room made at the altars by deliverance coming to those who were there, others would take the place, filling up the altar again. The work continued until late at night after a number were converted, backsliders reclaimed, several sanctified, and probably ten or twelve swept through to Pentecost. Saints were here from several places in Tennessee, Alabama, Georgia, Virginia and Indiana. The Lord honored us with His presence and glory, and indeed gave us a wonderful day - the most wonderful Fourth of July all day meeting I was ever in. There was such sweet fellowship among the saints and a holy reverence for God. Many prayers have gone up here for rain in the time of the latter rain. Zech. 10:1, and truly "There is a sound of an abundance of rain." 1 Kings 18:41. [*sic*]

CHAPTER 4

Water Baptism: Bath of Grace

Go therefore and make disciples of all the nations, baptizing them in the name of the Father and of the Son and of the Holy Spirit (Matthew 28:19).

Happy is our sacrament of water, in that by washing away the sins of our early blindness, we are set free and admitted into eternal life!

—Tertullian, *On Baptism*

Once, when our youngest son, Nathan, was about eight years old he started to enter our home after playing very hard all day. He was filthy. He was covered in dirt and sweat. His clothes were almost beyond salvaging, and he smelled bad. I met him at the door and told him to remove his clothes before he entered. Then, I said to him, "Go straight to the bathroom and get a good bath." With a look of protest on his face, he exclaimed, "A bath! Why do I need a bath?" He was perfectly content to live in his filth. About twenty minutes later, he walked out of the bathroom clean and smelling sweet. Now his presence was acceptable to live in our home once again.

Like a young child, we tend to be content with our own filthiness. We protest when it is suggested that we might need to clean up our lives. Jesus told the disciples, "I go to prepare a place for you" (John 14:2). If we desire to enter into our Father's house, we must be presentable; we must be clean. So that we may be cleansed, God has provided the sanctifying agents of the blood of Christ, the Holy

107

Spirit, and the Word of God. He has also provided water baptism. Water baptism is a *visible* sign of *invisible* grace. But it is more. Water baptism is a bath of grace in which the believer is spiritually cleansed in waters upon which the Holy Spirit, the Spirit of grace, is resting. Too often we have separated the experience of salvation from water baptism, because the decision to repent and the opportunity to be baptized are normally two events separated by time. But if salvation is understood as a series of crisis experiences along the *way of salvation*, instead of a single event, then water baptism becomes a significant salvific encounter. In this case, water baptism is a *visible* sign of *visible* grace, for the Spirit of grace should be evident in the new life of the believer, a life in which the "desire of the flesh" gives way to the "fruit of the Spirit" (Galatians 5:16-23). To put this in Pentecostal perspective, just as tongues speech is a visible (and audible) sign of the baptism in the Holy Spirit, so water baptism is a visible sign (initial evidence) of the new birth in Christ.

The Baptism of Jesus

Christian baptism as an act of worship and discipleship has its precedent in the Jordan baptism of Jesus by John the Baptist. Cleansing rituals common to Judaism were usually related to entry into the Temple or synagogue. John's baptism, however, was not about ritual cleansing. It was a baptism of repentance, which anticipated the Messiah's baptism of Spirit and fire. John did not baptize at the Temple complex in Jerusalem, but in the wilderness of the Jordan River. John's call was for Israel to return to the waters of the Jordan through which their ancestors walked as they entered the Promised Land. Jordan baptism symbolized death to the past and birth to the future. John invited the penitent to be baptized in water as a demonstration of spiritual cleansing that is imperative for participation in God's coming kingdom.

Jesus heard John's prophetic call and responded to his invitation for "water baptism." Even though it raises some interpretive difficulties, the baptism of Jesus was a major event in the early church tradition. The apostolic witness of the New Testament agrees that

Jesus was without sin.[114] If the purpose of Jesus' baptism was not for cleansing from sin, why was Jesus baptized? The answer is in John's pronouncement: "Behold, the Lamb of God who takes away the sin of the world!" (John 1:29). Many Jewish converts repented and were baptized by John in the Jordan, receiving cleansing from sin. As Jesus entered the Jordan River, the sinless One was baptized in the very waters contaminated by the sins of Israel. Jesus entered the baptismal waters of Jordan as High Priest to take on Himself the sins of humanity. By submitting to John's baptism of repentance, Jesus made a vicarious confession of sin for all humanity. Paul wrote, "He made Him who knew no sin to be sin on our behalf, so that we might become the righteousness of God in Him" (2 Corinthians 5:21).

Water baptism anticipates the cross. Immediately after He was baptized He entered into the wilderness temptation. Jesus spoke of His redemptive mission in terms of a baptism of suffering: "But I have a baptism to undergo, and how distressed I am until it is accomplished!" (Luke 12:50). Early Christian theologians associated Christ's baptism with his sufferings. Ignatius of Antioch (second century) wrote, "For our God, Jesus the Christ . . . was born and baptized in order that by his suffering he might cleanse the water."[115] Lactantius (third to fourth century) wrote:

> When He first began to reach maturity He was baptized by the prophet John in the river Jordan, that He might wash away in the spiritual layer not His own sins, for it is evident that He had none, but those of the flesh, which He bare; that as He saved the Jews by undergoing circumcision, so He might save the Gentiles also by baptism—that is, by the pouring forth of the purifying dew.[116]

Jesus' baptism in the Jordan was the beginning of His passion. With the Father's pronouncement, "This is My beloved Son, in whom I am well pleased" (Matthew 3:17), the journey to Calvary began.

---

[114] Acts 3:14; 2 Corinthians 5:21; Hebrews 4:15; 7:26; 1 Peter 2:22; 1 John 3:5.
[115] *The Apostolic Fathers*, 2nd edition. Edited and Revised by Michael W. Holmes. (Grand Rapids: Baker Book House, 1989), 92.
[116] *The Ante-Nicene Fathers, Vol. VI*, 115.

The New Birth

Once I baptized a man who had received Christ and was delivered from a life of chemical addiction. Afterwards, as we gathered together in the dressing room to dry off and change clothes, he looked at me and exclaimed, "I feel so clean!" A few months before being baptized, he had repented and accepted Christ as Lord. As a new believer, he probably did not understand all of the theological significance of being saved. But he intuitively knew that repentance and water baptism were corresponding events in the *way of salvation*. He knew that water baptism was more than a symbolic event.

Nicodemas approached Jesus and inquired about the kingdom of God. In the course of the conversation, Jesus said, "Truly, truly, I say to you, unless one is born of water and the Spirit he cannot enter into the kingdom of God" (John 3:5). In answering Nicodemas, Jesus spoke of new birth by using terms that are associated with the theme of the new covenant in the prophets—water and Spirit. As one example, let us consider the word of the Lord in Ezekiel:

> For I will take you from the nations, gather you from all the lands and bring you into your own land. Then I will sprinkle clean water on you, and you will be clean; I will cleanse you from all your filthiness and from all your idols. Moreover, I will give you a new heart and put a new spirit within you; and I will remove the heart of stone from your flesh and give you a heart of flesh. I will put My Spirit within you and cause you to walk in My statutes, and you will be careful to observe My ordinances (Ezekiel 36:24-27).

Six times in this Ezekiel text the Lord says, "I will." As Jesus told Nicodemas, salvation is from above; it is the work of God and is beyond human achievement. It is almost certain that Jesus had these words from Ezekiel in mind as He spoke with Nicodemas. In the Ezekiel text, as well as throughout Scripture, the Spirit and water are closely associated. In creation the Spirit of God hovered over the waters (Genesis 1:2). This led Tertullian to comment that the waters are the "seat of the Divine Spirit" and "that the Spirit of God, who hovered over (the waters), would continue to linger over the waters of the baptized."[117] During the great Flood, Noah and his family rested safely upon the flood waters in the ark. In 1 Peter, this is interpreted as corresponding to the salvific waters of baptism (1 Peter 3:20-21). As the Israelite slaves were delivered from Egypt, they passed through the waters of the Red Sea and were baptized into Moses.[118] The wilderness generation passed through the waters of the Jordan River to enter the Promised Land (Joshua 3:1ff). Jeremiah refers to the Lord as "the fountain of living waters" (Jeremiah 17:13). Jesus told the Samaritan woman," . . . whoever drinks of the water that I will give him shall never thirst; but the water that I will give him will become in him a well of water springing up to eternal life" (John 4:14). When Jesus said that one must be born of the Spirit and water he was using a well-established tradition that associated the Spirit of God with the life-giving properties of water. So then, is water merely a metaphor for the Spirit? Or, is water, touched by the Spirit, an agent of the Spirit in creation and redemption? When Jesus told Nicodemas that new birth comes by water and the Spirit, did He mean to suggest the waters of baptism? The best way to answer these questions is to see how the early Christians interpreted the words of Jesus in the life of the church.

There can be little doubt that the church of Acts associated water baptism with initial repentance and belief in the Lord Jesus Christ. Peter proclaimed, "Repent, and each of you be baptized in the name of Jesus Christ for the forgiveness of your sins; and you will receive the gift of the Holy Spirit" (Acts 2:38). Throughout Acts, all salvific acts—preaching, healing, exorcising, and baptizing—are done "in the name of Jesus Christ" because the crucified Jesus has been exalted as "Lord and Christ" by God the Father (Acts 2:32-36). Peter insists that ". . . there is no other name under heaven given among men by which we must be saved" (Acts 4:12, NKJV). The "name" represents the authority of the person. To be baptized "in the name of Jesus" affirms His authority over all earthly and spiritual powers. It is also an expression of the believer's submission and allegiance to the lordship of Christ.

---

[117] *The Ante-Nicene Fathers, Vol. III*, 670.
[118] Exodus 14:22, 29; 15:8; Job 4:9; Psalm 78:13; 1 Corinthians 10:1-2.

The early church practiced water baptism because they believed it to be associated with repentance, the forgiveness of sins, and the gift of the Holy Spirit. Repentance is not simply the confession of sin; it must also include presenting oneself for baptism. This is in continuity with the baptism of John the Baptist and the teaching of Jesus. On the Day of Pentecost, about three thousand people responded to Peter's sermon and were promptly baptized (Acts 2:41). At Samaria, Philip baptized "men and women" as they responded to the gospel (Acts 8:12). Later, Philip baptized the Ethiopian eunuch after he confessed, "I believe that Jesus Christ is the Son of God" (Acts 8:26-39). After seeing the risen Christ on the road to Damascus, Saul of Tarsus was baptized, probably by Ananias (Acts 9:10-18). The Gentile converts at Caesarea were baptized at Peter's command (Acts 10:24-48). Lydia and her household were baptized by Paul at Philippi (Acts 16:11-15). Also, the prison guard at Philippi, and his family, were baptized by Paul and Silas after hearing the gospel (Acts 16:25-34). At Corinth, Crispus, the ruler of the synagogue, and many other Corinthians received the Lord and were baptized by Paul (Acts 18:8). At Ephesus, twelve new believers were baptized after hearing the gospel of Jesus Christ (Acts 19:1-5). The example of the church in Acts tells us that the early Christians baptized all new converts. The possibility of repentance without baptism is not considered in the practice of the apostolic church. This suggests that the first Christians believed water baptism to be a significant event in the *way of salvation.*

Because the Acts of the Apostles is a primary source for Pentecostal theology, Pentecostals should be careful to follow the example of the apostolic church in the practice of water baptism. The proper understanding of baptism was one of the issues discussed at the seventh annual General Assembly of the Church of God.

> **Question.** Is water baptism obligatory when one is freed from all evil habits and sanctified?
>
> **Answer.** *Yes, all should be baptized* (italics mine), even if they have been baptized with the Holy Ghost before they were baptized with water. Acts 10:47, 48.

> **Question.** Can the Church of God fellowship one who has not taken on the Lord in baptism?
>
> **Answer.** Water baptism is not a door into the church, and is an act of obedience after one has been converted, hence the fellowship is unbroken, *provided such a one will be baptized at the first opportunity, and not reject the ordinance* (emphasis mine).[119]

This is a significant development when we realize that the moderator of the General Assembly, Bishop A.J. Tomlinson, had a strong Quaker heritage.[120] Quakers reject sacraments in favor of a spiritual baptism, that is, the mystical experience of the "inner light." Bishop Tomlinson was very influential in shaping the theology of the infant Church of God. The Quaker "spiritual baptism" and the Pentecostal baptism in the Holy Spirit could have been understood as corresponding spiritual experiences. Sacraments could have been viewed as unnecessary rituals. However, Pentecostals are committed to the Bible as the rule of faith. In the Bible, the baptism in the Holy Spirit is not a substitute for water baptism. Early Pentecostals were not anti-sacramental. They believed that water baptism is "obligatory" and that all converts should be "baptized at the first opportunity." Tomlinson wrote that a believer could be baptized anytime after conversion, but the scriptural evidence suggested that there was to be "no delay about water baptism after conversion." For Tomlinson, water baptism was "an essential ordinance of righteousness."[121] This conviction was shared by the early members of the Church of God. The *Book of Doctrines,* a book of church order published under the auspices of the General Assembly, suggested that those who did not

---

[119] *General Assembly Minutes 1906-1914: Photographic Reproductions of the First Ten General Assembly Minutes,* (Cleveland, TN: White Wing Publishing House, 1992), 139.

[120] A.J. Tomlinson, "Promptness in Obedience," *Church of God Evangel* (October 6, 1917), 1. Tomlinson offers his testimony of how "I got the veil of Quakerism off me." He said, ". . . I began to study my Bible in earnest. I suddenly found myself one cold day in November face to face with water baptism. I was alone with God, but I fought it out and submitted. I said, 'Lord, this is the first time in life that I have ever seen that your book teaches that everyone must repent and be baptized. I'll obey as quickly as possible."

[121] *Book of Doctrines,* 57-58.

receive water baptism were disobedient to God's Word and would find themselves "in a backslidden condition."[122] This was the sentiment of most early Pentecostals. W.J. Seymour's *The Apostolic Faith* stated that "baptism is not a saving ordinance, but is essential because it is a command of our Lord."[123] Water baptism is so "essential" that it is listed in Seymour's "principles of the doctrine of Christ" which seems to be an early Pentecostal way of salvation.[124] Donald Gee, a prominent Assemblies of God leader, did not view water baptism as necessary for salvation. But he warned that refusal to be baptized was a serious offense "because such an attitude of willful neglect and rebellion reveals a condition of the heart toward God that may make us doubt the possession of that grace, which, through repentance and faith, can alone bring us salvation." Even as Gee denied the salvific effect of water baptism, he affirmed a relationship between water baptism and salvific grace. Also, he admitted that in the primitive church "an unbaptized Christian was unknown and unthought of, and for that reason it was possible to use 'baptized' and being 'in Christ' as synonymous terms."[125] Water baptism was more than "mere form" for early Pentecostals. A.J. Tomlinson spoke of water baptism as a deeply moving, even ecstatic experience:

Oh, if you could realize the sweet thoughts of deeper consecration and devotion as you go down into the water, perhaps with a little burden, and prayer. And the faithful minister taking you by the hand leads you down where there is water deep enough, and lifts his hands toward heaven and says: "In obedience to the command of our Lord and Savior Jesus Christ, I baptize you, my brother, in the Name of the Father, and of the Son, and of the Holy Ghost. Amen!"

And down, down you go, buried with Christ in baptism, but as surely you rise again, the light falls full upon your face. The feeling of consecration is complete, and instead of the

---

[122] *Book of General Instructions for the Ministry and Membership,* 4.
[123] "The Ordinances Taught by Our Lord." *The Apostolic Faith* (September 1907), 2.
[124] *The Apostolic Faith* (October 1907), 4.
[125] Donald Gee, "Baptism and Salvation." *The Pentecostal Evangel* (March 22, 1953) 5, 10-12.

hesitant, just a little burdened and downcast step, all the world seems clothed in the brightness of the sun, the faces of the Christians shine as the firmament, sparkling with the fire of God's Love, for they realize just how you feel—and all seems happiness, you are light as a feather—you have been buried with Christ in baptism in the symbol, and you have risen in newness of life. And about all you can say, is "Glory to God in the highest."[126]

The testimony of early Pentecostals regarding water baptism may be summarized as follows:

- The doctrine of baptismal regeneration was rejected. However,
- Baptism is "essential" or "obligatory" for all new coverts in obedience to the Word of God.
- Failure to follow the Lord in baptism is "willful neglect" and may lead one to apostasy.
- Water baptism can be an ecstatic or spiritual experience, which leads the new believer to "deeper consecration."

We can appreciate the early Pentecostals' careful consideration of water baptism, even if it is sometimes ambiguous. If water baptism is indeed an "obligatory" and "essential" sacrament that leads to "deeper consecration," then we must admit that, in some manner, water baptism is a means of grace. Rodman Williams has written that water baptism is "an act of repentance" that is "immediately related to salvation." It is a "visible and tangible action" which may be a "channel of grace in which the putting off of the old self and the putting on of the new occurs." Further, water baptism is the "physical counterpart" to the spiritual occurrence of union with Christ, but is does not of itself effect union with Christ.[127]

If water baptism is to be understood as an effectual means of grace, we must hear once again the words of Peter: "Repent, *and* . . . be baptized in the name of Jesus" (Acts 2:38). Genuine repentance

---

[126] *Book of Doctrines*, 62-63.
[127] J. Rodman Williams, *Renewal Theology, Volume 3* (Grand Rapids: Zondervan Publishing House, 1992), 224-225.

will be expressed in water baptism, if we follow the biblical model. Both repentance and water baptism must be acts of faith, for faith in Christ is the effectual cause of regeneration. This is affirmed in the writings of the apostle Peter:

> For Christ also died for sins once for all, the just for the unjust, so that He might bring us to God, having been put to death in the flesh, but made alive in the spirit; in which also He went and made proclamation to the spirits now in prison, who once were disobedient, when the patience of God kept waiting in the days of Noah, during the construction of the ark, in which a few, that is, eight persons, were brought safely through the water. Corresponding to that, *baptism now saves you*—not the removal of dirt from the flesh, but an appeal to God for a good conscience—through the resurrection of Jesus Christ (1 Peter 3:18-21, emphasis mine).

Peter insisted that water baptism is, in some manner, salvific. Water baptism is a physical and visible means of grace. Just as the ark was a physical and visible means of grace for the redemption of humanity from the flood, so water baptism is a means of grace for those who have placed their faith in the death and resurrection of Jesus Christ.

"In Christ"

Water baptism is participation "in Christ." According to the apostle Paul, baptism is a paradigm for the believer's participation in the redemptive work of Christ. To be saved is to be "in Christ," and the church is the "body of Christ."[128] In the teaching of Paul, baptism is an important motif for understanding Christ's redemptive work. Paul's audience was familiar with the rite of baptism since most of his hearers had been baptized. Therefore, the analogy between water baptism and being "in Christ" was significant in the early Christian community. In the baptism of John the Baptist, Christ took upon Himself the sins of humanity. Likewise, in water baptism the redeemed participate in Christ's death, burial, and resurrection.

---

[128] Romans 12:5; 1 Corinthians 12:27; Ephesians 4:12.

In water baptism, the believer dies (Romans 6:3). Sharing in the death of Christ is essential to Christian life. Jesus' baptism by John the Baptist anticipated the cross. When believers are baptized "in Christ," they share His cross. Paul proclaimed, "I have been crucified with Christ" (Galatians 2:20). He also wrote that "our old self was crucified with *Him*, in order that our body of sin might be done away with, so that we would no longer be slaves to sin" (Romans 6:6). Death in Christ breaks the power of sin in our mortal bodies. Because the power of sin is broken, death is no longer master over humanity.

The association with the cross and water baptism was not lost on the early Christians. The noncanonical Epistle of Barnabas (second century) states: "Notice how he (the prophet) pointed out the water and cross together. For this is what he means: blessed are those who, having their hope on the cross, descended into the water."[129] Ambrose, the fourth-century Bishop of Milan, asked, "For what is water without the cross of Christ?"[130] Sharing in the death of Christ was more than a metaphor for early Christians. Martyrdom for the sake of the gospel occurred often. Stephen and James were martyred by those who sought to destroy the church (Acts 7:54-60; 12:1-2). The earliest traditions tell us that both Peter and Paul were executed in Rome. By the third century, martyrdom was referred to as the "baptism of blood."[131] Cyprian wrote:

> Let us only who, by the Lord's permission, have given the first baptism to believers, also prepare each one for the second; urging and teaching that this is a baptism greater in grace, more lofty in power, more precious in honor—a baptism wherein angels baptize—a baptism in which God and His Christ exult—a baptism after which no one sins any more —a baptism which completes the increase of our faith—a baptism which, as we withdraw from the world, immediately associates us with God. In the baptism of water

---

[129] *The Apostolic Fathers*, 177.
[130] *The Nicene and Post-Nicene Fathers, Second Series, Vol. X*, 319.
[131] *The Ante-Nicene Fathers, Vol. III*, 636.

is received the remission of sins; in the baptism of blood the crown of virtues.[132]

Apparently, in Cyprian's view "first baptism" (water baptism) antici- pated a "second baptism," the baptism of blood—martyrdom.

Embracing martyrdom seems far removed and alien to many Christians today, especially when compared to the martyrdom often promoted by the followers of radical Islam. The martyrdom of the early Christians was not a tactic of guerilla warfare, but an embracing of the sufferings of Christ the Lord. Paul desired to know Christ in "the fellowship of His sufferings" (Philippians 3:10). This was not lost on early Pentecostal missionaries. In 1920, Mattie Ledbetter, an Assemblies of God missionary to China, wrote the following report:

> The Chinese were all so glad to see us home from the coast and the meetings seem very precious. God pours on the Spirit upon us often in prayer services. Several more profess salvation and are asking for baptism. Water baptism in China certainly means martyrdom, the persecutions are so great.[133]

The German theologian, Dietrich Bonhoeffer issued a profound call to Christian discipleship. He wrote,

> The cross is laid on every Christian. The first Christ- suffering which every man must experience is the call to abandon the attachments of this world. It is that dying of the old man which is the result of his encounter with Christ. As we embark upon discipleship we surrender ourselves to Christ in union with his death—we give over our lives to death. Thus it begins; the cross is not the terrible end to an otherwise god-fearing and happy life, but it meets us at the beginning of our communion with Christ. When Christ calls a man, he bids him, "Come and die."[134]

---

[132] *The Ante-Nicene Fathers, Vol. V,* 497.
[133] "Baptism May Mean Martyrdom," *The Pentecostal Evangel* (November 13, 1920), 9.
[134] Dietrich Bonhoeffer, *The Cost of Discipleship* (New York: Simon and Schus- ter, 1995), 89.

During the years of Hitler's Germany, Bonhoeffer and other German Christians resisted the Nazi government. Many friends encouraged Bonhoeffer to leave Germany, but he refused. He knew he was called to suffer with German Christians during the war. Bonhoeffer taught in illegal seminaries and was a leader in the Confessional Church Movement. He was eventually arrested and accused in a conspiracy to assassinate Hitler. On April 9, 1945, he was executed by hanging at the Nazi concentration camp at Flossenburg. An eye witnesses to his execution, the camp doctor, remarked, "I have hardly ever seen a man die so submissively to the will of God."[135]

In water baptism, the believer is buried with Christ (Romans 6:4). When the lifeless body of the crucified Lord rested in the tomb, the earliest Christian traditions tell us that Jesus descended into Hades. This tradition is supported in the words of 1 Peter: ". . . by whom also He went and preached to the spirits in prison" (3:19, *NKJV*). Hades is the abode of the dead. The descent into Hades establishes that Jesus Christ suffered the totality of human death. Even in death, Jesus "had to be made like His brethren in all things, so that He might become a merciful and faithful High Priest" (Hebrews 2:17). In Hades, Jesus anticipated His resurrection and took possession of the keys of Hades and Death (Revelation 1:18). The power of death cannot be victorious. Water baptism is a real burial that signifies the death of a life corrupted by sin and anticipates resurrection to new life. Burial signifies the reality of death; the old life has passed. In burial, we can take nothing of this present age. The body of corruption fades into dust. Cyril of Jerusalem (fourth century) compared the baptismal pool to the sepulcher in which Christ was buried—a place of dying and being born, both grave and mother.[136] Burial is a transition from this present age to the age to come (Romans 8:18).

In water baptism, the believer shares in the resurrection of Christ, being raised to walk "in newness of life" (Romans 6:4). Death and burial anticipate resurrection. Remember Paul's proclamation: "I have been crucified with Christ; it is no longer I who live, *but Christ*

[135] Edwin Robertson, *The Shame and the Sacrifice* (New York: Macmillian Publishing Company, 1988), 277.
[136] *The Nicene and Post-Nicene Fathers Second Series Vol. VII*, 147.

lives in me" (Galatians 2:20). Being baptized "in Christ" means that believers are in union with Christ. The Holy Spirit and the power of the resurrected Christ are present within all believers. Therefore, believers can anticipate their own resurrection. Paul wrote, "But if the Spirit of Him who raised Jesus from the dead dwells in you, He who raised Christ from the dead will also give life to your mortal bodies through His Spirit who dwells in you" (Romans 8:11). This is the ultimate hope of Christian faith. Christians can joyfully respond to Christ's call to "Come and die" because of the certain hope of eternal life. Water baptism anticipates the "glory that is to be revealed" (Romans 8:18-23). This is why Christian martyrs can face death with joyful anticipation. We find such a witness in the life and martyrdom of Polycarp, a second-century bishop of the church in Smyrna. He was executed by burning with fire in about A.D. 156. The proconsul sought to excuse Polycarp because of his advanced age and encouraged Polycarp to denounce his faith in Christ. Polycarp replied, "For eighty-six years I have been his servant, and he has done me no wrong. How can I blaspheme my king who saved me?"[137] As his hands were being bound in preparation for execution, Polycarp prayed:

> O Lord God Almighty, Father of your beloved and blessed Son Jesus Christ, through whom we have received knowledge of you, the God of angels and powers of all creation, and of the whole race of the righteous who live in your presence, I bless you because you have considered me worthy of this day and hour, that I might receive a place among the number of martyrs in the cup of your Christ, to the resurrection to eternal life, both of soul and of body, in the incorruptibility of the Holy Spirit. May I be received among them in your presence today, as a rich and acceptable sacrifice, as you have prepared and revealed beforehand, and have now accomplished, you who are the undeceiving and true God. For this reason, indeed for all things, I praise you, I bless you, I glorify you, through the eternal and heavenly high priest, Jesus Christ your beloved Son, through who to you

---

[137] *The Apostolic Fathers*, 139.

with him and the Holy Spirit be glory both now and for the ages to come. Amen.[138]

Through the centuries, Christians have found the courage to face the difficulties of life and death because of the hope in Christ that is affirmed in water baptism. In October of 1940, my great grandfather, J.M. Tomberlin, was dying of colon cancer. He had been sick for many months and was often carried into church services on a cot. As he lay on his deathbed at home, he called his children and grandchildren to his bedside. He looked into their faces and said, "Youngins, this religion will do to die by." The many months of pain and suffering caused by cancer did not challenge his faith. This hope is an expression of the baptismal grace of sharing in Christ's resurrection.

Washing

Water baptism is a spiritual bath. Ananias encouraged Saul of Tarsus to be quickly baptized so that his sins could be *washed* away (Acts 22:16). Paul warned the Corinthians that the unrighteous—the sexually immoral, idol worshipers, thieves and liars—will not inherit the kingdom of God. Then Paul proclaimed, "Such were some of you; but you were washed, but you were sanctified, but you were justified in the name of the Lord Jesus Christ and in the Spirit of our God"(1 Corinthians 6:9-11). He wrote to Titus that Christians are saved "by the washing of regeneration and renewing by the Holy Spirit" (Titus 3:5). Later he wrote to the Ephesians that Christ would sanctify and cleanse His church "by the washing of water with the word" (Ephesians 5:26). The writer of Hebrews encourages us to "draw near with a sincere heart in full assurance of faith, having our hearts sprinkled clean from an evil conscience and *our bodies washed with pure water*" (Hebrews 10:22, emphasis mine). Some New Testament scholars suggest that these texts refer not to water baptism, but to a spiritual cleansing which is effected by the Holy Spirit. This ignores the fact that the Holy Spirit is the effective agent in water baptism. It also ignores the fact that water and the Spirit are

---

[138] *The Apostolic Fathers*, 140-141.

closely associated in human salvation throughout the Scriptures. To make a distinction between the salvific activity of the Holy Spirit and water baptism is alien to the thought of the apostles. Nothing in the New Testament suggests that water baptism alone is sufficient for human salvation. There must be repentance and a confession of faith before one is baptized. Tertullian wrote, "That baptismal washing is a sealing of faith, which faith is begun and is commended by the faith of repentance. We are not washed in order that we may cease sinning, but because we have ceased, since in heart we have been bathed already."[139] The "washing of regeneration" is wholly the work of the Holy Spirit. Again, Tertullian wrote,". . . for the Holy Spirit, who is about to come upon us, by the washing away of sins, which faith, sealed in (the name of) the Father, and the Son, and the Holy Spirit, obtains."[140] Tertullian affirms that the "washing away of sins" is obtained by faith through the agency of the Holy Spirit in association with the baptismal waters.

Some early Pentecostals cautiously affirmed the efficacy of water baptism. E.N. Bell wrote that water baptism "certainly does, in some sort of a sense, wash away our sins." He declared that those who denied the need for water baptism were false teachers. Bell then explained the "sense" in which baptism washes away sins: "So then, our sins are actually taken away through the blood of Christ by the power of the Holy Ghost, and they are figuratively washed away in water baptism." For Bell, "figuratively" meant "likeness." In baptism, believers share in the likeness of Christ's death, and also in the likeness of Christ's resurrection (Romans 6:5). Bell denied that the believer shares "in the real and actual death of Jesus Christ" but affirms that the believer rises from the baptismal waters "alive unto God." Bell's explanation here is muddled. It seems that he is suggesting that in baptism believers share "figuratively" in Christ's death, but "actually" in His resurrection. Bell affirmed the primacy of the blood and Spirit in the remission of sin. He does not support the doctrine of baptismal regeneration, but he sought to affirm the efficacy of water baptism, *in some sense,* in the washing away of

---

[139] *The Ante-Nicene Fathers, Vol. III,* 662.
[140] *The Ante-Nicene Fathers, Vol. III,* 672.

sins. For Bell, the sacramental forms of the church represented "the pictures of realities, the symbols of glorious truth."[141]

G.R. Beasley Murray, a Baptist theologian, has written:

> ... baptism cannot be reduced to a bare sign anymore than the cross of Christ can be described as a 'mere symbol'; the sacrament is the meeting of God and man in grace and faith, a spiritual transaction that cannot but have spiritual consequences for one engaged in it.[142]

Water baptism is a sacrament, a means of salvific grace, because it is so closely associated with the work of the Holy Spirit and the death and resurrection of Christ. It is a spiritual bath which looks to the resurrection of the body. We must keep in mind the nature of human salvation. We tend to think in terms of the "salvation of the soul." But the Christian view of human redemption is not limited to the spirit and/or soul. The whole human person—body, soul, and spirit—is redeemed and anticipates resurrection. Yes, the Holy Spirit is the effective agent in the washing of the person. Likewise, the Spirit resting upon the waters is the effective cause in water baptism. Creation reflects an essential and causal relationship between the Spirit and matter. Creation and the Spirit are not closed to each other, but open. We do not have to decide in terms of "either/or," that is, water or the Spirit. Water has its origin in the creative work of the Spirit. We can affirm the concept of "both/and," that is water and the Spirit. Sergius Bulgakov has written, "The world has doors that are open to the spirit, to superphysical action, which, in relation to the limited laws of this world alone, is *miracle*."[143] This is the nature of water baptism. In presenting our bodies for water baptism, we present our whole self—body, soul, and spirit. Salvation is about a clean conscience and pure heart. It is also about our bodies being a temple of the Holy Spirit (1 Corinthians 6:19). Tertullian wrote:

---

[141] E.N. Bell, "Baptized Once for All." *Weekly Evangel* (March 27, 1915), 1, 3.

[142] G.R. Beasley-Murray, *Baptism in the New Testament* (London: Paternoster Press, 1972, 1997), 209.

[143] Sergius Bulgakov, *The Bride of the Lamb* (Grand Rapids: Eerdmans Publishing Co., 2002), 401-402.

> The flesh, indeed, is washed, in order that the soul may
> be cleansed; the flesh is anointed, that the soul may be
> consecrated; the flesh is signed (with the cross), that the
> soul too may be fortified; the flesh is shadowed with the
> imposition of hands, that the soul also maybe illuminated
> by the Spirit; the flesh feeds on the body and blood of
> Christ, that the soul likewise may fatten on its God. They
> cannot then be separated in their recompense, when they
> are united in their service. [144]

The cleansing of the spiritual heart of a person has a sanctifying
effect upon the physical body because spirit, soul, and body are
three components of the human self. Spirit and water are a means
of salvific grace whereby human spirit and body are cleansed so that
the whole human person—body, soul, and spirit—may be a temple
of the Holy Spirit.

BAPTISM IN THE HOLY SPIRIT

Water baptism anticipates the baptism in the Holy Spirit. John
the Baptist spoke of the Messiah as one who would baptize "in the
Holy Spirit and fire" (Matthew 3:11). When John baptized Jesus in
the Jordan River, the heavens opened and the Holy Spirit descended
upon Him. While most English translations describe a peaceful
event, the Greek text describes something altogether different. The
Gospel of Mark records the descent of Spirit upon Jesus with these
words: "And at once, as he was coming up out of the water, he saw
the heavens torn apart and the Spirit, like a dove, descending on
him" (Mark 1:10, *NJB*, emphasis mine). The descent of the Spirit
upon Jesus threatened the stability of the present cosmological
order and anticipated the coming eschatological kingdom. Because
Jesus embodies all humanity, the descent of the Spirit upon Him
at His baptism anticipates the Jerusalem Pentecost event, which
is characterized by a "rushing mighty wind" and "tongues of fire"
(Acts 2:1-4).

---

[144] *The Ante-Nicene Fathers Vol. III*, 551.

In his Pentecost message, the apostle Peter declared that the goal of Christ's redemptive work is "the gift of the Holy Spirit" (Acts 2:38-39). Jesus' crucifixion and resurrection anticipate Pentecost. In the preaching of the apostles, to be saved is to be born of the Spirit. It is the Holy Spirit who makes the blood of Jesus efficacious, regenerates penitent sinners, sanctifies the believer, effects adoption into the family of God, and by whom believers receive glorification.[145] Water baptism is the Christian rite that represents the believer's regeneration by the Spirit and anticipates the fullness of the Spirit. Water baptism alone does not affect the new birth; neither does it confer the Holy Spirit. Cornelius' household received the Spirit with the evidence of speaking in tongues, prior to being baptized in water (Acts 10:44-48). While water baptism should not be minimized, reception of the Spirit is by faith. Peter *commanded* Cornelius and his household to be baptized in water *after* they had received the Spirit. God is free to bestow the Spirit as God wills. In this context, water baptism is a sacramental ritual signifying the church's affirmation of God's saving acts.

The relationship between water baptism and Spirit baptism is clearly demonstrated in Paul's mission at Ephesus.

> He said to them, "Did you receive the Holy Spirit when you believed?" And they said to him, "No, we have not even heard whether there is a Holy Spirit." And he said, "Into what then were you baptized?" And they said, "Into John's baptism." Paul said, "John baptized with the baptism of repentance, telling the people to believe in Him who was coming after him, that is, in Jesus." When they heard this, they were baptized in the name of the Lord Jesus. And when Paul had laid his hands upon them, the Holy Spirit came on them, and they began speaking with tongues and prophesying (Acts 19:2-6).

The promise of Pentecost is "Repent, and each of you be baptized in the name of Jesus Christ for the forgiveness of your sins; and you will receive the gift of the Holy Spirit" (Acts 2:38). The baptism of

---

[145] John 3:5; Romans 8:11-19; 1 Corinthians 6:11; 2 Thessalonians 2:13; Titus 3:5; 1 Peter 1:2.

John the Baptist did not anticipate the gift of Spirit. Because the Ephesian believers had received the baptism of John, they had not received the gift of the Holy Spirit. But John anticipated the One who "is mightier than I . . . . He will baptize you with the Holy Spirit" (Matthew 3:11). For the earliest Christians, the baptism of Jesus in the Jordan River was the paradigm for all Christian baptisms. It was expected that as the believers came up out of the baptismal waters, the Holy Spirit would descend upon them. Christian water baptism was more than a ritual washing; it was an encounter. After the Ephesian believers received water baptism "in the name of Jesus," Paul laid his hands on them and "the Holy Spirit came on them, and they began speaking with tongues." There is an undeniable correspondence between being water baptized in the name of Jesus and receiving the gift of the Holy Spirit.[146]

The relationship between water baptism and Spirit baptism was not lost in the thought of some early Pentecostals. Speaking in reference to the baptism of Jesus, Stanley H. Frodsham wrote:

> The Holy Spirit came down like a dove on Jesus immediately (after) He was baptized, and we should look for every one to receive the like gift immediately (as) they come out of the water. Chrysostom in the 4th century wrote "Whoever was baptized, in apostolic days straightway spake with tongues." This was the initial physical evidence that they had received the baptism of the Holy Ghost.[147]

The Apostolic Faith, the newspaper for the Azusa Street Mission, reported on baptismal services in which the baptismal candidates were Spirit-baptized.

---

[146] P.W. Evans has written that in the apostolic church water baptism "affords the fitting occasion" for reception of Holy Spirit. He writes, "How did the Church arrive at that doctrine? It has been suggested that the prevalence of such evidences of the coming of the Spirit as *glossolalia,* commonly manifested on baptismal occasions, provided the basis for the doctrine." *Sacraments in the New Testament* (London: The Tyndale Press, 1946). Internet: http://www.theologicalstudies.org.uk/pdf/sacraments_evans.pdf

[147] Stanley H. Frodsham, "Baptism," *The Christian Evangel* (28 June 1919), 12. Frodsham's citation from John Chrysostom is probably from *Homilies on the Acts of the Apostles, Homily 24. The Nicene and Post-Nicene Fathers Vol. XI,* 155.

On Thanksgiving Day a baptismal service was held at the
Pentecostal Mission on Maple and Eighth Streets, where
there is a baptistry. Twenty-four were baptized by immersion. The Spirit of God was upon the people. The candidates for baptism were filled with the Spirit and shouted
and praised God as they came out of the water.[148]

Baptismal services took place on the banks of the River
Assimboine at this place 23 persons receiving baptism
by immersion. It was a sacred occasion. The Holy Ghost
witnessed through the speaking in tongues of those who
were baptized.[149]

Likewise, *The Christian Evangel*, the newspaper for the Assemblies
of God, reported on a baptismal service in Ramsey, Illinois:

The last Sunday of the meetings three followed the Lord in
the ordinance of baptism according to Matt. 28:19. The Lord
put his seal of approval on the service by pouring out His
Spirit on the candidates and they could hardly get out of the
water, the power of God was on them in such a wonderful
way.[150]

One believer (probably Homer Tomlinson) testified that his own
experience of water baptism was a powerful and moving Pentecostal
event.

In the year 1908 when I myself was baptized 128 went down
into the water the same day. Without a single exception they
came up beaming with the light of God upon their faces—
and a shout in their hearts, and many broke out in praises,
even speaking in other tongues as on the day of Pentecost,
about which we have studied previously. There is nothing like
obedience to make your soul feel the Pentecostal blessing.
In fact, there have been many instances of which I myself
have heard when those who followed the Lord obediently
in water baptism, were baptized with the Holy Ghost and

---

[148] *The Apostolic Faith* (December 1906), 1.
[149] "Pentecost in Winnipeg, Manitoba." *The Apostolic Faith* (June to September, 1907), 1.
[150] *The Christian Evangel* (July 12, 1919), 15.

began to speak in other tongues as they came up out of the
water—just as Jesus received the Holy Ghost immediately
after He was baptized in Jordan.[151]

Many first-generation Pentecostals experienced Spirit baptism
as they were baptized in water. And, it seems that they expected
this to be normative for all believers.

A second generation Church of God leader, D.C. Boatwright, wrote
that water baptism after repentance is essential if one's salvation is
to be "enjoyed in the fullest measure." Although Boatwright rejected
that water baptism imparted *saving* grace, he insisted that baptism
was essential to "fulfill all righteousness," that is, to be obedient
to the command of Christ. It could be inferred that Boatwright,
with his contemporaries, understood water baptism in terms of
sanctifying grace. If the new convert was to enjoy salvation in its
fullest measure—sanctification and Spirit baptism—then the new
convert must walk in obedience to the Scriptures and be baptized in
water. Full obedience to God's Word is where "the Christian's power
lies." Further, Boatwright suggested a correspondence between water
baptism and Spirit baptism. He said, "I honestly believe that one
reason so many find it difficult to receive the baptism with the Holy
Ghost is because they have not taken this profound truth seriously
enough." In his view, submission to water baptism as an act of
obedience was, in some manner, preparatory for Spirit baptism.[152]

There is a rich tradition in the early church that links reception
of the *charismata* to water baptism. Building upon the theology
of Justin and Irenaeus before him, the third-century theologian
Tertullian believed water baptism to be a charismatic event. Just as
the Holy Spirit hovered over the waters of creation, the Spirit rests
upon the baptismal waters of new creation, awaiting the penitent
sinner.[153] He wrote:

---

[151] *Book of Doctrines*, 60.
[152] D.C. Boatwright, "Water Baptism," *Church of God Evangel* (22 October 1949), 8.
[153] *The Ante-Nicene Fathers, Vol. III*, 670.

> Therefore, you blessed ones, for whom the grace of God is waiting, when you come up from the most sacred bath of the new birth, when you spread out your hands for the first time in your mother's house with your brethren, ask your Father, ask your Lord, for the special gift of his inheritance, the distributed charisms, which form an additionally underlying feature [of baptism]. Ask, he says, and you shall receive. In fact, you have sought, and you have found: you have knocked, and it has been opened to you.[154]

Commenting on Tertullian's statement Kilian McDonnell has written:

> The most obvious sense of the words indicated that, at least for some of the neophytes, there is some observable phenomena, something experiential, perhaps the first expression of a charism, which leads the onlooker to conclude that prayer has been answered. Tertullian is not speaking in a vacuum. The presence and exercise of the charisms is a fact of ecclesial life in the second and third centuries.[155]

The "distributed charisms" of which Tertullian speaks correspond to the inventory of spiritual gifts offered by the prophet Isaiah (11:1-3) and the apostle Paul (1 Corinthians 12:8-11). Tertullian taught that the presence of the *charismata* within the church is essential to establish Christian authenticity. These early charismatic theologians believed that there is a vital link between water baptism and the fullness of Spirit. Tertullian wrote, ". . . not that in the waters we obtain the Holy Spirit, but in the water . . . we are cleansed, and prepared for the Holy Spirit . . . for the Holy Spirit, who is about to come upon us."[156] The baptismal waters have a sanctifying effect in preparing the believer for the reception of the Holy Spirit, "who is about to come upon us." This is what happened when Paul preached at Ephesus—new believers were baptized in the Spirit shortly after

---

[154] Tertullian, *On Baptism*, 20. Translation by Kilian McDonnell, *Christian Initiation and Baptism in the Holy Spirit: Evidence from the First Eight Centuries* (Collegeville, MN: The Liturgical Press, 1991), 98.
[155] McDonnell, *Christian Initiation and Baptism in the Holy Spirit*, 104.
[156] *The Ante-Nicene Fathers, Vol. III*, 672.

being baptized in water (Acts 19:5). The words of Jesus in Mark's Gospel suggest that "signs" may be associated with water baptism.

> He who has believed and has been baptized shall be saved; but he who has disbelieved shall be condemned. These signs will accompany those who have believed: in My name they will cast out demons, they will speak with new tongues; they will pick up serpents, and if they drink any deadly poison, it will not hurt them; they will lay hands on the sick, and they will recover" (Mark 16:16-18).

We must keep in mind that water baptism anticipates baptism in the Holy Spirit in the *way of salvation*. Pentecostals have long affirmed that signs follow baptized believers, specifically tongues speech. Frank Macchia has suggested that tongues speech is a sacrament in which the believer encounters God through an experience that is "unmediated and direct." Tongues speech is a "visible/audible" sacramental sign that accents the "free, dramatic, and unpredictable move of the Spirit of God." As a sacramental sign, tongues speech is "theophanic," that is, it points to "a church life characterized by a fervent expectation for the signs and wonders of God's Spirit." Macchia presents tongues speech as the primary sacrament in Pentecostal Christianity.[157] Following Macchia, Kenneth Archer has suggested that tongues speech should be considered a sacramental sign which corresponds to Spirit baptism. Spirit baptism is a sacrament of charismatic empowerment which is often marked by "ecstatic praise and compassionate weeping for the lost and hurting." As a sacramental sign, "tongues is the expression of the mystical experience of union with and participation in God's triune being."[158]

Water baptism and Spirit baptism are related salvific experiences in the *way of salvation*, but they are not concomitant. As we have seen, Spirit baptism may precede water baptism as an event in time. A believer may be baptized in the Spirit upon rising out of the

---

[157] Frank D. Macchia, "Tongues as a Sign: Towards a Sacramental Understanding of Pentecostal Experience," *Pneuma: The Journal of the Society for Pentecostal Studies*, 15, 1 (Spring 1993) 61-76.
[158] Archer, "Nourishment for our Journey," 79-96.

baptismal waters as Tertullian suggested. But just as regeneration and Spirit baptism are distinct experiences in the way of salvation, so is water baptism and Spirit baptism. Water baptism anticipates Spirit baptism; and it may serve an as analogy for Spirit baptism. But water baptism is not Spirit baptism.

Church Membership

Most Pentecostals do not view water baptism as a "door into the church." This demonstrates the disconnect between soteriology and ecclesiology that is prominent in most Evangelical and Pentecostal churches. As we have discussed earlier, if life in the church is to be meaningful in the Pentecostal *way of salvation,* then Pentecostals must allow for a causal relationship in repentance, new birth, water baptism, and church membership. Early adherents of the Church of God believed water baptism and church membership to be essential in the "divine order" of salvation. J.L. Thornhill wrote:

> The expression born into the kingdom; baptized into the body; then joined or added to the church is divine order. . . It was an apostolic practice in the early church.[159]

The church teaches, nourishes, supports, and graciously disciplines believers so that believers may be properly discipled. Membership in the church must be understood as the ongoing sanctification of the believer in the *way of salvation.*

In Acts, we find that repentance, water baptism, and membership in the church are significant and interrelated events in the *way of salvation.* "So then, those who had received his word were baptized; and that day there were added about three thousand souls" (Acts 2:41). The church is the fellowship of the baptized. Baptism is the sacramental sign through which believers enter. Water baptism incorporates the believer into the body of Christ which is the church—a single body with many members (1 Corinthians 12:14, 20, 27). Christ himself is the head of the body (Ephesians 4:15; 5:23). To be outside of the church is to be outside of the body of

---

[159] J.L. Thornhill, "The Church of God – The Pillar and Ground of the Truth," *The Church of God Evangel* (April 28, 1923), 1.

Christ. Paul wrote, "For by one Spirit we were all baptized into one body—whether Jews or Greeks, whether slaves or free—and we were all made to drink of one Spirit" (1 Corinthians 12:13). One might object that Paul here is speaking of Spirit baptism, not water baptism. But we have already observed that throughout the New Testament, the Holy Spirit is the effective agent in water baptism and that water baptism anticipates Spirit baptism. In this context, Paul is referring to Spirit-infused water baptism. Further, water baptism is participation "in Christ," and the church is the "body of Christ." Paul often uses the Greek verb *baptizo* to speak of water baptism and Spirit baptism because the two are related experiences in the *way of salvation*. The pledge of water baptism is fulfilled in Spirit baptism. Since water baptism corresponds to membership in the body of Christ, we must define the church.

The church is a community in covenant with God bound together by a common confession and encounter that Jesus Christ is Lord. The foundation of the Christian faith is the confession of Peter: "You are the Christ" (Mark 8:29). It is this confession of faith that is the basis of human salvation.

> If you confess with your mouth Jesus as Lord, and believe in your heart that God raised Him from the dead, you will be saved (Romans 10:9).

> And we know that the Son of God has come, and has given us understanding so that we may know Him who is true; and we are in Him who is true, in His Son Jesus Christ. This is the true God and eternal life(1 John 5:20).

The earliest creedal statements of the Christian church were baptismal confessions. The earliest baptismal confession is recorded by Luke:

> Now as they went down the road, they came to some water. And the eunuch said, "See, here is water. What hinders me from being baptized?" Then Philip said, "If you believe with all your heart, you may." And he answered and said, *"I believe that Jesus Christ is the Son of God"* (Acts 8:36-37, NKJV).

The confession "Jesus is Lord" is inspired by the Holy Spirit. When Peter confessed, "You are the Christ," Jesus responded, "Blessed are you, Simon Barjona, because flesh and blood did not reveal this to you, but My Father who is in heaven" (Matthew 16:17). Paul wrote, ". . . no one can say that 'Jesus is Lord' except by the Holy Spirit" (1 Corinthians 12:3). This confession is the life-seed of the church. From this confession all spiritual life springs forth.

By the beginning of the third century, the church developed formal baptismal creeds that were to be affirmed by the baptismal candidate. The following baptismal creed is from *The Apostolic Traditions* of Hippolytus.

> When each of them to be baptized has gone down into the water, the one baptizing shall lay hands on each of them, asking, "Do you believe in God the Father Almighty?" And the one being baptized shall answer, "I believe." He shall then baptize each of them once, laying his hand upon each of their heads.
>
> Then he shall ask, "Do you believe in Jesus Christ, the Son of God, who was born of the Holy Spirit and the Virgin Mary, who was crucified under Pontius Pilate, and died, and rose on the third day living from the dead, and ascended into heaven, and sat down at the right hand of the Father, the one coming to judge the living and the dead?" When each has answered, "I believe," he shall baptize a second time.
>
> Then he shall ask, "Do you believe in the Holy Spirit and the Holy Church and the resurrection of the flesh?" Then each being baptized shall answer, "I believe." And thus let him baptize the third time.[160]

The purpose of this type of baptismal creed is to form a binding covenant between two parties, in this case, a covenant of faith. This practice has its precedent in ancient Roman contractual law.[161] When the baptismal candidate answers, "I believe," to the questions

---

[160] Hippolytus, *The Apostolic Tradition*, 21.12-18. Translation by Kevin P. Edgecomb. Internet: http://www.bombaxo.com/hippolytus.html.
[161] Hippolytus, *On The Apostolic Tradition*, Translation by Alistair Stewart-Sykes, 121-122.

of faith, the candidate makes a public affirmation that the faith and teaching of the church is accepted. This is a binding covenant between the candidate and the church.

The church is a visible communion. Being baptized into the body of Christ—the church—is more than a "mystical" or "spiritual" reality. Water baptism is a visible event that signifies being incorporated into the visible church. There can be no church without humans who have made the confession that "Jesus Christ is Lord." Jesus said, "For where two or three have gathered together in My name, I am there in their midst" (Matthew 18:20). This is a visible gathering of worshiping believers. The church is to be a witness to the world. The church is how the world *sees* Christ. Jesus said, "By this all men will know that you are My disciples, if you have love for one another" (John 13:35). Christian love is demonstrated by visible acts of mercy to the hungry, poor, strangers, and prisoners (Matthew 25:31-46). The church is a divine-human institution, a living body that exists as a visible reality in this world.

The church is a visible community that exists as a single corporate entity with a diversity of members. The church is comprised of male and female, Gentile and Jew, and rich and poor. In this diverse community there is to be no distinction.[162] This is a testimony to the unity of humanity in Christ. However, we must admit that the church has not always demonstrated this unity. If we carefully examine ourselves, we will find that too often we have been a divided community. Paul warned against the church's tendency to be schismatic. The Corinthian believers were divided by their allegiance to charismatic church leaders and by economic class(1 Corinthians 1:10-15; 10:18-22). Paul insisted that these divisions do not reflect the essential unity of the church as the one body of Christ. Of course, the Corinthian church has not been the only church to suffer schism. The conflicts between the Catholics and the Montanists of the third century, the East and West of the eleventh century, and the Catholics and Protestants of the sixteenth century, all serve as

---

[162] Acts 15:6-9; Romans 10:12; Galatians 3:28; James 2:1-4.

reminders that the church has failed to demonstrate unity. This is in spite of our Lord's prayer for the unity of His church:

> I do not ask on behalf of these alone, but for those also who believe in Me through their word; that they may all be one; even as You, Father, are in Me and I in You, that they also may be in Us, so that the world may believe that You sent Me. The glory which You have given Me I have given to them, that they may be one, just as We are one; I in them and You in Me, that they may be perfected in unity, so that the world may know that You sent Me, and loved them, even as You have loved Me (John 17:20-23).

The church is an egalitarian community. Water baptism affirms the universal priesthood of all believers. Water baptism is the primary sacrament of the church. All believers come to Christ in the same manner: by a call from the Holy Spirit and through the waters of baptism. As the primary sacrament, all members of the church, whether bishops or laity, enter through the same door. Tertullian advised that water baptism should be administered with the permission of the bishop and with great reverence. But he also insisted that, ". . . even laymen have the right; for what is equally received can be equally given . . . baptism, which is equally God's property, can be administered by all."[163] Water baptism is an egalitarian sacrament—the common experience and confession of all believers. Early Pentecostals embraced this sentiment.

Even as Tertullian insisted that laypersons can administer the rite of baptism, he also insisted that the episcopal leadership of the church should be honored. Within the egalitarian community God, through Christ and the Spirit, has established leaders to serve the church. This is a functional hierarchy. The leaders of the church are the bishops, pastors, elders, and deacons who fulfill the ministry of apostles, prophets, pastors, teachers, and evangelists. These offices and ministries are God's gifts to the church. The Holy Spirit distributes the gifts according to God's will. God calls and empowers ministers to guide the church. The church discerns and affirms the

---

[163] *The Ante-Nicene Fathers, Vol. III*, 677.

ministry gifts through ordination. The leaders serve by teaching and guiding the church as shepherds. Submission to ordained leaders is an essential spiritual discipline in the life of the church.[164]

Because water baptism corresponds with church membership in the *way of salvation,* pastors and church leaders should insist that those who present themselves for baptism likewise join the church; and those who seek church membership should be baptized. Christian practice should be a reflection of Christian theology.

Discipleship

In commissioning His apostles, Jesus established baptism as the initiation rite for those answering His call to salvation and discipleship (Matthew 28:19-20). Jesus said, "He who has believed and has been baptized shall be saved; but he who has disbelieved shall be condemned" (Mark 16:16). Believing and baptism are faith responses to the call of salvation. They are the initial salvific experiences along the *way of salvation.* The way of salvation also includes being a disciple. The Greek word *mathetes* literally means "learner." To be a disciple is to be instructed in the faith. In commissioning His apostles, Jesus said:

> "Go therefore and *make disciples* of all the nations, *baptizing them* in the name of the Father and the Son and the Holy Spirit, *teaching them* to observe all that I commanded you; and lo, I am with you always, even to the end of the age" (Matthew 28:19-20, emphasis mine).

Disciple-making requires "baptizing them" *and* "teaching them."

Early in the history of the Christian church, converts were required to prepare for baptism through a series of spiritual disciplines, such as fasting, prayer, and instruction in the Faith. *The Teaching of the Lord to the Gentiles by the Twelve Apostles,* or the Didache, is a first-century baptismal manual used to instruct new converts in the Faith and guide church elders in the proper observance of sacraments. The appearance of the Didache coincides

---

[164] 2 Thessalonians 3:14; Hebrews 3:17; 1 Peter 2:13.

with the inclusion of Gentiles within the Christian church. According to the Acts of the Apostles, the inclusion of the Gentiles was a controversial issue and led to the Jerusalem Council (Acts 15). The leaders of this council, under direction of the Holy Spirit, determined that Gentile converts were not required to submit to a "double conversion," that is, from paganism to Judaism, and then from Judaism to Christianity. Although this decision affirms the universal nature of Christ's redemptive work, it posed a challenge to the church. Jewish converts accepted Christ in the framework of the Messianic expectations of Judaism, so the practice of immediately baptizing Jewish converts was not problematic. However, most Gentile converts seeking membership in the Christian church were not familiar with the theological and ethical traditions of the Old Testament. Gentiles converted to Christ from pagan and idolatrous cultures. Pagan religious practices included temple prostitution and eating meat consecrated to idols.[165] Also, the sexual ethics of the Hellenistic world were contrary to the sexual ethics of the Old Testament. Homosexuality, incest, and abortion were almost unheard of in Jewish culture, but they were common practices in pagan cultures. In order to address these moral issues, the Didache contained prohibitions not found in the New Testament.

> The second commandment of the teaching is: You shall not murder; you shall not commit adultery; you shall not corrupt boys; you shall not be sexually promiscuous; you shall not steal; you shall not practice magic; you shall not engage in sorcery; you shall not abort a child or commit infanticide.[166]

The church elders who composed the Didache found it necessary to take a clear stand on such issues. Therefore, immediate baptism of pagan converts became problematic. Consequently, an extensive ethical and theological instruction process was established. Through this teaching protocol, pagan converts could experience transformation by "the renewing of [their] minds" (Romans 12:2), which in

---

[165] Acts 15:29; 21:25; 1 Corinthians 6:15-16; 10:28; 15:29.
[166] *The Apostolic Fathers*, 150.

effect gave birth to a Christian counterculture. For these believers, Christian baptism was initiation into a new way of life, a new community, a new culture, and a new age (2 Corinthians 5:17).

Pentecostals should give serious consideration to a structured pre-baptismal training for converts. As converts enter the church from a postmodern or non-Christian culture, they will need instruction in the faith to establish a firm foundation. The church faces a present danger. There is a high rate of Biblical illiteracy among adults. Most Christians do not have adequate knowledge about their faith to be able to discern truth from fiction. Nor can they defend orthodox doctrines about Jesus Christ against onslaughts from cults or other religions. The divorce rate among evangelical marriages is not significantly different than that of non-church families. Our young people are being influenced and nurtured by a pop culture that celebrates sexual immorality, self-indulgence, and extravagance. The church may be facing a crisis of faith in which our children forget the Lord (Judges 3:7; 1 Samuel 12:9).

Developing a structured program of discipleship training will be a challenge for a Pentecostal culture which favors spontaneity and resists formal education. Pentecostals should affirm that Christian discipleship begins with an initial sanctifying *encounter* and continues in a sanctifying *process.* This sanctifying process is the nurture of the church. Believers are sanctified by the Holy Spirit, the blood of Christ, and the Word of God. To be educated in the theology and ethics of the Christian faith is a sanctifying process. The church as a Spirit-formed and Spirit-filled community is endowed with Spirit-inspired teachers for this very purpose. Spirit-inspired teachers assure the transformation and acculturation of new believers in the church. Justin Martyr (second century) said, "For instruction leads to faith, and faith with baptism is trained by the Holy Spirit."[167] If the church fails in this ministry, there is high probability that water baptism will become a formal rite rather than a transforming encounter.

---

[167] *The Ante-Nicene Fathers, Vol. II,* 217.

The Baptismal Formula

Early Pentecostal proclamation was Christocentric. Jesus Christ is Savior, Sanctifier, Healer, Spirit Baptizer, and soon coming King. As is often the case in renewal movements, early enthusiasm can lead to the development of questionable, even heretical theology. During the formative years of the movement, Pentecostalism was threatened by a major theological controversy. After the Azusa Street revival, some leaders began espousing a "new issue" relating to the use of Jesus' name. Because miracles were being performed "in Jesus name," it was suggested water baptism should also be performed in the name of Jesus only. Proponents of this practice looked to scriptural examples in Acts.

- Repentant sinners are saved and baptized in the name of Jesus (Acts 2:38; 8:12, 16; 10:48; 16:31; 19:5).
- Believers received the gift of the Holy Spirit in the name of Jesus (Acts 2:38).
- The sick are healed in the name of Jesus (Acts 3:6, 16; 4:10, 30).
- Demons are exorcised in the name of Jesus (Acts 16:18).
- Believers were persecuted for the name of Jesus (Acts 5:40; 15:26; 21:13).
- Christians worshiped in the name of Jesus (Acts 19:17).

This led to a "new revelation" concerning the nature of God. According to those labeled "oneness" Pentecostals, the names "Father, Son, and Spirit" did not represent three eternally distinct persons who share one divine essence, but a threefold manifestation of one divine being. While it appeared to be a "new issue," it was nothing more than a revival of a third-century heresy known as "modalism." Modalism denies that God exists eternally as Father, Son, and Spirit. Rather, through the ages, God is revealed in various temporary modes. The scope of this book prohibits a full discussion of the many theological implications of this controversy. Therefore, discussion will be limited to the significance of Trinitarian baptism, "Father, Son and Spirit," as opposed to baptism in the name of Jesus or "Jesus only."

Pentecostals should insist upon the Trinitarian baptismal formula, because it is supported by the earliest Christian documents. Although apostolic ministry was done "in the name of Jesus Christ," it was not at the exclusion of the Father and the Holy Spirit. Jesus Christ is affirmed as Son and Savior by the Father and the Spirit through miracles, the greatest of which is the resurrection.[168] The Spirit is the "promise of the Father" and is given through the Son.[169] Salvation is consistently presented in terms of Trinitarian redemptive activity.[170]

The Trinitarian baptismal formula is preferred in order that the Father, Son, and the Holy Spirit are equally glorified in human redemption. The Trinitarian baptismal formula dates from the earliest Christian documents, both canonical and noncanonical. The Trinitarian formula found in the Didache is identical with that given by Jesus in Matthew.

Matthew 28:19	Didache 7:1
Go therefore and make disciples of all the nations, *baptizing them in the name of the Father and of the Son and of the Holy Spirit...*	And concerning baptism, baptize as follows: after you have reviewed all these things, *baptize into the name of the Father, and of the Son, and of the Holy Spirit...*[1]

This leads some scholars to suggest that Matthew and the Didache are dependant upon an earlier liturgical source. Further, in the writings of the church fathers and the Protestant reformers, there is a unanimous witness to the use of the Trinitarian baptismal formula, which suggests there was never an *orthodox* alternative.

Pentecostals should insist upon the Trinitarian baptismal formula, because it affirms the deity of Jesus Christ. In early Jewish

---

[168] Acts 2:22-24, 32, 36; 3:15, 18, 21-22, 26; 4:10; 5:30-32; 7:55-56; 10:34-43; 13:30, 36-37; Matthew 3:16-17; 17:5; John 12:28; Romans 1:4; 1 Peter 3:18.

[169] Luke 11:13; John 14:26; 15:26; Acts 1:4; 2:17, 33; 15:8; Galatians 4:6; Ephesians 4:7, 11; Titus 3:4-6.

[170] Matthew 28:19; Romans 1:1-4; 2 Corinthians 13:14; Ephesians 2:18; 2 Thessalonians 2:13-14; Hebrews 9:14; 1 Peter 1:12; 3:18.

Christianity, the deity of the Father and the Spirit was assumed, even if the personal distinctions between them were not. The inclusion of "and of the Son" in the early baptismal creed was an effort to insist upon the deity of Jesus and His ontological equality with God the Father. The early theologians affirmed the dogma of the Holy Trinity in order to protect Jewish monotheism, as well as offer an explanation as to how Jesus, the son of Mary, could also exist eternally as God the Son. Oneness Pentecostalism denies the eternal sonship of Christ, which also ultimately denies His personal distinction as God the Son. In effect, the "hyper-Christology" of oneness Pentecostalism actually denies the essential nature of the Incarnation as the permanent union between God and humanity. D.A. Reed has written,

> Oneness theology generally teaches that the sonship, being human, will cease in the eschaton. With the mediatorial work of Christ completed, he will return to the form in which he existed prior to the creation, or simply be known as the Almighty God. The humanity and sonship ultimately become dispensable in order that Christ may ultimately reign as the Lord of Glory. The Trinitarian doctrine of eternal differentiation between Father and Son is replaced by a functional and temporal sonship.[171]

Pentecostals should insist upon the Trinitarian baptismal formula, because it affirms the deity and personal distinction of the Holy Spirit. In the modalist theology of "oneness" Pentecostalism, the personal distinction and deity of the Holy Spirit is diminished. The ontological equality of the Spirit with the Father and the Son is vitally important in redemption. The Spirit effected the Incarnation (Matthew 1:18, 20; Luke 1:35); anointed and empowered Jesus for His messianic ministry (Matthew 3:16; Luke 3:22; 4:1); was active in the resurrection of Jesus (Romans 8:11); and proceeds from the Father and from (or through) the Son (John 14:26; 15:26; Acts 2:33). Through the redemptive activity of the Holy Spirit, penitent

---

[171] *The New International Dictionary of Pentecostal and Charismatic Movements,* s.v. "Oneness Pentecostalism."

sinners receive the full blessing of salvation.[172] The Spirit creates the redemptive community (2 Corinthians 13:14). If the Holy Spirit is less than God, then Jesus, the child of Mary, is less than God, and the whole economy of redemption is without effect.

The question Pentecostal pastors should ask is, "Should those who have been baptized 'in the name of Jesus' be rebaptized 'in the name of the Father, and of the Son, and of the Holy Spirit?'" Ambrose wrote that unless the believer "be baptized in the Name of the Father, and of the Son, and of the Holy Spirit, he cannot receive remission of sins nor gain the gift of spiritual grace."[173] John of Damascus wrote, ". . . those who were not baptized into the Holy Trinity, these must be baptized again."[174] However, Ursinus, a fifth century monk, suggested that the rebaptism of those "who have been baptized either in the name of Christ alone or in the name of the Father and of the Son and of the Holy Spirit" is unnecessary.[175] Baptism "in the name of Jesus" is attested in the Acts of the Apostles as a biblical baptismal formula. Although it is not universally recognized as orthodox, it should not be labeled as heretical. The Christology of the "oneness" Pentecostals reflects a variation of ancient heresies. But we should remember that throughout Christian history "men have been frequently condemned for denying the deity of Christ, but rarely for denying the distinction between the Father and the Son."[176] However, the theological implications are numerous and very problematic. If water baptism is to properly reflect the Trinitarian economy of salvation as revealed in the New Testament and confessed by the church, the Trinitarian baptismal formula is to be preferred. Furthermore, the Trinitarian baptismal formula is preferred because it is universally recognized and witnesses to the unity of the church.

---

[172] Romans 5:5; 8:2, 14-15; 1 Corinthians 6:11; Galatians 5:22-23; Ephesians 1:13; 3:16; 2 Thessalonians 2:13; Titus 3:5; Hebrews 6:4; 9:14; 1 Peter 1:2.
[173] *The Nicene and Post-Nicene Fathers, Second Series, Vol. X*, 319.
[174] *The Nicene and Post-Nicene Fathers, Second Series, Vol. IX*, 78.
[175] *The Nicene and Post-Nicene Fathers, Second Series, Vol. III*, 391.
[176] Arthur C. McGiffert, quoted by Jaroslav Pelikan in *The Emergence of the Catholic Tradition* (Chicago: The University of Chicago Press, 1971), 182.

Some early Pentecostals sought to remain faithful to the teaching of Holy Scriptures and embrace both baptismal formulas. In a response to the "Jesus only" controversy, E.N. Bell wrote that there are "scriptural varieties" of the baptismal formula and that any scriptural formula is proper as long as it is "done in good faith" and not to the exclusion of other biblical formulas.[177] The *Book of Doctrines,* published by the Church of God, offers two baptism formulas to be used by ministers.

> In obedience to the command of our Lord and Savior Jesus Christ, I now baptize you, my brother, in the name of the Father, and of the Son, and of the Holy Ghost. Amen.

> Upon your confession of faith in the Lord Jesus Christ, I now baptize you, Brother Davis, in the name of the Father, and of the Son, and of the Holy Ghost.[178]

Finally, when a pastor is presented with the question of rebaptism, the teaching and preference of the church should be considered. For example, the official position of the Church of God is that water baptism administered by other churches should be accepted as valid "provided they have been baptized in the name of the Father, and of the Son, and of the Holy Ghost."[179]

The Mode of Water Baptism

The Greek word *baptízō* (to baptize) has its root in the word *bápto* which means "to dip in or under," "to dye," "to immerse," "to sink," "to drown," "to bathe," and/or "wash." From the Biblical language, there can be little doubt that the proper mode of water baptism is immersion. Further, since water baptism is participation in the death, burial, and resurrection of Jesus Christ, the physical and visual impact of complete immersion in water suggest it to be the normative mode.[180]

---

[177] E.N. Bell, "Scriptural Varieties on Baptismal Formula." *Weekly Evangel* (July 3, 1915), 1.
[178] *Book of Doctrines,* 65.
[179] *Minutes of the 71st General Assembly of the Church of God* (Cleveland, TN: Pathway Press, 2006), 82.
[180] Not all Pentecostals insisted on immersion. *The Discipline of the Pentecostal Holiness Church* (1908) stated, "All candidates for baptism shall have the right of choice

The earliest noncanonical reference we have to the mode of water baptism is found in the Didache.

> Now concerning baptism, baptize as follows: after you have reviewed all these things, baptize "in the name of the Father and of the Son and of the Holy Spirit" in running water. But if you have no running water, then baptize in some other water; and if you are not able to baptize in cold water, then do so in warm. But if you have neither, then pour water on the head three times "in the name of the Father and Son and Holy Spirit."[181]

Commenting on this text, Aaron Milavec makes the following observations: First, total immersion is preferred. Second, in cases where there was not sufficient water for immersion, pouring water over the head is sufficient. The action of the water flowing down over the body approximated "running waters." Finally, pouring water over the head "three times" suggests that the baptismal candidate is soaked.[182]

There is continuity in the practice of baptism in the Didache (first century) with that in *The Apostolic Tradition* (third century). The practices of invoking the Trinitarian formula and threefold immersion remain fixed in the early centuries of the church. However, these early traditions allow for alternative modes of baptism when there is not sufficient water for immersion.

On occasion, I have been asked to perform baptisms where immersion was not practical. The first such occasion occurred when a paraplegic man asked to be baptized. Not only was he paralyzed from the waist down, but he was a rather large individual. As we discussed how to accommodate his desire to be baptized, I suggested pouring water over his head. He replied, "Pastor, that's fine. But I want to get really wet." On the designated Sunday morning, he came forward to the altar in his wheelchair. We anointed him with oil, and prayed for him. Then, after saying the Trinitarian formula for

---

between the modes of baptism as practiced by the various evangelical denominations." The *Discipline* allowed for immersion and sprinkling (13-14, 27-29).
[181] *The Apostolic Fathers*, 153.
[182] Aaron Milavec, *The Didache: Faith, Hope, and Life of the Earliest Christian Communities, 50-70 C.E.*, (New York: The Newman Press, 2003), 264.

baptism, I poured a large pitcher of water over his head, getting him thoroughly wet. As the water flowed over his body, he lifted his hands and began to offer spontaneous praises to God.

On another occasion, I was asked to baptize an elderly lady as she was dying in a hospital bed. She was over eighty years old when she became a Christian. About six months after conversion, she became sick with pneumonia. As I visited her in the hospital one day, she said, "Pastor, you know I've never been baptized. I want to be baptized before I die." I knew that she would not survive her illness. She did not have the strength to sit up in bed. I took a cup of water and poured it over her forehead speaking the names of the Holy Trinity. She responded with a smile. Just two days later, on Christmas Eve, she passed into eternity.

Even as we are committed to immersion as the proper mode for water baptism, pastors should be open to other modes when immersion is not practical. For those who might object, I remind them of the thief on the cross. With no opportunity to receive baptism, Jesus promised that the thief would enter Paradise. This biblical example, along with the early tradition of the church, suggests that when necessary there is some freedom in baptismal practices.

POSTBAPTISMAL SIN

By the fourth century, it became common for believers to postpone baptism until just before death. Baptism was understood to be the rite of initiation and was to be administered only once. Should a believer fall into sin, rigorous rites of penance were required for the remission of sin. Some Christians, following Hebrews 6:1-6, believed that there could be no forgiveness for postbaptismal sins. Baptism just before death assured these believers of their righteous standing before God.

Other situations arose that caused many to ponder whether believers should be baptized more than once. Should believers who lapsed during persecution be rebaptized when returning to the faith? If a believer is baptized by a schismatic bishop or priest, should that believer be rebaptized by a bishop in good standing with the church catholic? Cyprian insisted that those who had received baptism from a heretic should receive the true baptism that can be given only by the one true church. But he did not consider this to be a rebaptism, for there can be only one true baptism administered by the one true church.[183] Augustine suggested that baptism administered by a priest or bishop who is ordained in proper apostolic succession is valid even if the officiating minister has become a heretic and schismatic. He wrote:

> It is not the Christian sacraments, but the crime of schism, which makes you a heretic . . . . For from the Catholic Church are all the sacraments of the Lord, which you hold and administer in the same way as they were held and administered even before you went forth from her. The fact, however, that you are no longer in that Church from which proceeded the sacraments which you have, does not make it the less true that you still have them. You are at one with us in baptism, in creed, and in the other sacraments of the Lord. But in the spirit of unity and bond of peace, in a word, in the Catholic Church itself, you are not with us.[184]

Augustine insisted that the validity of the sacrament is in the high priesthood of Christ rather than in the personal holiness of the minister. For Augustine, to suggest that a heretic, schismatic, or apostate should be rebaptized when returning to the true church is itself heretical because it implies that the high priesthood of Jesus Christ is insufficient. In fact, rebaptism has been generally opposed by the church throughout the centuries.

Some Pentecostals hold to a different view. When Jesus rebuked the church at Ephesus for falling from their "first love" he challenged them to "Remember therefore from where you have fallen; repent and do the first works" (Revelation 2:5, NKJV). This is interpreted to mean that when a believer falls into a "season of sinfulness," or apostasy; restoration into fellowship with Christ requires rebaptism. Water baptism is among the "first works." This seems to be a hermeneutical stretch. There is no explicit suggestion in the New Testament that a believer who has fallen into sin should be rebaptized. Throughout

---

[183] *The Ante-Nicene Fathers, Vol. V,* 379ff.
[184] *The Nicene and Post-Nicene Fathers, Vol. I,* 398.

church history, water baptism has always been understood as a single, unrepeated initiatory event. As a rule, exceptions to this have been among schismatic groups. The Donatists insisted that Christians who lapsed during persecution must be rebaptized. Oneness Pentecostals have insisted that those who have been baptized in the name of the Father, Son, and Spirit must be rebaptized "in the name of Jesus Christ." I do not mean to suggest that the rebaptism of a fallen convert is a sinful or heretical practice. But it may be unnecessary. When a fallen one is restored, it may be that one's repentance and restoration is a sign of continuing baptismal grace. (As we will discuss in chapter six, footwashing might be the preferred sacrament for post-baptismal sin.) The Spirit of grace continues to abide and strive with fallen believers, calling them to repentance and restoration. This is a sign that apostasy is not without remedy. This should not be interpreted as embracing the doctrine of unconditional eternal security. But neither should we embrace a doctrine of unconditional *insecurity*. Even as the writer of Hebrews acknowledges the possibility of apostasy, he speaks to us of the "full assurance of faith."

> Let us draw near with a sincere heart in full assurance of faith, having our hearts sprinkled clean from an evil conscience and our bodies washed with pure water (Hebrews 10:22; also 3:14; 6:11).

It may be that the question of rebaptism is best answered by the conscience of the restored believer after consultation with one's pastor.

CELEBRATION OF WATER BAPTISM

Services where converts are baptized should be among the most joyful celebrations of Pentecostal worship. When a sinner bows at the altar in repentance, all heaven rejoices (Luke 15:1-10). It is a mistake to perceive a baptismal service simply as an addendum to a regularly scheduled worship service. Celebrating water baptism should never be an afterthought. When scheduling a baptismal service, repentant sinners should be central to the purpose of the celebration. The music, prayers, sermon, and sanctuary decor should reflect the meaning of baptism—passing from death into life. Through careful planning, the baptismal service can reflect the joy of the occasion with dignity and reverence.

If baptism is to be a memorable event, it would be helpful to schedule baptismal services that correspond with important dates on the Christian calendar. Though few Pentecostal congregations follow a liturgical calendar, such a practice is an excellent way to guide in worship. This practice is especially useful in planning worship that involves the celebration of sacraments. One of the oldest traditions of the Christian church is baptizing new converts on Easter as a way to celebrate the resurrection of Jesus. The apostle Paul uses water baptism as a paradigm for a believer's redemptive experience. In water baptism, a believer shares in the death, burial, and resurrection of Christ. Therefore, to schedule a baptismal service at Easter is a most appropriate practice. Tertullian suggested that other appropriate times for water baptism are Passover and Pentecost. Passover is especially solemn, because in baptism, the believer is identified with the Lord's passion. Pentecost is appropriate, because water baptism anticipates baptism in the Spirit. After suggesting certain solemn days for baptism, Tertullian wrote, "every day is the Lord's; every hour, every time, is apt for baptism: if there is a difference in the solemnity, distinction there is none in the grace."[185]

For maximum effect, this observance should be planned well in advance of the actual date. Planning should begin with scheduling and announcing the date(s). Sufficient time should be allotted for baptismal candidates to adequately prepare and to send invitations to family and friends. When planned appropriately, sacramental worship can be an excellent opportunity for baptismal candidates to present Christ to non-Christian friends and family members.

Prior to a baptismal service, pastors should arrange a time for discussion and instructions with those presenting themselves for baptism. This could be in the form of a "New Believer's Class" or other venue, but it is vitally important for new believers to develop a foundational understanding of the Christian faith.

---

[185] *The Ante-Nicene Fathers, Vol. III*, 678.

COVENANT OF BAPTISM

Pastor: Do you believe in God the Father Almighty, Creator of heaven and earth?

Response: Yes, I believe.

Pastor: Do you believe in Jesus Christ, His only Son, our Lord, who was conceived by the Holy Spirit and born of the Virgin Mary; who suffered under Pontius Pilate, was crucified, died and was buried; who on the third day rose from the dead; who ascended into heaven and is seated at the right hand of God the Father; who will come again to judge the living and the dead?

Response: Yes, I believe.

Pastor: Do you believe in God the Holy Spirit, the Lord and giver of life, who proceeds from the Father, and by whom we are baptized into Christ? Do you believe in the holy Christian church, the communion of the saints, the forgiveness of sins, the resurrection of the body and life everlasting?

Response: Yes, I believe.

Pastor: Do you now publicly confess that you have repented of your sins and accepted Jesus Christ as your Savior?

Response: Yes, I do confess Jesus Christ as Lord.

Pastor: Do you now pledge, that with God's help, you will continually devote yourself to the apostle's teaching, to the fellowship of the church, to the breaking of bread, and to prayer?

Response: Yes, I do pledge to be a faithful Christian.

Adapted from: *The Book of Common Prayer* (New York: The Church Hymnal Corporation, 1979), 304-305; *The Book of Worship* (Nashville: The United Methodist Publishing House, 1965), 9-10; and the Nicene Creed.

On the day of the scheduled baptismal service, baptismal candidates may be asked to sit in an area reserved for friends and family. At the designated time, candidates should be invited forward to the altar and face the congregation. At the altar, the pastor, or church elder, presents the baptismal candidates to the congregation and officiates the Covenant of Baptism. This provides candidates an opportunity to publicly and formally testify to their faith in Christ.

Instead of using the covenant, the pastor may wish to give each baptismal candidate a few minutes to share their testimony of conversion and faith in Christ.

Following the "Covenant of Baptism," and/or the testimony, the pastor and church elders may anoint each candidate with oil and "lay hands" on each candidate as prayer is offered. Since water baptism anticipates Spirit baptism, it is appropriate to offer prayer on behalf of the candidates for the baptism of the Holy Spirit. In a sacramental altar service, candidates for baptism come forward to present themselves to God and the church. They have publicly affirmed faith in Christ. They have been anointed with oil, and prayer has been offered that they might be "filled with all the fullness of God" and be "sent forth in the power of the Spirit." Some candidates may have experienced the sanctifying power of the Spirit and may have been baptized in the Holy Spirit.

BAPTISMAL PRAYER

We thank You, Almighty God, for the gift of water. Over which the Spirit moved in Creation. Through which you delivered the Hebrew's out of Egyptian bondage into Canaan, the land of promise.

We thank You for Your Son, Jesus, who was baptized by John in the water of Jordan. Upon whom the Spirit descended in the form of a dove to anoint and to lead those who believe and obey from the bondage of sin into everlasting life.

We thank You, Holy Father, for the water of baptism. In submission, we are buried with Christ in death. In rising, we share with Christ in resurrection. Therefore, by obedience to Your Word, we joyously bring into fellowship these who have openly confessed faith in Christ.

Now sanctify by Your Spirit these who have been cleansed by the washing of regeneration and birthed to new life in Christ.

To God the Father, Jesus His Son and the comforting Holy Spirit, be honor and glory, now and forever. Amen.

From: *The Book of Common Prayer*, 306-307.

As a conclusion to altar worship, the pastor and candidates should prepare for water baptism. Many churches provide baptismal robes for the purpose of maintaining sacredness for the service and modesty for the candidates. Upon entering the baptismal pool, the pastor may offer a baptismal prayer.

Then each candidate is led into the water and baptized in the name of the Father, and of the Son, and of the Holy Spirit. As a sign of spiritual identification, worshipers in the congregation often express spontaneous praise and affirmation. This is more than formal liturgy, ritual, or ceremony; it is worship in the Holy Spirit.

This is a time of celebration and rejoicing. The service should be filled with singing and praise to God for His mighty saving love. The selected songs should reflect the various theological themes associated with water baptism: Holy Trinity, celebration of new birth, anticipation of the fullness of the Holy Spirit, discipleship, and fellowship in the church. Classic songs and hymns appropriate to the occasion could be . . .

Philip Doddridge, "**O Happy Day**," *Church Hymnal* (Cleveland, TN: Pathway Press, 1951, 1979) 86.

Fanny J. Crosby, "**I Am Thine, O Lord**," *Church Hymnal,* 362.

R. H. McDaniel, Charles H. Gabriel, "**Since Jesus Came Into My Heart**," *Church Hymnal,* 269.

Elisha A. Hoffman, John H. Stockton, "**Glory to His Name**," *Hymns of the Spirit* (Cleveland, TN: Pathway Press, 1969) 17.

John W. Peterson, "**Heaven Came Down**," *The Celebration Hymnal* (Word Music / Integrity Music, 1997) 510.

Doris Akers, "**Sweet, Sweet Spirit**," *The Celebration Hymnal,* 391.

Stephen R. Adams, "**Where the Spirit of the Lord Is**," *The Celebration Hymnal,* 385.

Daniel Iverson, Lowell Alexander, "**Spirit of the Living God**," *The Celebration Hymnal,* 389.

David Sapp, "**There Is a River**," *Best of the Gaither Vocal Band,* Spring House, EMI, 2004.

There are many contemporary songs and hymns that reflect the themes of water baptism. Some suggestions are:

Donna Adkins, "**Glorify Thy Name**," *The Celebration Hymnal,* 9.

Paul Baloche, "**Our God Saves**," *Our God Saves,* Sony, 2007.

John Wimber, "**Spirit Song**," *The Celebration Hymnal,* 384.

Darrell Evans, "**Trading My Sorrows**," *Trading My Sorrows: The Best of Darrell Evans,* Sony, 2002.

"**Let the River Flow**," *Let the River Flow, Sony, 2002*

"**Fields of Grace**," *Trading My Sorrows: The Best of Darrell Evans,* Sony, 2002.

Charlie Lowell, "**There Is a River**," *Jars of Clay: Good Monsters,* Essential, 2006.

Joseph Sabolick, "**Reign**," *Integrity's iWorship Next,* Integrity Music, 2004.

Ben Fielding, Morgan, Reuben, "**Mighty to Save**," *Hillsong Live: Mighty to Save,* Sony, 2002.

Brian Doerksen, "**The River**," *It's Time,* Integrity Music, 2008.

Robin Mark, "**Take Us to the River**," *The Best Worship Songs Ever,* Virgin / EMI, 2004.

CHAPTER 5

The Lord's Supper: Bread Of Life, Cup Of Blessing

And when He had given thanks, He broke it and said, "This is My body, which is for you; do this in remembrance of Me." In the same way He took the cup also after supper, saying, "This cup is the new covenant in My blood; do this, as often as you drink it, in remembrance of Me" (1 Corinthians 11:24-25).

O nce, I was leading a worship service for ministerial candidates. The worship service followed a session in which I taught on the sacraments of the church. At the conclusion of the session, I invited the participants to the altar to pray for one another. As we anointed and laid hands on the participants, the Holy Spirit began to move. I offered the bread and cup as people wept, shouted, and worshiped in tongues. It was evident to all that we were in the "real presence" of God. A few days later, a colleague who participated in that holy meal said to me, "I left that service feeling so full." Jesus said, "Blessed are those who hunger and thirst for righteousness for they shall be filled (Matthew 5:6).

The meal is a prominent theological motif throughout the Scriptures. In the midst of the Garden of Eden, God provided the Tree of Life and the Tree of the Knowledge of Good and Evil (Genesis 2:9). The fruit of the Tree of Life was a holy meal, a meal of grace, blessing, and eternal life. The fruit of the Tree of the Knowledge of Good and Evil was an unholy meal that poisoned humanity and resulted in death. During Israel's wilderness journey, God provided manna from heaven, even though the people yearned for the food of Egypt (Numbers 11:4-6). When the prophet Elijah hid by the Brook Cherith during a drought and famine, the Lord sent ravens to bring him bread and meat (1 Kings 17:1-6). The psalmist's description of the Word of God was that it tasted as sweet as honey (Psalms 19:10; 119:103). Isaiah prophesied an eschatological banquet hosted by the Lord to which all the people of the earth are invited (25:6-8).

The feeding miracles are prominent in the Gospels. These miracles provide theological motifs that introduce Jesus as the fulfillment of Jewish Messianic expectations. The feeding miracles of Moses occurred in a barren wilderness, whereas the feeding miracles of Jesus took place in the grassy meadows of Galilee (Matthew 14:19; Mark 6:39). The manna God provided Israel was fresh for a day and then spoiled. The feeding miracles of Jesus reflect no such tendencies; leftovers were collected to be used in feeding others or perhaps a later meal. These miracle stories not only look back on redemption's history, but they also look forward and anticipate the consummation of redemption to be fulfilled at a future eschatological banquet.

Mark presents two feeding miracles, one for Israel (6:34ff), the other for Gentiles (8:1ff), to demonstrate the universal character of Jesus' redemptive mission. Matthew's account of the feeding miracles occurs in the context of Jesus' healing ministry (Matthew 14:14; 15:30, 31). The feeding miracles in the synoptic Gospels are in anticipation of the Lord's Supper. In each story, Jesus took bread, broke bread, gave thanks and ate as an act of remembrance. Luke begins his Gospel by referring to the significance of the messianic meal and concludes with a celebration of the symbolism of the messianic meal (Luke 1:53; 24:41-43). John presents the messianic meal in terms of Eucharistic theology. Jesus, God incarnate, is the sinless sacrificial Lamb (John 1:14, 29). John's record of a feeding miracle occurs during Passover when the Pascal Lamb became a meal of remembrance, as well as advance celebration of the imminent death of Jesus as the last Lamb (Exodus 12:8; John 6:4). John provides further theological insight of the feeding miracle in the discourse where Jesus identified Himself as the "bread of life" and "living bread which came down from heaven" (John 6:31-58). Although John does not make a formal presentation of the Eucharist, the last supper Jesus shared with His disciples constituted a paschal meal (John 13:1ff).

The gospel stories of Jesus' table fellowship are significant in the understanding of the Lord's Supper. Jews, Gentiles, and sinners, "the poor and the maimed and the lame and the blind" were all welcomed (Luke 14:21). Jesus was anointed for His substitutionary death at the sacramental Table (Matthew 26:6-12; Mark 14:3-8). Jesus is present at the Table and the Table is a place where sinners find mercy and receive forgiveness (Luke 7:37-50). Jesus' disciples discovered the Table to be a place where discipleship was formed and their faith challenged. All Jesus' disciples, past and present, share the cup of Christ's redemptive sufferings at the Table (Matthew 20:22, 23; Mark 10:38, 39). It is at the Table of the Lord that the disciples are taught the true nature of discipleship—disciples are to be servants (Mark 14:29, 30). Peter and Judas both experienced judgment at the Lord's Table.[186] In Mark's account of the Last Supper, the Twelve were confronted by Jesus and exposed as lacking in their devotion to Him (Mark 14:29-30). In Luke, the Table is where the resurrected Christ revealed Himself to His disciples who were slow to comprehend the reality of the resurrection (Luke 24:13-35). In John, during a meal with the resurrected Christ, Peter finds forgiveness for his threefold denial of Christ (John 21:15-17). The Table of the Lord is a place where the fallen are received and restored by our Lord.

The Lord's Supper in the Apostolic Church

The significance of the Lord's Supper[187] among early Christian communities has significant implications for Pentecostal worship. Paul's first letter to the church at Corinth is primary to Pentecostal

---

[186] Matthew 26:33-35; Luke 22:21, 31-34; John 13:18, 26-27.

[187] There are four designations in the New Testament: the Lord's Supper (1 Corinthians 11:20); Communion (1 Corinthians 10:16, *NKJV*—from the Greek word *koinōnia*); the Table of the Lord (1 Corinthians 10:21); and Eucharist (1 Corinthians 11:24—from the Greek word *eucharisteō*, which translates into English as "having given thanks").

theology, especially as it relates to the *charismata*—the spiritual gifts. It is interesting how Paul moved to a discussion of the *charismata* immediately after concluding a discussion regarding the Lord's Supper. This suggests that liturgical rites and charismatic manifestations were significant issues in the earliest Christian churches. Paul does not object to "a *form* of godliness," but to a form of godliness in which the power of God is denied (2 Timothy 3:5). In his instructions regarding the *charismata* Paul wrote, "But all things must be done properly and in an orderly manner" (1 Corinthians 14:40). Paul insists that liturgy and *charismata* be governed by a dual concern for "order *and* power" (1 Corinthians 11:34; 14:40). Religious practices should manifest the Spirit's *power*, and charismatic manifestations should demonstrate the Spirit's *order*. Sometimes, Pentecostals struggle with the tension that exists between manifestations of the Holy Spirit and the maintenance of order in worship. Some Pentecostals believe that any effort at maintaining order quenches the Spirit's fire. Pentecostal pastors are charged with the responsibility to lead worship in which the Spirit is not quenched and the worshiper is free to respond to the moving of the Holy Spirit. In doing so, the pastor must be aware that sometimes a *lack of order* can quench the Holy Spirit.

The celebration of the Lord's Supper was a central feature of worship for the early church (Acts 20:7). Like other first-century Christian churches, the Corinthian church met regularly, probably weekly, to celebrate the Lord's Supper. Paul offered the following instruction about worship: "Therefore when you meet together, it is not to eat the Lord's Supper, for in your eating, each one takes his own supper first" (1 Corinthians 11:20-21). Some scholars suggest that in most early churches the celebration of the Eucharist was preceded by the agape feast, which was a common fellowship meal. At the agape feast there was often discrimination between the rich and poor. This was an offense to the nature of Christian fellowship. Paul's instructions to the Corinthian church regarding the separation of the agape feast from the Eucharist may have been the beginning of separating the two for all churches. The Corinthians' practice of joining the agape feast with the Eucharist was an innovation that displeased Paul.[188] Paul's objection was not their regularity in observing the Lord's Supper. He objected to the improper manner by which they observed the Lord's Supper. Again, Paul's concern is for power *and* order. Their improper worship denied the power of the holy meal to bring the people of God into a holy communion. It should be noted, however, that Paul affirms the Lord's Supper as essential and normative in early Christian worship. Paul proposes two things in this Corinthian discourse: first, to reestablish proper order in worship and, second, to return to the earlier tradition of the Lord's Supper(1 Corinthians 11:23-26). For Paul, proper observance of the Lord's Supper was normative to Christian worship.

SACRAMENT OF UNITY

The celebration of the Lord's Supper calls the church to unity with Christ. Paul's criticism of the Corinthians was directed at disorderly worship and relational divisions. The first issue Paul addressed was their division (1 Corinthians 1:10-13). The Corinthian church was divided over issues regarding spiritual authority, and other social, cultural, and economic issues. The Corinthian church consisted of Jews and Gentiles, rich and poor, slave and free. Their diversity, which should have been a testimony to the power of the gospel to heal social brokenness, violated the very purpose of their gathering. Instead of demonstrating unity in Christ, the Lord's Supper became a reflection of the brokenness of their fellowship. Paul's rebuke was harsh: "You come together not for the better, but for the worse. . . . Do you despise the church of God?" (1 Corinthians 11:17, 22). To Paul, a broken and divided church is an offense to the reconciling power of the cross and an offense to the body and blood of Christ in the Eucharist (1 Corinthians 1:11-18; 11:27). His rebuke was a call to unity that demonstrates the transformative power of the gospel that heals the brokenness of human community.

A few years ago I was called by a local school official to help establish a program of conflict resolution for students who often demonstrated angry and violent behavior. This was precipitated by

---

[188] Gregory Dom Dix, *The Shape of the Liturgy* (New York: Continuum, 2003), 96-102.

a fight at school between two teenaged girls. These two had a history of hostility toward each other, and one day as they passed in the hall, angry words led to a full-blown "nail-clawing, hair-pulling" brawl. Teachers intervened, and eventually these two were in the office of the school counselor. In the ensuing conversation, the counselor discovered that both girls attended church regularly. As they began to talk about their church, and their love of Jesus, they began to be calm and civil to each other. For these two young ladies, their love of Jesus overwhelmed their hatred of each other. The conflict and reconciliation of these two girls could serve as a model for the unity of the church. For those familiar with church history, the unity of the church has been an ontological ideal that has difficulty finding concrete expression. Beginning with strife between Jesus' own apostles, and continuing in the various schisms throughout two millennia, the church continues to suffer from self-inflicted wounds of division.

The advent of the modern Pentecostal/Charismatic Movement is a testimony to the kind of unity that may be forged in the power of the Holy Spirit. Pentecostalism transcends ethnic and social cultures as well as diverse ecclesiastical and theological traditions. That which unifies diverse Pentecostal groups is a common encounter with the Holy Spirit which is expressed in a variety of worship forms—the most common of which is tongues speech. However, Pentecostalism is by no means a model of Christian unity. It seems that those who testify to fullness of the Spirit can also quench and grieve the Holy Spirit when issues of unity are involved. The unity that defined the Azusa revival was short-lived. Pentecostalism fragmented along cultural and ethnic lines.

The Christian church is universal in scope. The unity of the church is demonstrated in that all Christians are in fellowship with a singular Bishop—the Lord Jesus Christ (1 Peter 2:25; 5:4). The unity of the church must be an expression of devotion to Jesus Christ as Lord and His command that believers are to love one another. In spite of this bond of unity, the Table of the Lord has become a source of tension and ironically, a symbol of Christian schism. For example, charismatic Catholics are forbidden to sit at the

Table with charismatic Protestants. The Roman Catholic Church recognizes Protestants as brothers and sisters. Referring to the Protestants as "separated," the Catholic Church acknowledges that Protestants are "brought up in the faith of Christ, and the Catholic Church accepts them with respect and affection as brothers.... All who have been justified by faith in Baptism are incorporated into Christ; they therefore have a right to be called Christians, and with good reason are accepted as brothers in the Lord by the children of the Catholic Church."[189] However, Catholics and Protestants are forbidden to celebrate Holy Communion together. According to the *Catechism of the Catholic Church,* "Ecclesial communities derived from the Reformation and separated from the Catholic Church, have not preserved the proper reality of the Eucharistic mystery in its fullness, especially because of the absence of the sacrament of Holy Orders. It is for this reason that, for the Catholic Church, Eucharistic intercommunion with these communities is not possible." There is, however, an exception to this rule: "When . . . a grave necessity arises, Catholic ministers may give the sacraments of Eucharist. . . to other Christians not in full communion with the Catholic Church, who ask for them of their own will, provided they give evidence of holding to the Catholic faith regarding these sacraments and possess the required dispositions."[190] It should be noted that this allows Protestants to receive Holy Communion from Catholic priests, but this is not reciprocal. Catholics are forbidden to receive Holy Communion from Christian ministers who are not in communion with the Bishop of Rome.

Some Protestant churches have made the Table of the Lord a place of separation by practicing a "closed Communion." The Westminster Larger Catechism closes the Table of the Lord to children and those who lack sufficient mental capacity to examine themselves. The position of the Lutheran Church—Missouri Synod is representative of the doctrine of closed Communion:

---

[189] *Catechism of the Catholic Church,* 216.
[190] *Catechism of the Catholic Church,* 353-354.

On the basis of the New Testament's attitude toward heterodoxy, however, we concluded that the corporate unity
implied in the very act of the Lord's Supper itself could
scarcely ignore the presence of contradictory confessions . . . [therefore] communion fellowship with those who
adhere to heterodox confessions (that of Rome, or of the
Reformed) is out of the question.[191]

It seems that the bread and cup of Holy Communion no longer
represent the brokenness of Christ's body for human redemption.
Rather the bread and cup seem to better reflect the brokenness and
spilled blood of Christ's communion—the church. Those who share
the common confession that "Jesus is Lord" and embrace a common
encounter in the Holy Spirit should lead the effort to bring all believers
together at the Lord's Table in the unity of the Holy Spirit.

A Celebration of Christ's Death

The celebration of the Lord's Supper summons the church to
a celebration of the sacrificial death of Christ. Jesus met with His
disciples on the eve of His passion to eat a meal. Although some
debate as to whether the Last Supper was *the* Passover meal, there
can be little doubt Passover is the theological motif that informs the
church's understanding of the Eucharist.[192] In fact, it was Jesus, the
Lamb of sacrifice, who reinterpreted and fulfilled Passover through
His sacrificial death. N.T. Wright has written:

Jesus' last meal with his followers was a deliberate double
drama. As a Passover meal (of sorts), it told the story of
Jewish history in terms of divine deliverance from tyranny,
looking back to the exodus from Egypt and on to the great
exodus, the return from exile, that was still eagerly awaited.
But Jesus' meal fused this great story together with another
one: the story of Jesus' own life, and of his coming death.
It somehow involved him in the god-given drama, not as

---

[191] *Admission to the Lord's Supper: Basics of Biblical and Confessional Teaching.*
(St. Louis: The Lutheran Church—Missouri Synod, 2000), 31-32.
[192] Matthew 26:17-29; Mark 14:12-25; Luke 22:8-23; John 1:29, 36; 19:13-16;
1 Corinthians 5:7.

spectator, or as one participant among many, but as the central character.[193]

Passover and the Eucharist may be contrasted in that the former is the "First Supper," and the latter is the "Last Supper." The Passover meal served to tutor many generations of Hebrews about their national redemption and miraculous deliverance from Egyptian slavery (Exodus 12:25-27). Without the Passover, succeeding generations would have been born in bondage. Therefore, Passover was more than a historic remembrance of an event that liberated their ancestors; it was a continuing redemptive event celebrating the liberation of successive generations. The Passover as the "First Supper" anticipates the "Last Supper," the meal in which Jesus, as High Priest, offered Himself as the sacrificial lamb for the redemption of all humanity. When Christians gather at the Table of the Lord, it is to remember the sacrificial death of Christ and, thus, the past event becomes present. It is not simply to recall a past redemptive event; it reminds believers that they are participants in an ongoing redemptive event.

W.J. Seymour believed the Lord's Supper was the "Christian Passover." He wrote, "the passing over the Red Sea . . . was a type of the blood of Jesus Christ that gives us victory over all the powers of the enemy." Just as the Exodus Passover was deliverance for the children of Israel, the Lord's Supper as Passover points to "our great deliverance," that is, the coming of the Lord. Just as the Exodus Passover reminded the Israelites of God's redemptive love, the Lord's Supper is a memorial of God's redemptive love in Jesus Christ. Just as the children of Israel were nourished by the body of the lamb, the Lord's Supper is healing and health to all believers who partake by faith. Seymour proclaimed, "Our souls are built up, for we eat His flesh and drink His blood."[194]

---

[193] N.T. Wright, *Jesus and the Victory of God.* (Minneapolis: Fortress Press, 1996), 554.

[194] W.J. Seymour, "The Ordinances Taught By Our Lord." *The Apostolic Faith* (September 1907), 2. "Salvation and Healing." *The Apostolic Faith* (December 1906), 2.

"This Is My Body"

The Lord's Supper is a simple yet profound meal whose common elements, the loaf and the cup, carry controversial theological implications in the Christian church. The statement of Jesus, "This is my body . . . this is my blood," has been the subject of much debate. Because many Pentecostals reject the primacy of the Eucharist in worship, there has been limited discussion among Pentecostals as to how Christ is present in the Eucharist.

Yet in the early church, the celebration of the Lord's Supper was a primary act of worship. Justin Martyr describes the weekly worship of second-century Christians.

> And on the day called Sunday, all who live in cities or in the country gather together to one place, and the memoirs of the apostles or the writings of the prophets are read, as long as time permits; then, when the reader has ceased, the president verbally instructs, and exhorts to the imitation of these good things. Then we all rise together and pray, and, as we before said, when our prayer is ended, bread and wine and water are brought, and the president in like manner offers prayers and thanksgivings, according to his ability, and the people assent, saying Amen; and there is a distribution to each, and a participation of that over which thanks have been given, and to those who are absent a portion is sent by the deacons. And they who are well to do, and willing, give what each thinks fit; and what is collected is deposited with the president, who succors the orphans and widows and those who, through sickness or any other cause, are in want, and those who are in bonds and the strangers sojourning among us, and in a word takes care of all who are in need.[195]

But how is Christ present in the bread and cup? Christ's presence in the bread and cup is firmly based on the Incarnation. Gnostic foes of early Christians denied the possibility of the immortality of the flesh and hence the necessity, even the possibility, of the Incarnation. Because they denied the Word became flesh, it would logically follow

---

[195] *The Ante-Nicene Fathers, Vol. I*, 186.

that the Gnostics rejected the presence of Christ in the Eucharist. Irenaeus explained that the salvation of the flesh (the resurrection of the body) and the real presence of Christ in the Eucharist may be properly understood only in terms of the Incarnation.

> But vain in every respect are they who . . . disallow the salvation of the flesh, and treat with contempt its regeneration, maintaining that it is not capable of incorruption. But if this indeed does not attain salvation, then neither did the Lord redeem us with His blood, nor is the cup of the Eucharist the communion of His blood, nor the bread which we break the communion of His body. . . . the Eucharist, which is the body and blood of Christ; so also our bodies, being nourished by it, and deposited in the earth, and suffering decomposition there, shall rise at their appointed time, the Word of God granting them resurrection to the glory of God, even the Father, who freely gives to this mortal immortality, and to this corruptible incorruption.[196]

The Incarnation is the redemptive event of history. For mankind to be redeemed, the Eternal Word assumed human nature (flesh, soul, and spirit). Jesus Christ, the "enfleshed Word," offered Himself to be "broken and poured out" for the redemption of all people. Anyone receiving the Eucharist received nothing less than the flesh and blood of Christ. The bread and cup of the Eucharist are understood to be an extension of the Incarnation. According to early church theologians, if the Eucharist is anything less than the real flesh and blood of Christ, it is without saving grace. In his *First Apology*, Justin Martyr wrote:

> They abstain from the Eucharist and from prayer, because they confess not the Eucharist to be the flesh of our Savior Jesus Christ, which suffered for our sins, and which the Father, of His goodness, raised up again. Those, therefore, who speak against this gift of God, incur death. For not as common bread and common drink do we receive these; but in like manner as Jesus Christ our Savior, having been made flesh by the Word of God, had both flesh and blood for our salvation, so likewise have we been taught that the food

---

[196] *The Ante-Nicene Fathers, Vol. I,* 528.

which is blessed by the prayer of His word, and from which
our blood and flesh by transmutation are nourished, is the
flesh and blood of that Jesus who was made flesh.[197]

This early Eucharistic theology can be summarized in three
statements:

- Jesus Christ is at once fully God and fully human.
- Through prayer and the Word, the elements of the
  Eucharist are the flesh and blood of Jesus Christ.
- By receiving the Eucharist, humans are nourished to eternal
  life which is resurrection to immortality in a body of flesh
  and blood.

By the time of the Reformation, the Roman Catholic Church
had expanded this earlier view of the Eucharist into the doctrine of
"transubstantiation." The Council of Trent defined transubstantiation
in the Eucharist as "the body and blood, together with the soul and
divinity, of our Lord Jesus Christ and, therefore, the whole Christ is
truly, really, and substantially contained" in the consecrated bread
and wine.[198] The transubstantiated bread and wine are understood
to be a continuing sacrifice of Christ, presented to God the Father
by the officiating priest and administered to communicants. During
mass, the priest presents the bread and wine and offers the Epiclesis,
that is, the invocation of the Holy Spirit. "The Epiclesis . . . is the
intercession in which the priest begs the Father to send the Holy
Spirit, the Sanctifier, so that the offerings may become the body
and blood of Christ and that the faithful, by receiving them, may
themselves become a living offering to God."[199] The Holy Spirit effects
the transubstantiation so that bread and wine become the flesh and
blood of Christ while maintaining their physical properties. Once
consecrated, the transubstantiation of the bread and wine "endures
as long as the Eucharistic species subsist." Therefore, the logical
consequence is that the elements of the meal, as the body of Christ,
have themselves become objects of adoration.

---

[197] *The Ante-Nicene Fathers, Vol. I*, 185.
[198] *Catechism of the Catholic Church*, 346.
[199] *Catechism of the Catholic Church*, 287.

The Protestant reformers took issue with this doctrine. Martin Luther rejected transubstantiation, but he affirmed the "real presence" of Christ in the holy meal. He insisted that Christ's body is "in, with, and under" the bread and wine in the Eucharist. In *The Larger Catechism*, Luther wrote:

> The true body and blood of our Lord Jesus Christ, in and under the bread and wine which we Christians are commanded by the Word of Christ to eat and to drink . . . the sacrament is bread and wine, but not mere bread and wine, such as are ordinarily served at the table, but bread and wine comprehended in, and connected with, the Word of God.

Subsequent Lutheran theologians referred to this doctrine as *consubstantiation*. The Lutheran doctrine of consubstantiation differs from transubstantiation in that Luther denied that the bread and wine "leave or lose their own natural substance." For Luther, the presence of Christ in the bread and wine was a matter of the authority of the Word.

> Therefore also it is vain talk when they say that the body and blood of Christ are not given and shed for us in the Lord's Supper, hence we could not have forgiveness of sins in the Sacrament. For although the work is accomplished and the forgiveness of sins acquired on the cross, yet it cannot come to us in any other way than through the Word. For what would we otherwise know about it, that such a thing was accomplished or was to be given us if it were not presented by preaching or the oral Word? Whence do they know of it, or how can they apprehend and appropriate to themselves the forgiveness, except they lay hold of and believe the Scriptures and the Gospel?[200]

Also, Luther's doctrine of the ubiquity of Christ—ubiquitarianism—insists that the physical body of Christ is not limited to one place. In particular, Luther insisted that the humanity of Christ, as well as his divinity, is omnipresent.

---

[200] Martin Luther, *The Larger Catechism* (Albany, OR: Ages Software, 1997), 90-93.

John Calvin rejected Luther's doctrine of consubstantiation. He wrote:

> The presence of Christ in the Supper we must hold to be such as neither affixes him to the element of bread, nor encloses him in bread, nor circumscribes him in any way (this would obviously detract from his celestial glory); and it must, moreover, be such as neither divests him of his just dimensions, nor dissevers him by differences of place, nor assigns to him a body of boundless dimensions, diffused through heaven and earth.

However, he affirmed that Christ's "flesh is the meat, his blood the drink, of my soul." For Calvin, Christ is present in the bread and wine of the Eucharist just as He is present in this age—through the advent of the Holy Spirit. Because "the whole kingdom of Christ is spiritual," Christ is present in the Eucharistic meal through "the incomprehensible agency of the Holy Spirit." Calvin wrote:

> Such I say is the corporeal presence which the nature of the sacrament requires, and which we say is here displayed in such power and efficacy, that it not only gives our minds undoubted assurance of eternal life, but also secures the immortality of our flesh, since it is now quickened by his immortal flesh, and in a manner shines in his immortality.

Calvin insisted that "Christ descends to us . . . that he may truly quicken our souls by the substance of his flesh and blood." His understanding of Christ's presence in the Eucharist differed from that of the Council of Trent and Martin Luther. Whereas, they insisted upon an Incarnational (or Christological) interpretation, Calvin understood Christ's presence as Pneumatic, that is, in terms of a spiritual reality in this temporal and material age.

> This kingdom is not limited by any intervals of space, nor circumscribed by any dimensions. Christ can exert his energy wherever he pleases, in earth and heaven, can manifest his presence by the exercise of his power, can always be present with his people, breathing into them his own life, can live in them, sustain, confirm, and invigorate them, and preserve them safe, just as if he were with them in the body; in fine,

can feed them with his own body, communion with which he transfuses into them. After this manner, the body and blood of Christ are exhibited to us in the sacrament.[201]

With this Pneumatic understanding of Holy Communion, Calvin continued to affirm the salvific efficacy of the holy sacrament.

The Swiss reformer Ulrich Zwingli moved beyond both Luther and Calvin in his understanding of the Lord's Supper. For Zwingli, the church "celebrates" the Lord's Supper as a memorial event, and the bread and wine *signify* the presence of Christ. Unlike Luther and Calvin, Zwingli sought to remove any consideration of salvific efficacy of holy sacraments and insisted that salvation was a result of the unmediated impartation of salvation by the Holy Spirit. As a reflection of his theology, Zwingli changed the way in which the Lord's Supper was observed. Instead of weekly observances, the Lord's Supper was observed only four times a year. He changed the emphasis of the sacrament as central to the altar. Instead of serving communicants the meal at the altar, the bread and wine were distributed to congregants where they were seated. Care should be exercised before suggesting Zwingli robbed the Eucharist of all significant meaning. In his *Exposition of the Faith*, Zwingli wrote:

> By this commemoration all the benefits that God has displayed in His Son are called to mind. And by the signs themselves, the bread and wine, Christ is as it were set before our eyes, so that not merely with the ear, but with the eye and palate we see and taste that Christ who the soul bears within and in whom it rejoices.[202]

Although Zwingli broke with the early fathers, the Roman Catholic Church, Luther, and Calvin, it seems he could not bring himself to deny Holy Communion as a powerful and mysterious event in the life and worship of the church.

---

[201] John Calvin, *The Institutes of the Christian Religion*, (Oak Harbor, WA: Logos Research Systems, Inc., 1997), 4:17:18, 19, 24, 28, 32, 33.
[202] Ulrich Zwingli, *Exposition of the Faith* (1536) in *Zwingli and Bullinger*. (Louisville: Westminster John Knox Press, 1953, 2006), 248.

It was the later Anabaptist theologians who ultimately denied any sacramental presence or salvific efficacy in the Lord's Supper. The real issue for Anabaptists was not the presence of Christ in the bread and wine; it was the presence of Christ, that is, the witness of the Spirit, in the life of the worshiping community. When the church came together to partake of the memorial supper, they did so in a holy communion with each other and with Christ. The manifestation of Christ's presence was in the unity, love, and peace of the community.

We should learn to appreciate the deep struggles and rich dialogue of church theologians through the ages. They preached and wrote from their own particular historical, political, and pastoral contexts. We should carefully consider each view, even if we have profound disagreements. Each view expresses the deep devotion of the theologians and the traditions they represent. It is a sad irony that the very act of worship that should draw Christians to unity has become an issue that sometimes separates brothers and sisters.

Partakers of Divine Nature

In the celebration of the Lord's Supper, believers are partakers of the divine nature. It should be of interest to Pentecostals that each theological tradition, from Roman Catholic to the Anabaptist, affirms the Holy Spirit as the effective agent in the celebration of the Eucharist. The person and work of the Holy Spirit was active in the birth, ministry, and crucifixion of Jesus. The Eternal Word was "enfleshed" by Spirit in the womb of the Virgin Mary (Matthew 1:18; Luke 1:35). It was through the Spirit that Jesus ministered as the anointed One of God (Luke 4:1, 14, 18). Jesus was raised from the dead by the Spirit, and by the Spirit His sacrifice for sin is eternally efficacious.[203] Through Christ's priestly ministry, humanity is sanctified so we can receive the Spirit (Hebrews 10:22; 1 Peter 1:2). The Holy Spirit comes through the intercession of Jesus.[204] Through the Spirit, Christ comes to believers in the bread and cup. John of Damascus (seventh and eighth centuries) wrote:

---

[203] Acts 2:24; Romans 8:11; Hebrews 9:14.
[204] John 14:16-17; 15:26; 16:7; Acts 2:33.

> You ask how the bread becomes the Body of Christ, and
> the wine . . . the blood of Christ. I shall tell you: the Holy
> Spirit comes upon them and accomplishes what surpasses
> every word and thought . . . . Let it be enough for you to
> understand that it is by the Holy Spirit, just as it was of the
> Holy Virgin and by the Holy Spirit that the Lord, through
> and in himself, took flesh.[205]

Some early Pentecostals used a "drinking" metaphor when speaking of the essence of the Pentecostal encounter. David Wesley Myland said that being baptized in the Holy Spirit was like swallowing "God liquidized."[206] Pentecostals have affirmed that God's energies can be transferred to material objects, or that God's anointing is tangible, that is, "touchable." Therefore, Pentecostals should have little difficulty in understanding the Eucharist as worship in which the believer can touch and taste the divine.

Although early Pentecostals resisted liturgical rites in worship, they embraced the Lord's Supper with great devotion. A.J. Tomlinson wrote that partaking of the Lord's Supper is one of "the most sacred and hallowed moments in the entire Christian life."[207] Reporting on an Eucharistic observance, he wrote,

> As the bread was broken and mention made of the broken
> body of Jesus, He seemed to manifest His presence in the
> midst. As I stood there in the presence of God and before
> the large audience with the broken bread; a piece in each
> hand, I seemed to get a broader view of the Christ and
> wonderful scheme of redemption than ever before.[208]

Tomlinson's reflection suggests an encounter that is much more than a memorial. Christ is present and the "broken bread" reveals the mystery of redemption. In an early Sunday school lesson "from

---

[205] John of Damascus, *The Orthodox Faith.* Quoted in *Catechism of the Catholic Church*, 287.

[206] David Wesley Myland quoted by Douglas Jacobsen in *Thinking in the Spirit.* (Indianapolis: Indiana University Press, 2003), 122.

[207] *Book of Doctrines*, 69.

[208] A.J. Tomlinson, "Fourth of July at the Tabernacle," *The Evening Light and the Church of God Evangel* (15 July 1910), 1.

a Pentecostal viewpoint," the writer offers an explanation of how believers partake in the divine nature at the Lord's Table.

> As we come to the communion table, behind the symbol and the sign, we are to see our precious Savior and to appropriate and partake of Him. It is His desire to communicate Himself to us and as we partake in faith, discerning Him whilst we feed, we receive life for our spirits, souls, and bodies.

> As the showbread was placed anew, every Sabbath, on the table before the Lord . . . so the Lord's death was shown, or announced afresh at the Lord's table [sic] on the first day of every week in the primitive Church. We need to continue steadfastly in the apostles' doctrine and fellowship and in the breaking of bread.[209]

J. Roswell Flower, an early leader in the Assemblies of God, wrote an article on "the sacrament of the Lord's Supper" that is wonderfully sacramental. Flower wrote that the Lord's Supper is a "visible means" of promoting "the maintenance of spiritual life through personal communion with God" and that the Lord's Supper feeds the believer's "spiritual nature for a healthy growth in the Spirit." When Flower writes about the cup and the loaf of the holy meal, it is evident that he believes there is more here than mere symbol. Concerning the cup he writes:

> When the fruit of the vine was being partaken of, we have been conscious of melting, weeping, praising, and adoring among those receiving it . . . . The fruit of the vine speaks to us of the spilled Blood in which we see our sins forgiven . . . . We grasp it readily and our hearts are broken again and again in deep appreciation of the benefits of Calvary.

As he writes concerning the significance of the bread, his words portray a deep sacramental devotion:

> . . . (the bread) was composed of fine flour. This speaks to the perfection of the humanity of Christ . . . . And the flour was mingled with oil. The oil, of course, speaks of the Holy

---

[209] E.N. Bell, editor. "The Lord's Supper," *The Christian Evangel* (12 July 1919), 12.

Ghost. Here we have the mingling of the perfect human nature of the Lord Jesus with the Divine.

As to the significance of the believer's participation in this sacrament, Flower writes:

> Just as the manna must be gathered daily to sustain life, so we too must draw nigh daily to partake of Christ; we must hold daily communion with Him if we are to be sustained by His life . . . . May God grant a deepening of our life of communion with Him, for a fuller manifestation of His life in us.[210]

I am not suggesting that early Pentecostals held to a Catholic or Lutheran view of the Eucharist. They often outright rejected such views. Even as they rejected the traditional Eucharistic theology of transubstantiation and consubstantiation, neither did they fully embrace the traditional Anabaptist view. It seems that early Pentecostal leaders intuitively knew that there is a "presence" inherent in the holy meal. Baptism in the Holy Spirit brought into their lives a "real presence" that anointed the sacred acts of worship. This understanding of "real presence" became associated with the Lord's Supper. It is evident that Pentecostals understood that at the Table, through the power of the Holy Spirit, Christ is present. D.W. Kerr wrote:

> There is nothing old or stale about this memorial feast, the fruit of the vine is not old, the shed blood is not aged, the bread is not stale, the Lord's body is not a mere thing of the past, the way is new and living. The thing most striking about the character of the feast is its presentness, not its pastness or its futureness. It has a present aspect, there is a sign of warmth, the blood is not cold and coagulated but flowing fresh from the wounded side of Jesus . . . . Here is the present tense of Calvary. We have come to a place of freshness, the result of Calvary. What is it? Life and life more abundant!

---

[210] J. Roswell Flower, "The Broken Bread: A Meditation on the Lord's Supper." *The Pentecostal Evangel*, 942 (2 April 1932), 2-3.

The Pentecostal encounter of the Holy Spirit baptism led early leaders of the movement to revise much of the received Christian tradition. Sometimes, they lacked the theological language to clearly express what they were experiencing or thinking. This became especially evident when they wrote about the sacraments.

> Faith can grasp mysteries that are unexplainable. Faith enters into a realm far beyond the sphere of understanding, and can extract the good and joy out of what soars high above our reasonings. We have no need to preach a doctrine of consubstantiation nor of transubstantiation; we just receive Jesus' words and act on them. "Whoso eateth my flesh and drinketh my blood, hath everlasting life."[211]

This is the language of mystery—a supernatural truth that defies reasonable explanation. To demonstrate this, let us consider the writings of William A. Cox:

> The communion is *not a mere form*. It is *more than a memorial*. I believe God has given us the fellowship of the holy communion so that we may draw nigh to Him, and not only draw nigh but also receive from Him the supply of our every need (emphasis mine).

He continues by rejecting the doctrines of consubstantiation and transubstantiation, and says, "We believe it is a memorial, a symbol." He seems to be struggling to properly express his view. But then he begins to associate participation in Holy Communion with the indwelling of Jesus Christ and baptism in the Holy Spirit, and his language regarding the "symbols" of the meal becomes very sacramental.

> It (the Lord's Supper) is not an empty service, it does not mean simply being served with a little bread and wine on the first Sunday of the month—it is a means of fellowship with God, through Jesus, by the Spirit, and we have a right to come to it expecting God to meet us. Indeed we have a

---

[211] D.W. Kerr, "The Message of the Sacrament." *The Weekly Evangel* (28 October 1916), 4.

right to expect to draw so near to God that whatever our need may be at that moment, whether spiritual or physical, He will supply it.

. . . when we eat of the divine body of the Lord Jesus, the living Bread which came down from heaven. . . He quickens the spiritual man; He revives the physical; He heals our diseases, and gives us strength to live by. By eating Jesus, the Bread of life, we have life in our physical bodies.

. . . if we eat the flesh of Jesus, and drink His blood, we shall live by Him. So when you want to be healed, just take a great big meal of Jesus.

Communion was not thought to be a dead, traditional rite. To partake of the holy meal is transformative—"the very nature of the individual is changed . . . strengthened and empowered by the very life and body of the Lord Jesus Christ."[212] Believers were encouraged, ". . . while we are taking Communion, let us get into the Spirit and draw from God."[213] Here we discover the distinction between a Pentecostal understanding of "real presence" and the traditional Pneumatic view held by Calvin and Wesley. The traditional Pneumatic view may be defined in terms of a reasonable faith. The Spirit is present because the Word is proclaimed. Faith is an exercise of the reason. Although Pentecostals embrace the preeminence of the proclaimed Word, faith is more than an exercise of reason. Faith is experiential and an experiential faith is accompanied by spiritual manifestations that may be perceived by the physical senses.

Cecil Knight, a Pentecostal leader of a later generation, wrote that the observance of Holy Communion should be a "vital part of the church's life in worshiping the Risen Christ." Knight believed the bread and cup are more than symbols. He wrote:

---

[212] "The Spiritual Import of the Lord's Supper." *The Weekly Evangel* (May 4, 1918), 8. The author speaks of "the wonderful divine alchemy" of the Lord's Supper. It seems that the "alchemy" refers to the transformation of the nature of the participant, rather than a transformation of the bread and cup. However, it is clear that the author attributes "supernatural power" associated with the meal.
[213] William A. Cox, "The Lord's Table." *The Pentecostal Evangel* (25 May 1929), 3, 8-9.

> There is deep spiritual meaning in the Lord's Supper. The
> participant does not merely look at the symbols; *he receives
> spiritual food.* Just as the bread and the fruit of the vine
> will nourish and invigorate the body of man, so *Christ,
> through Communion, sustains and quickens the soul.* When
> a Christian truly worships Christ in the Lord's Supper, *he is
> ministered to by the Holy Spirit*, thereby receiving strength
> and a deep abiding peace (emphasis mine).

In Holy Communion there is a real presence—Christ and Spirit—
whose presence in the celebration are a means of grace—sustenance,
strength, and peace.[214]

The Trinitarian economy of salvation is reflected in a Pentecostal
understanding of the Eucharistic meal. In chapter three, we discussed
how Christ and the Spirit are present in the sacraments and suggested
that Gregory Palamas' theology of the "divine energies" offers a
theological precedent. Due to the "transfer of divine energies," when
communicants consume the consecrated bread and cup of the
Eucharist, they partake of the energies of the Son and the Spirit. This
understanding of the "real presence" differs from Catholic, Lutheran,
and Anabaptist interpretations. This Pentecostal interpretation
suggests the real presence of Christ in the Eucharist in terms of a
dyadic relationship between the Son and the Spirit.[215] That is, in
the economy of salvation, the work of the Son and the Spirit are
interdependent. The believer encounters one through the activity
of the other. According to Hebrews, Christ our High Priest, offered
Himself as a spotless sacrifice to God "through the eternal Spirit"
(Hebrews 9:14). The bread and cup of the Eucharist are gifts of Christ

---

[214] Cecil B. Knight, "Communion: A Sign and a Seal." *Church of God Evangel* (22
March 1971), 16-17.

[215] Sergius Bulgakov speaks of the Son and the Spirit as a "dyadic union," that is,
"two hypostases abiding together without separation and without confusion."
The Comforter, 249. The "dyadic union" of the Son and the Spirit are ancient
concepts. Clement of Alexandria wrote "And the blood of the Lord is twofold.
For there is the blood of His flesh, by which we are redeemed from corruption;
and the spiritual, that by which we are anointed. And to drink the blood of Jesus,
is to become partaker of the Lord's immortality; the Spirit being the energetic
principle of the Word, as blood is of flesh" (*The Ante-Nicene Fathers Vol. II*, 242).

through the Spirit. The "real presence" in the Eucharist is more than Pneumatic, it is Christo-Pneumatic. The Eucharist is possible only by virtue of Pentecost. The Spirit makes Christ really present in the bread and cup. In view of the emphasis in Pentecostal theology upon the Son and the Spirit, it seems inappropriate for Pentecostals to limit sacramental discussions to Zwinglian or Anabaptistic theological positions. With the Anabaptists, Pentecostals gladly affirm the presence of Christ and the witness of the Spirit in the worshiping community. With emphasis on the miraculous, it seems logical that Pentecostals would be willing to affirm the presence of Christ and the Spirit in the bread and cup of the holy meal. These two views are not mutually exclusive.

The Medicine of Immortality

In the Gospel of Matthew, we find that the feeding miracles are performed in the context of Jesus' healing ministry. The first feeding miracle and the miracle of Jesus walking on the water occur between Matthew's reporting of Jesus healing the sick. Just before the feeding miracle, Jesus "saw a large crowd, and felt compassion for them and healed their sick" (Matthew 14:14). Immediately after Jesus walked on the water, He and His disciples arrived at Gennesaret where "the men of that place recognized Him, they sent word into all that surrounding district and brought to Him all who were sick; and they implored Him that they might just touch the fringe of His cloak; and as many as touched it were cured" (Matthew 14:35-36). Likewise, the second feeding miracle at the Sea of Galilee occured in the context of Jesus' healing ministry (Matthew 15:29-38). In both feeding miracles, Jesus was concerned for the well-being of the multitudes. He was moved with compassion and concerned that the people might faint, or grow weary, for their lack of sustenance. Also, in both instances, Jesus commanded His disciples to feed the multitude, and Jesus offered a blessing (Matthew 14:19) and a prayer of thanksgiving for the loaves and fishes. The Greek word for "giving thanks" is *eucharistéo* (Matthew 15:36). In healing the sick and providing food for the weary, Jesus was

restoring *shalom* to the people of God. Jesus is the Anointed One
who restores and satisfies the sick and hungry. The healing ministry
of Jesus is one of the thematic emphases of Matthew's Gospel. Citing
the prophet Isaiah, Matthew wrote:

> When evening came, they brought to Him many who were
> demon-possessed; and He cast out the spirits with a word,
> and healed all who were ill. This was to fulfill what was
> spoken through Isaiah the prophet: "He Himself took our
> infirmities and carried away our diseases" (Matthew 8:16-
> 17; Isaiah 53:4-5).

Jesus' healing miracles were signs of the coming of the kingdom
of God in which the powers of sin and death are destroyed. Healing
miracles are not an end unto themselves. They are signs that point
to the resurrection of the dead. In both feeding miracles, Jesus
blessed, or eucharized, the meal and then gave the loaves and fishes
to His disciples for distribution to the multitudes. Later, when Jesus
gathered His disciples to share His last Passover meal, He gave
thanks (*eucharistéo*) for the bread and cup and passed the bread
and cup to His disciples.

> While they were eating, Jesus took some bread, and after a
> blessing, He broke it and gave it to the disciples, and said,
> "Take, eat; this is My body." And when He had taken a cup
> and given thanks, He gave it to them, saying, "Drink from
> it, all of you; for this is My blood of the covenant, which
> is poured out for many for forgiveness of sins" (Matthew
> 26:26-28).

This meal, the Lord's Supper, is offered for the salvation of humanity. This is the ultimate feeding miracle in which Jesus has offered
His own body on the cross, and in the bread and cup, for human
salvation.

Bishop Ignatius of Antioch referred to the bread of the Eucharist
as the "medicine of immortality, the antidote we take in order not
to die, but to live forever in Jesus Christ."[216] Ignatius used the Greek

---

[216] *The Apostolic Fathers*, 93.

phrase *pharmakon athanasias* which was a technical medical term that referred to a healing ointment.[217] This was a metaphor that was adopted by later bishops of the early church. Irenaeus said that in the Eucharist "the substance of our flesh is increased and supported" and because of the nourishing power of the Eucharist, the bodies of believers, even though they suffer decomposition in the earth, shall be raised in immortality.[218] Cyprian spoke of "the true medicine derived from the atonement." The context of this statement suggests that Cyprian was speaking in reference to the Eucharist.[219] Augustine suggested that all forms of miracles and healings were caused by means of the sacraments.[220] All humans suffer from a terminal disease—sin. Because of our sinfulness, we are corrupt. This corruption is demonstrated in a multitude of diseases— physical, psychological, and spiritual. The early church believed that by partaking in the Eucharist, believers receive "medicine" that heals. In the bread and cup of the Eucharist, believers partake of the flesh and blood of the Great Physician. The healing ministry of Christ continues through the holy meal.

Early Pentecostals enthusiastically affirmed the ancient understanding of the Eucharist as therapeutic. Actually, it is here in associating the Lord's Supper with divine healing that Pentecostals completely embraced the holy meal as a sacrament—a means of grace in which Christ is present.

> The Lord Jesus is brought very near in the observance of the Lord's Supper. The redemptive work for the body is often attested to, as the communicants partake in faith, drinking His blood, and eating His flesh, the Lord healing them of sicknesses and delivering them of infirmities. Praise His precious name forever.[221]

---

[217] Willy Rordorf and Others, *The Eucharist of the Early Christians* (New York: Pueblo Publishing Company, 1978), 61. Also, William R. Schoedel, *Ignatius of Antioch: A Commentary on the Letters of Ignatius of Antioch* (Philadelphia: Fortress Press, 1985), 97-99.

[218] *The Ante-Nicene Fathers Vol. 1*, 528.

[219] *The Ante-Nicene Fathers Vol. 5*, 441.

[220] *Nicene and Post Nicene Fathers, First Series, Vol. 2*, 485.

[221] J. Roswell Flower, "The Lord's Supper." *Word and Witness* (August 1915), 5.

This theme is common in the writings of early Pentecostals, and continues to be present among many Pentecostals today. Holy Communion is often presented as a means of grace that has a twofold purpose. The cup represents the blood of Jesus Christ which is shed for the remission of sins. The broken bread represents the body of the Lord, which was broken for the healing of the physical body.

> This meal is intended not only for our spiritual, but our physical benefit. Here is good news for the sick. You are invited to a meal for your health. As you are eating in faith you can receive healing for your body.[222]

Pentecostals often referred to the Lord's Supper as "God's medicine." It was suggested that some believers left the Lord's Table sick and afflicted because they did not properly discern "in the bread His perfect body broken for their imperfect bodies." Early Pentecostal periodicals included testimonies of believers who were healed as they participated in the Lord's Supper.[223] Pentecostal Communion services are not to be mere ritual. They are salvific encounters with God in which believers are brought into God's presence so that they may receive spiritual nourishment for their souls and medicine for their physical bodies.

Worship That Is Prophetic

The celebration of the Lord's Supper is a prophetic act of worship. The active presence of Spirit in worship is at the heart of Pentecostal belief and practice. From the outset, Pentecostals viewed themselves as a prophetic people. They were prophetic in their call for prayer and repentance; purity and holiness; renewal of the *charismata* and an emphasis on the imminent return of Christ.

---

[222] D.W. Kerr, "The Message of the Sacrament," 4.
[223] "Virtue in the Perfect Body of Jesus." *The Apostolic Faith* (February-March 1907), 2. E.R. Trussell, "The Lord's Supper," *Confidence* (April 1915), 70. E.N. Bell, "The Lord's Supper," *The Christian Evangel* (12 July 1919), 12. Don Mallough, "The Twofold Meaning of Communion" *The Pentecostal Evangel* (29 January 1956), 3, 21-22. John W. Everett, "Healing at the Communion Table," *The Pentecostal Evangel* (18 February 1968), 13.

Worship in the Pentecostal church can and should be a prophetic experience. As worshipers sing and pray, and as the Spirit is manifested in worship, there may be shouts of praise, expressive dancing, and/or ecstatic tongues. When sinners are present, the Holy Spirit "convicts" or "confronts" with a call to repentance. Worshipers experiencing the presence of God, identify with the prophet Isaiah, who cried, "Woe is me, for I am ruined! Because I am a man of unclean lips, and I live among a people of unclean lips; for my eyes have seen the King, the Lord of hosts" (Isaiah 6:5). The apostle Paul experienced a sense of the same as he wrote, "But if all prophesy, and an unbeliever or an ungifted man enters, he is convicted by all, he is called to account by all; the secrets of his heart are disclosed; and so he will fall on his face and worship God, declaring that God is certainly among you" (1 Corinthians 14:24-25). The presence of God in worship is a prophetic call whereby sins are disclosed, sinners are convicted, and God is exalted.

In the same manner, celebration of the Lord's Supper is a prophetic act of worship. When instructing the Corinthians regarding proper observance of the Lord's Supper, Paul speaks of spiritual accountability.

> Therefore whoever eats the bread or drinks the cup of the Lord in an unworthy manner, shall be guilty of the body and the blood of the Lord. But a man must examine himself, and in so doing he is to eat of the bread and drink of the cup. For he who eats and drinks, eats and drinks judgment to himself if he does not judge the body rightly. For this reason many among you are weak and sick, and a number sleep. But if we judged ourselves rightly, we would not be judged. But when we are judged, we are disciplined by the Lord so that we will not be condemned along with the world (1 Corinthians 11:27-32).

Here, Paul uses words that "belong to the semantic domain of the law and the courtroom."[224] Consider the following words:

- *anaxiōs*, vs. 27; cf. 6:2—unworthy
- *enochos*, vs. 27—guilty

---

[224] Raymond F. Collins, *First Corinthians*, Sacra Pagina (Collegeville, MN: The Liturgical Press, 1999), 436.

- *dokimazō*, vs. 28—examine, scrutinize
- *krima*, vv. 29, 34—judgement
- *diakrinō, vv. 29, 31; krinō, vv. 31-32*— judge
- *paideuō*, v. 32—disciplined
- *katakrinō*, v. 32—condemn

Paul insists that self-examination and the discipline of the Lord are integral aspects of sacramental worship. It is through self-examination that worshipers escape the Lord's discipline and judgment. When Isaiah stood at the temple altar, he became intensely aware of personal sins. Similarly, when a publican prostrated himself before God, he accurately discerned his spiritual deficiency (Luke 18:13). Both Isaiah and the publican encountered God's holiness, discerned their sinfulness, and experienced the grace and power of God.

The Scriptures are replete with examples of those who discerned their spiritual condition incorrectly and encountered the discipline and judgment of the Lord. Judgment begins at the "household of God" (1 Peter 4:17). The boastful Pharisee trusted his own righteousness, and was not justified before God (Luke 18:11). Ananias and Sapphira discovered too late they could not hide sin from the discerning Spirit and suffered swift judgment (Acts 5:1-11). To be "in covenant" with God means that individuals present themselves in accountability to the whole body. Paul commanded the Corinthians to discipline those in the church guilty of immorality, lest the whole church suffer the judgment of one person's sin. The Table of the Lord can be a place where the Spirit reveals sin and thus brings the guilty to repentance. Anyone who approaches the Table of the Lord unrepentant or irreverently risks the Table of Life becoming a table of death. The purpose of such discipline and judgment is redemptive. The hope is that the offending one might be saved.[225] When approaching the Lord's Table, a worshiper who fails to self-judge correctly will be judged by the sovereign Lord.

---

[225] 1 Corinthians 5:1-5; 11:32; Hebrews 12:5-11; Revelation 3:19.

Qoheleth's ancient warning is appropriate: "Guard your steps as you go to the house of God and draw near to listen rather than to offer the sacrifice of fools; for they do not know they are doing evil" (Ecclesiastes 5:1).

The postapostolic church developed the practice of "closed Communion" in which those who were not baptized, or those who became apostate, were excluded from the Table. The Didache says, "But let no one eat or drink of your Eucharist except those who have been baptized into the name of the Lord, for the Lord has also spoken concerning this: 'Do not give what is holy to dogs!'"[226] Also, *The Apostolic Tradition* states "Let everyone take care that an unbeliever does not taste of the Eucharist."[227] However, Paul does not state that sinful individuals should be refused the Table of Lord, but that everyone who approaches the Lord's Table should do so with great care. The Table of the Lord, as a means of grace, is a place where the Spirit reveals sin and brings the guilty to repentance. The church should never refuse grace to a sinner who comes to the Table.

A colleague in ministry once shared the testimony of his conversion. He had been attending church for some time, but had not accepted Christ as Lord. One Sunday morning, during the observance of Communion, he experienced the conviction of the Holy Spirit and the call to salvation. He rose from his seat and approached the altar. As he received the bread and cup of Holy Communion, he repented and accepted Christ as Lord. He testified, "From that day to this, I have loved Communion." For this believer, the celebration of the Lord's Supper is indeed a meal of grace. His experience is a modern answer to an ancient Eucharistic prayer: "If anyone is holy, come. If anyone is not, convert!"[228]

The Eucharist is a meal of confession and reconciliation. As believers approach the Table of the Lord, they must come in unbroken fellowship. Sometimes this requires times of private and

---

[226] *The Apostolic Fathers*, 154.

[227] *The Apostolic Tradition*. Translation by Paul F. Bradshaw, *The Apostolic Tradition: A Commentary* (Minneapolis: Augsburg Fortress Publishers, 2002), 37.

[228] Didache 10:6. Translation by Aaron Milavec, *The Didache*, 35.

public confession. Relationships within family and church cannot be healed without sincere confession. The Didache suggests that one of the best opportunities for reconciliation is the observance of Holy Communion.

> On the Lord's own day gather together and break bread and give thanks, having first confessed your sins so that your sacrifice may be pure. But let no one who has a quarrel with a companion join you until they have been reconciled, so that your sacrifice may not be defiled.[229]

The issue is holiness—a holy church that offers holy worship. Jesus said, "Therefore you are to be perfect, as your heavenly Father is perfect" (Matthew 5:48). Paul encouraged, "Let us cleanse ourselves from all defilement of flesh and spirit, perfecting holiness in the fear of God" (2 Corinthians 7:1). Each believer must strive for perfection. When sinfulness is discovered, the only remedy is confession. The Christian church must be a holy fellowship. Quarrels within the fellowship demonstrate the presence of lust and greed (James 4:1-2). Jesus is coming for "a glorious church, not having spot or wrinkle or any such thing, but that she should be holy and without blemish" (Ephesians 5:27). The writers of the Didache share Paul's concern for accountability. The weekly Eucharist offers an opportunity for believers to examine their own lives, as well and the spiritual health of the community. As the church gathers around the altar, or Table of the Lord, sinful believers may come seeking mercy. We must understand that sincere confession is not a license to sin. Confession is placing ourselves under subjection to spiritual elders who will offer prayers on our behalf as well as hold us accountable. Confession is not an excuse for sin, but seeking deliverance from sin. This is often a painful process and many tears will be shed, but the outcome is joy and eternal life.

The Lord's Supper is prophetic because it anticipates the Marriage Supper of the Lamb (Revelation 19:9). Paul said, "For as often as you eat this bread and drink the cup, you proclaim the Lord's death *until He comes*" (1 Corinthians 11:26). The return of Christ is the blessed

---

[229] *The Apostolic Fathers*, 157.

hope of the church (Titus 2:13). The resurrection of the body is the hope of every Christian(1 Corinthians 15:16-19). The Eucharistic prayer found in the Didache expresses the eschatological hope of early Christians:

> Remember your church, Lord, to deliver it from all evil and to make it perfect in love; and gather it, the one that has been sanctified, from the four winds into your kingdom, which you have prepared for it; for yours is the power and glory forever. May grace come, and may this world pass away. . . Maranatha![230]

At the Table of the Lord, believers participate in an eschatological meal that anticipates the resurrection of the body and the new heaven and earth. The bread and cup of Christ express the deepest hopes of humanity. Pentecostalism is an eschatological movement. The outpouring of the Holy Spirit and the renewal of spiritual gifts are prophetic signs that God has inaugurated the "last days." Pentecostals anticipate the imminent return of the Lord. Because of the eschatological emphasis in Pentecostal theology, celebration of the Lord's Supper should be a primary element of Pentecostal worship.

Celebration of the Lord's Supper

"While we are taking Communion, let us get into the Spirit and draw from God."
—William A. Cox

The Lord's Supper was a normative event celebrated weekly, or perhaps, daily in the early church. The challenge for Pentecostal pastors—who seek to conform to the New Testament pattern of worship—is to integrate the celebration of the Lord's Supper into regular worship in a way that encourages worshipers to encounter the Holy Spirit. In many Protestant and Pentecostal churches, the Lord's Supper is served by elders to congregants who are either standing or seated throughout the sanctuary. This tradition dates to the practice of Ulrich Zwingli, and later, to the Anabaptists. This

---

[230] *The Apostolic Fathers*, 155.

method does nothing to encourage the worshiper to understand the Lord's Supper as an altar call. For Pentecostals, worship is defined as a "Spirit-movement" and is expressed in terms of movement—the lifting of hands, clapping, shouting, dancing, and many other physical activities. One of the most significant movements in the Pentecostal worship service is the altar call. As the Holy Spirit moves during worship, Pentecostal worshipers are encouraged to move to the altar. Hence, it is natural for Pentecostals to respond to an invitation to come to the altar to receive Holy Communion. This was the preferred method of many first-generation Pentecostals.

> On Saturday night, July 30, after the sermon by Brother Latimer, *the saints assembled at the altar for the sacrament*, afterwards came the good old time love feast of feet washing (emphasis mine).[231]

The Lord's Supper should be celebrated as an altar call where worshipers present themselves as "a living sacrifice, holy, acceptable to God" (Romans 12:1) and receive the body and blood of Jesus.

Frequent celebration of the Lord's Supper can be incorporated into Pentecostal worship in a variety of ways. One of which is to celebrate the Supper during the "praise and worship" portion of a worship service. As worshipers sing, congregants are directed to move to the altar where elders serve the bread and cup. After receiving the Supper elements, congregants may return to their seats to conclude the service. In this manner, the celebration of the Lord's Supper is not an interruption of the worship service, but a natural movement and essential part of worship.

Because the altar call is usually the climax of Pentecostal worship, a pastor may wish to incorporate the Lord's Supper as a closing altar call. After an invitation to sinners and/or those desiring prayer for healing or other needs, a pastor may call all worshipers to the altar for a time of prayer. The bread and cup may be offered to all worshipers who come forward to pray, or after worshipers have prayed. This

---

[231] Turner Brogdon, "Report of a Georgia Meeting," *Church of God Evangel* (August 20, 1921), 2.

option provides the opportunity to employ another way to celebrate the Lord's Supper.

The celebration of Holy Communion is essentially a prayer service, in which believers receive into themselves the body and blood of Christ through the Holy Spirit, who animates and inspires Christian worship. Here are some suggestions for the order of a Communion service.

SONGS OF CELEBRATION

It is appropriate for the Pentecostal worship leader to select and prepare songs/hymns that contribute to participative worship. Celebration of the Lord's Supper lends itself to a wide variety of worship expressions: laments for sin, rejoicing for forgiveness, thanksgiving for reconciliation and joyful anticipation of the Lord's return. Therefore, this service should be planned with much prayer and sensitivity to the leadership of the Holy Spirit. The songs and hymns for the celebration of the Lord's Supper should reflect the themes of: remembrance, Atonement, nourishment, healing, confession, fellowship, and the second advent of Christ. If this observance and celebration is understood to represent the entirety of Pentecostal proclamation, then almost any song from "Amazing Grace" to "Victory in Jesus" is appropriate. However, there are some classic hymns and songs that are especially appropriate for Pentecostal worship:

> C.C. Widmeyer, S.H. Bolton, "**Come and Dine**," *Hymns of the Spirit,* (Cleveland, TN, Pathway Press, 1969) 144.

> Milton Bourgeois, "**Rise and Be Healed**,"*The Celebration Hymnal* (Word Music/Integrity Music, 1997) 711.

> . S.J. Henderson, D.B. Towner, "**Saved by the Blood**," *Hymns of the Spirit,* 70.

> V.B. "Vep" Ellis, "**Let Me Touch Him**," *Hymns of the Spirit,* 284.

Also, there are some wonderful contemporary worship songs and hymns that will enrich the Eucharistic occasion:

> Wayne Watson, "**People of God**," *The Celebration Hymnal,* 427.

Shawn Lewis, "**Altar of God**," *Glory Revealed: The Word of God in Worship*, Reunion, 2007.

David Nasser, Mac Powell, "**By His Wounds**," *Glory Revealed: The Word of God in Worship*, Reunion, 2007.

Leeland Dayton Mooring, Marc Byrd, Steve Hindalong, "**Carried to the Table**," *Sound of Melodies*, Essential, 2006.

Claire Cloninger, Martin J. Nystrom, "**Come to the Table**," *Come to the Table*, Sparrow, 1991.

Michael Card, "**Come to the Table**," *The Ultimate Collection*, Sparrow, 2006.

Don Moen, "**I Am the God That Healeth Thee**," *Give Thanks*, Integrity/Epic, 1991.

Kathryn Scott, "**Hungry (Falling on My Knees)**," *Satisfy*, Vertical Music, 2003.

Brenton Brown, Glenn Robertson, "**All Who Are Thirsty**," *The Best Worship Songs Ever*, Virgin/EMI, 2004.

Public reading of Scripture, and/or a short meditation or homily by the pastor or elder is appropriate for this occasion.

REFLECTIONS ON HOLY COMMUNION

1 Corinthians 11:24-32

I. As we worship God in Holy Communion, we are brought face to face with the grim reality of the death of our Lord as a sacrifice for sin (1 Corinthians 11:24).

II. As we worship God in Holy Communion, we are brought face to face with the darkness of our sinful lives and the joyous reality of our redemption (1 Corinthians 11:28).

III. As we worship God in Holy Communion, we affirm the spiritual union of all believers together with Christ(1 Corinthians 10:16-17).

IV. As we worship God in Holy Communion, we celebrate the resurrection of our Lord and we anticipate His glorious appearing at the end of this age (1 Corinthians 11:26).

After the pastor or elder shares the message, a call to prayer should be announced. The model for this prayer is "The Lord's Prayer" (Matthew 6:9-13). Use of the Lord's Prayer during the celebration of sacraments is a tradition that dates back to the first century.[232] This should not be understood as the recitation of a formal prayer. By using the Lord's Prayer as a model, the pastor or elder leads the congregation in a time of *Spirit-directed* prayer.

There is evidence to suggest that early Eucharistic services included spontaneous moves of the Holy Spirit. The Apostle Paul associates the Greek word *eucharistéō* (the Eucharistic blessing) with "praying in the Spirit" (1 Corinthians 14:16-17). The Didache describes the Eucharist as "Spirit-sent food and drink for life forever through your servant Jesus Christ."[233] The local prophets within the Didache community were encouraged to offer Spirit-inspired Eucharistic prayers. Concerning the charismatic nature of Eucharistic prayer in the early church, Aaron Milavec has written:

> The prayer and gestures of the eucharistic celebrant might have been engaging, true, and profound—provoking deep longings and offering fervent hope. The prophets . . . . began with the closing eucharistic petitions of saving, perfecting, and gathering the church and transformed these into living and breathing expectations that those present were able to "taste and see"—provoking tears and trembling and jubilation. The prophetic eucharistizing, therefore, was the sweet dessert that culminated the eucharistic meal.[234]

If the celebration of Holy Communion is to be a Spirit movement, pastors and congregations should nurture the expectation that these services are Spirit-empowered events.

---

[232] Didache 8:2.
[233] Didache 10:3. Translation by Aaron Milavec, *The Didache*, 33.
[234] Aaron Milavec, *The Didache*, 434.

INVITATION TO PRAYER

In this manner, therefore, pray: Our Father in heaven, Hallowed be Your name.

Offer a prayer of worship and adoration.

Your kingdom come. Your will be done on earth as it is in heaven.

Offer an intercessory prayer for the power of God's Kingdom to be manifested in all the earth.

Pray for the salvation of souls

Pray for the unity and mission of the church

Pray for the fullness of the Holy Spirit

Pray for laborers for the harvest

Pray for those in spiritual authority

Pray for those who need healing and deliverance

Pray for broken families to be mended

Pray for those who govern in the world.

Give us this day our daily bread.

Offer a prayer for God's daily blessings to be on your family and extended community.

And forgive us our debts, as we forgive our debtors.

Offer a prayer of repentance and reconciliation to examine our relationship with God and others.

And do not lead us into temptation, but deliver us from the evil one.

Offer a prayer of empowerment in spiritual warfare.

For Yours is the kingdom and the power and the glory forever. Amen.

Offer an affirmation of the sovereignty of God to accomplish God's will in us.

Remember, movement to the altar is the heart of Pentecostal worship. Through the years, I have observed many believers as they approached the altar to receive the holy meal. Many people who don't frequently respond to an altar call will come to receive the Eucharist. As they come to the Table they do so prayerfully and reverently. They move to the altar with the community. Often they tarry at the altar prayerfully reflecting upon the significance of the

Eucharist. They come to the altar, not to receive the bread and cup, but to encounter God through Christ and the Spirit.

CELEBRATION OF HOLY COMMUNION
from
*The Book of Common Prayer**

Holy and gracious Father: In your infinite love you made us for yourself; and, when we had fallen into sin and become subject to evil and death, you, in your mercy, sent Jesus Christ, your only and eternal Son, to share our human nature, to live and die as one of us, to reconcile us to you, the God and Father of all.

He stretched out his arms upon the cross, and offered himself, in obedience to your will, a perfect sacrifice for the whole world.

TAKING THE BREAD

On the night he was handed over to suffering and death, our Lord Jesus Christ took bread; and when he had given thanks to you, he broke it, and gave it to his disciples, and said, "Take, eat: This is my Body, which is given for you. Do this for the remembrance of me.

TAKING THE CUP

After supper he took the cup of wine; and when he had given thanks, he gave it to them, and said, "Drink this, all of you: This is my Blood of the new Covenant, which is shed for you and for many for the forgiveness of sins. Whenever you drink it, do this for the remembrance of me."

The minister receives the Sacrament in both hands, and then delivers it to the people.

**Book of Common Prayer* (New York: Oxford University Press, 1990) 362-363.

The worship ideas offered here are guides; they are not attempts to establish a "Pentecostal liturgy." To suggest the need for a Pentecostal liturgical recitation is inconsistent with the wonderful spontaneous, Spirit-movement characteristic of Pentecostal worship.

Consideration should be given to the physical preparation of the bread and cup. Use of a single cup and a single loaf is preferred by many when administering the elements to the congregants. This provides a strong visual component for worshipers. If a congregation prefers using individual cups, the pastor may still desire to pour the "wine" from a larger single cup into smaller individual cups. Or, the leader may choose to distribute the bread to worshipers at the altar. Then the worshipers may come to the one cup, dip the bread into the cup, and then consume the "flesh and blood" of Christ.

The content of the cup, wine or grape juice, has become a point of contention for some Christians. One of the great issues of concern for the nineteenth century Holiness Movement was the prohibition of alcoholic beverages. Because of the strong social influence of the Holiness Movement, the use of pasteurized grape juice, instead of wine, in Communion services has become common since the late 1860s. Most Pentecostals use nonalcoholic wine, or pasteurized grape juice for the cup.

The loaf, representing the body of our Lord, should be a single loaf of bread which provides a uniformly recognizable visual image. Of course, any type of loaf may be used, but the presiding leader will learn that round Mediterranean pita bread works perfectly. Or, a pastor might wish to use the larger "Eucharistic host" commonly used in liturgical churches. The "host" is especially prepared bread for use in Communion. It is about five inches in diameter and scored so it can easily be broken into small pieces.

The use of the single cup and the single loaf in the Eucharistic service projects a strong theological message—all Christians receive salvation and spiritual nourishment from one Lord (Ephesians 4:5). This can be a profound visual statement about the unity of the Christian faith and to the unity of the church. Those who prepare Communion should approach their task with reverence and care. The elements of Communion, once consecrated, constitute more than bread and cup. It is a pastor's responsibility to inform the congregation regarding the true nature and proper observance of Communion. A congregation that expects commercially produced wafers and grape juice from a bottle, or a prepackage item, may project a low view of this sacred observance. However, when congregations are properly informed of the charismatic nature of sacramental worship, they approach the Table of the Lord as an act of spiritual worship.

The Book of Doctrines

Issued in the Interest of The Church of God

Copyright 1922

Church of God Publishing House

Cleveland, Tennessee

The Lord's Supper (from pages 69-70)

Those who have not participated in the service of the Lord's Supper have missed some of the most sacred and hallowed moments in the entire Christian Life. The heart melts completely in contemplation of the death and suffering of Christ. In deep contrition, and repeated regret that our hearts could ever have been so far away from Him, we beg and implore, Father, forgive us our trespasses as we forgive those who trespass against us. Usually the heart is softened in the deepest gratitude and devotion, and often we break into tears. When we think how Christ suffered in His agonizing prayer in Gethsemane, our sorrow is often too deep for tears. Surely nothing could take the place of the Lord's Supper. As the unleavened bread is broken can we not hear the beat of the hammer that drove the nails into His hands and His feet? And the spear piercing His side? And as we behold the wine in the cup, does it not better than anything else in the world bring thoughts of the shed blood of Christ- the tears in the Garden that were as great drops of blood? And the blood that trickled down, and flowed from His hands and His feet, and gushed from His side and He bowed His head, and said, "It is finished." May the day not come when we shall forget Calvary and the sacrifice for sin that was made there for the whole world. And could that include even me? It could, and that is the thought that fills our heart as we partake of the body and blood of the Lord is symbol and remembrance until He comes. Even so come Lord Jesus!

CHAPTER 6

ƒootwashing:
The ƒellowship oƒ
The Towel

If I then, the Lord and the Teacher, washed your feet, you also ought to wash one another's feet. For I gave you an example that you also should do as I did to you" (John 13:14-15).

"The feet washing service is one among the most beautiful and attractive services that we have... There may be something deeper in feet washing than we will ever know in this world."

—A.J. Tomlinson

ƒ ootwashing is a sacred act of worship that has a special significance in my spiritual journey. I believe it to be especially suited for Pentecostal worship. My experience has been that footwashing is the Spirit and church at play. Footwashing services are joyful occasions in which believers express love and devotion for each other. Believers wash each other's feet as they shout, pray, and speak in other tongues. In the midst of this symphony of praise, one can hear the sounds of water splashing. At times, it all seems a bit silly, like watching small children play under the water hose during a hot summer day. Maybe the appeal of footwashing is that as we come to "play in the Spirit," we become little children. By participating in footwashing, our pretense is stripped away. One may walk into a footwashing service as a respected attorney or professor, but in moments, the pretense of respected position is erased as believers worship in their bare feet, washing the feet of their brothers in Christ.

Footwashing has never been universally accepted as a sacrament, even among Pentecostals. But it has long been observed by the church as an occasional sacramental rite. There is evidence to suggest that some of the church fathers understood footwashing as a sacrament associated with water baptism. In *Homilies on the Gospel of John*, Augustine referred to footwashing as a "wonderful sacramental symbol" and a "lofty mystery."[235] Ambrose interpreted footwashing as a sacramental act that demonstrates the "mystery of humility."[236] Benedict (sixth century) included footwashing among the weekly disciplines to be observed as an example of loving service.[237] In 694, the Seventeenth Synod of Toledo commanded all bishops and priests in a position of superiority to wash the feet of those subject to them.[238] Bernard of Clairvaux (twelfth century) recommended daily footwashing as a sacrament for the remission of sins.[239]

Today, some liturgical churches observe the practice of footwashing. It is normally associated with the observance of the Maundy Thursday of Holy Week. In this observance, the priest washes the feet of designated parishioners in remembrance of when Jesus washed His disciples' feet and as a sign that those ordained to Christian ministry follow the Lord as servant to God's people. Footwashing has also been incorporated into the services of installation for popes, bishops and other hierarchical church leaders. In the installation service, the newly ordained bishop will wash the feet of a priest, deacon, or layperson under his charge. The significance of footwashing in this context is to establish that all who serve in authority in the church must do so in the spirit of love and humility. Irenaeus, one of the earliest defenders of the apostolic succession of the bishops, insisted that ecclesiastical authority "consists in the preeminent gift of love, which is more precious than knowledge,

---

[235] *The Nicene and Post-Nicene Fathers, Vol. VII,* 303.
[236] *The Nicene and Post-Nicene Fathers, Second Series, Vol. X,* 95.
[237] *The Rule of St. Benedict,* 35:1-9.
[238] *Catholic Encyclopedia* s.v. "Washing of Feet and Hands."
[239] *New Schaff-Herzog Encyclopedia of Religious Knowledge* s.v. "Foot-washing."

more glorious than prophecy, and which excels all the other gifts of God."[240] Footwashing as a sacred act of worship demonstrates such loving service.

Throughout the history of the church, footwashing has often been adopted by renewal movements which have protested against the ecclesiastical hierarchy. The most notable of these groups are the Anabaptists. The earliest Anabaptists practiced footwashing in a literal sense. That is, footwashing was not observed in conjunction with communal worship, but was observed in the believer's home as they received guests. Menno Simons wrote, "Do wash the feet of your beloved brethren and sisters who are come to you from a distance, tired. Be not ashamed to do the work of the Lord, but humble yourselves with Christ, before your brethren, so that all humility of godly quality may be found in you."[241] Later, many Anabaptist churches adopted footwashing as an addendum to the observance of the Lord's Supper. Article thirteen of *The Confession of Faith in a Mennonite Perspective,* which was adopted by the General Conference of the Mennonite Church and Mennonite Churches in 1995, states:

> We believe that Jesus Christ calls us to serve one another in love as he did. Rather than seeking to lord it over others, we are called to follow the example of our Lord, who chose the role of a servant by washing his disciples' feet.
>
> Just before his death, Jesus stooped to wash the disciples' feet and told them, "So if I, your Lord and Teacher, have washed your feet, you also ought to wash one another's feet. For I have given you an example, that you also should do as I have done to you." In this act, Jesus showed humility and servanthood, even laying down his life for those he loved. In washing the disciples' feet, Jesus acted out a parable of his life unto death for them, and of the way his disciples are called to live in the world.
>
> Believers who wash each other's feet show that they share in the body of Christ. They thus acknowledge their frequent need of cleansing, renew their willingness to let go of pride

---

[240] *The Ante-Nicene Fathers, Vol. I,* 508.
[241] John C. Wenger, ed., *Complete Writings of Menno Simons: Circa 1496-1561* (Scottdale, PA: Herald Press, 1956), 417.

and worldly power, and offer their lives in humble service and sacrificial love.[242]

These words reflect an Anabaptist spirituality in which the observance of footwashing is understood as:

- A protest against hierarchy.
- A demonstration of Christlike humility.
- A rejection of the worldly power.
- A sign of Christian community.
- An expression of the believers' need for cleansing from sin.

Pentecostals share much in common with this Anabaptist spirituality.

For many Pentecostal churches, the sacrament of footwashing has been understood as significant to congregational spirituality and worship.[243] W.J. Seymour listed footwashing as one of the "three ordinances of the church." For Seymour, footwashing was a "type of regeneration" and was an act of devotion that led the participants to "humility and charity."[244] The first General Assembly of the Church of God declared that "Communion and feet washing are taught by the New Testament Scriptures . . . [therefore] in order to preserve the unity of the body, and to obey the sacred Word, we recommend that every member engage in these sacred services . . . one or more times each year."[245] Footwashing is understood to be one of the "sacred services" of the Church, ordained by the Scriptures. "Every member" is encouraged to observe this sacred service on the basis of fidelity to the "sacred Word" and the unity of the church. Also, even though the official statement suggests that footwashing be

---

[242] *Confession of Faith in a Mennonite Perspective* (Scottdale, PA: Herald Press, 1995).

[243] Pentecostal churches which affirm footwashing as sacramental include: Church of God (Cleveland, TN); Church of God in Christ; Pentecostal Church of God; Church of God of Prophecy; Pentecostal Free-Will Baptist Churches; and others. The International Pentecostal Holiness Church "allows its members liberty of conscience in the observance of foot washing."

[244] W.J. Seymour, "The Ordinances Taught By Our Lord." *The Apostolic Faith* (September 1907), 2.

[245] *General Assembly Minutes 1906-1914*, 9-11.

observed "one or more times each year" it was observed much more frequently. Footwashing was observed at revivals, camp meetings, and special services. A.J. Tomlinson wrote:

> The feet washing service is one among the most beautiful and attractive services that we have. To see a little crowd of devoted saints humbly bowing before one another in holy reverence to Jesus and performing this little service just because Jesus said we ought to do it, and does not explain or give the reason for it, it is a mark of devotion and sincerity worthy of the most commendatory remarks. . . . There may be something deeper in feet washing than we will ever know in this world.[246]

Judging from the early literature, it can be faithfully stated that footwashing was just as important to the spirituality of these early Pentecostals as was speaking in tongues.

The Descent of the Word

Footwashing witnesses to the descent of the eternal Word. The Gospel of John presents a high Christology. Jesus Christ is the eternal Word who assumed human flesh. There is no ambiguity in John's claims about Jesus. The descent and incarnation of the eternal Word is summarized in just a few words: "And the Word became flesh, and dwelt among us, and we saw His glory, glory as of the only begotten from the Father, full of grace and truth" (John 1:14). John declared that God the Word descended from the glory and power essential to His nature to assume our nature and dwell among us. The descent of the Lord is a theme common to the New Testament. Peter spoke of the descent of our Lord when he "made proclamation to the spirits now in prison" (1 Peter 3:19). In a beautiful early hymn of the church, Paul relates to us the heart of his Christology:

> . . . Christ Jesus, who, although He existed in the form of God, did not regard equality with God a thing to be grasped, but emptied Himself, taking the form of a bond-servant, and being made in the likeness of men. Being found in appearance as a man, He humbled Himself by becoming

---

[246] A.J. Tomlinson, "Obedience to Jesus," *Church of God Evangel* (May 5, 1917), 1.

obedient to the point of death, even death on a cross. For
this reason also, God highly exalted Him, and bestowed
on Him the name which is above every name, so that at
the name of Jesus every knee will bow, of those who are in
heaven and on earth and under the earth, and that every
tongue will confess that Jesus Christ is Lord, to the glory of
God the Father (Philippians 2:5-11).

The apostolic witness of the New Testament interprets the
Incarnation using terms denoting humility and service. The nature
of the Incarnation is expressed by the following Greek terms:

- *katabainō*—descended, came down in John 3:13; 6:38, 51;
  Ephesians 4:9-10

- *kenoō*—to make empty in Philippians 2:7

- *doulos*—slave, servant, bondservant in Philippians 2:7

- *tapinoō*—"to make low," humbled, humiliate in Matthew
  11:29; Philippians 2:8

- *diakoneō*—"to serve" in Matthew 20:28; Mark 10:45

- *ptōcheuō*—"to become extremely poor" in 2 Corinthians 8:9

The image of Jesus rising from the table, laying aside His garments, taking a towel, pouring water into a basin, bowing before
His disciples and washing their feet incorporates into one prophetic
action the significance of the Incarnation. The story of Jesus washing the feet of His disciples serves as the introduction to the story of
His impending death on the cross, which is the climax of the Word's
descent. Jesus said, "I am the good shepherd; the good shepherd lays
down His life for the sheep . . . . No one has taken it away from Me,
but I lay it down on my own initiative" (John 10:11, 18). In Christ's
own self-emptying He has revealed to us the glory of God. Clement
of Alexandria wrote, "The Lord ate from a common bowl, and made
the disciples recline on the grass on the ground, and washed their
feet, girded with a linen towel—*He, the lowly-minded God, and Lord
of the universe*" (emphasis mine).[247]

---

[247] *The Ante-Nicene Fathers, Vol. II*, 247.

Christians are called to emptiness, humility, self-denial, and voluntary poverty.[248] This is the spirituality of footwashing—the fellowship of the towel. This is a difficult spirituality for Christians who live in a culture of affluence, where spirituality is defined in terms of prosperity and success. One who wishes to enter into the fellowship of the towel must first experience the *kenosis,* the emptying of one's self. When a rich young ruler came to Jesus seeking eternal life, he was told to empty himself. Jesus said, "One thing you still lack; sell all that you possess and distribute it to the poor, and you shall have treasure in heaven; and come, follow Me" (Luke 18:22). When Peter confessed, "You are the Christ," Jesus told His disciples "If anyone wishes to come after Me, he must deny himself, and take up his cross and follow Me" (Mark 8:34). Paul challenged the believers at Philippi: "Do nothing from selfishness or empty conceit, but with humility of mind regard one another as more important than yourselves" (Philippians 2:3). Footwashing is more than a sacramental act of worship; it is a way of life. As a sacrament, participation in footwashing is to participate in the humiliation of our Lord.

The Cross

Footwashing interprets Christ's sacrificial death. One of the major distinctions between John's Gospel and the synoptic Gospels is that of the relationship between the Lord's Supper as presented in the Synoptics, and the footwashing as presented by John. The three synoptic Gospels relate the institution of the Lord's Supper in conjunction with the Passover.[249] John presents the footwashing in conjunction with the Passover (John 13:1). The footwashing story is not presented by John in order to replace the Eucharist, but as an interpretation of the Eucharist. Both the Lord's Supper and Jesus' washing of his disciples' feet are presented as redemptive events by the collective witness of the four Gospels. In the synoptic Gospels, Jesus offered bread and wine—His body and blood—to establish

---

[248] Matthew 10:39; 16:24-25; 19:21; Mark 8:34-35; 10:21; Luke 9:23-24; 17:33; 18:22; John 12:26; Acts 2:45; 4:34-37; Philippians 2:3-5; 3:7-8.
[249] Matthew 26:17-19; Mark 14:12-16; Luke 22:7-13.

the covenant of salvation. In John, Jesus washed the feet of His disciples so that they might be cleansed and be in fellowship with Him (John 13:8-10). Irenaeus wrote, "For He who washed the feet of the disciples sanctified the entire body, and rendered it clean."[250] Athanasius implied a relationship between the act of footwashing and the crucifixion. He wrote, ". . . in the same body in which He was when he washed their feet, He also carried up our sins to the Tree."[251] In the synoptic Gospels, the Lord's Supper anticipates the cross and represents Christ's sacrificial death. In the gospel of John, Jesus' washing of His disciples' feet interprets the cross as the climax of the Son's descent in service to humanity.

The footwashing event is presented in terms of Christ's saving love and death. It is a regenerative act in that as Jesus washed their feet, the disciples experienced a spiritual transformation. Unless the disciples allowed Jesus to wash their feet, they could have "no part" of Him (John 13:8). The significance of this event as redemptive cannot be discounted. For Christ's disciples, footwashing was not a matter of their individual consciences, but a matter of salvation. To have their feet washed by Jesus was to confess Him as "Teacher and Lord" (John 13:13). Also, Jesus commanded His disciples to wash one another's feet (John 13:14). By doing so, they affirmed each other as disciples of Jesus. Footwashing interprets the cross as Jesus having laid down His life for His disciples. Likewise, He commanded His disciples to lay down their lives for one another.

Sanctification

The Gospel of John does not present an explicit account of Jesus' own baptism, nor does John present the institution of the Lord's Supper. However, water baptism and the Eucharist serve as salvific themes throughout. John presents Jesus washing His disciples' feet and His corresponding command that they wash each other's feet in the theological context of baptism and the Eucharist. Footwashing interprets the Eucharist in terms of the descent of the Son and His sacrificial death. Footwashing compliments water baptism and

---

[250] *The Ante-Nicene Fathers, Vol. I*, 493.
[251] *The Nicene and Post-Nicene Fathers, Second Series, Vol. IV*, 578.

signifies the ongoing life of faith. John of Damascus seems to have understood these three sacramental acts as an interrelated means of receiving God's salvific grace. He wrote:

> We were therefore given a birth by water and Spirit: I mean, by the holy baptism: and the food is the very bread of life, our Lord Jesus Christ, Who came down from heaven. For when He was about to take on Himself a voluntary death for our sakes, on the night on which He gave Himself up, He laid a new covenant on His holy disciples and apostles, and through them on all who believe on Him. In the upper chamber, then, of holy and illustrious Zion, after He had eaten the ancient Passover with His disciples and had fulfilled the ancient covenant, He washed His disciples' feet in token of the holy baptism.[252]

Footwashing is not to be understood as the initial regenerative event and should not be confused with water baptism. Augustine said that footwashing was not an accepted custom throughout the church, because some had confused it with water baptism. However, he affirmed footwashing during the season of Lent that it "might make a deeper and more serious impression."[253] John presented water baptism as the first of the transformation rituals (John 3:3, 5). Footwashing is presented as a subsequent event which indicates a continuing relationship in which the believer moves from being a new convert to a bond-servant of the Lord. Whereas, water baptism is presented as a single, initial event corresponding to the new birth; footwashing is presented as an oft-repeated event corresponding to the believer's need of continual cleansing. The conversation between Jesus and Peter reflects the distinction between water baptism and footwashing:

> Peter said to Him, "Never shall You wash my feet!" Jesus answered him, "If I do not wash you, you have no part with Me." Simon Peter said to Him, "Lord, then wash not only my feet, but also my hands and my head." Jesus said to him, "He who has bathed needs only to wash his feet" (John 13:8-10).

---

[252] *The Nicene and Post-Nicene Fathers, Second Series, Vol. IX*, 82.
[253] *The Nicene and Post-Nicene Fathers, Vol. I*, 314.

The "bath" to which the Lord refers may be that of water baptism. Peter has made his confession of faith and has been "born of water and the Spirit." That which Peter and the disciples now require is not the initial bath of cleansing, but a subsequent cleansing. Jesus desires that His disciples be "completely clean" (John 13:10).

The problem of postbaptismal sin was an issue of great concern in the early church. The baptismal doctrine of the early church taught that water baptism was the initial act of Christian confession which cleansed the human soul of original sin and all sins committed up to the point of baptism. By the time of the conversion of Constantine, many converts to the Christian faith were not baptized as an initial act of Christian confession, but waited until just before death. This was done because some Christians had come to believe that there was no remedy for sins committed after Christian baptism. These early Christians appealed to specific statements in the apostolic writings that seem to support such a teaching.

> For if we go on sinning willfully after receiving the knowledge of the truth, there no longer remains a sacrifice for sins (Hebrews 10:26; also see 6:1-4).

> For if, after they have escaped the defilements of the world by the knowledge of the Lord and Savior Jesus Christ, they are again entangled in them and are overcome, the last state has become worse for them than the first (2 Peter 2:20).

> No one who abides in Him sins; no one who sins has seen Him or knows Him (1 John 3:6; also see 3:9; 5:18).

The early fathers did not want to trivialize God's grace or the seriousness of human sin. Clement of Alexandria wrote, "He, then, who has received the forgiveness of sins ought to sin no more. . . But continual and successive repentings for sins differ nothing from the case of those who have not believed at all, except only in their consciousness that they do sin."[254] It should be understood that the sins of concern here were "mortal sins," such as idolatry, sexual immorality, or murder. A "mortal sin" is considered to be so grave that it may lead

---

[254] *The Ante-Nicene Fathers Vol. II*, 360-361.

one to apostasy. In an effort to offer grace to those who had fallen into sin after baptism, and to exercise discipline within the Christian community, the early church established the practice of *exomologesis*, that is, "second repentance" or "public confession."[255] If a believer committed a mortal sin, the penalty could be excommunication from the church. However, if the offending member submitted to a period of restoration (penance), climaxing in the *exomologesis*, then the believer could be reconciled. During this time of penance, the offending member does not cease to be a Christian (or a member of the church). The offending member is not allowed to participate in certain aspects of church life, such as, partaking of the Eucharist or serving as deacon. The climax of the period of restoration is the *exomologesis*, a public and dramatic display that at once is a confession of sin and an act of reconciliation. The *exomologesis* in not a verbal confession of sin; it is a *somatic* (of the body) confession of sin which demonstrates the desire to be reconciled. In *exomologesis* the body assumes the posture of repentance. To many Protestants this may seem to be an example of justification by works. It is, in fact, the operation of the Spirit of grace within the community of faith. Tertullian explained that "... *exomologesis* is a discipline for man's prostration and humiliation, enjoining a demeanor calculated to move mercy."[256] Pentecostals have taught that sinners must "bear fruits in keeping with repentance" (Luke 3:8; 19:8-9). Repentance of fallen believers includes doing one's "first works" (Revelation 2:5). The Pentecostal *way of salvation* is the pursuit of holiness, which is, sharing in the moral excellence of God. The pursuit of holiness affects the whole human self—spirit, soul, and body. Therefore, the confession of sin includes a right disposition of the heart, a true confession of the mouth, and presenting the body as "a living and holy sacrifice, acceptable to God, which is your spiritual service of worship" (Romans 12:1).

---

[255] *The Ante-Nicene Fathers Vol. II,* 360-361; *The Ante-Nicene Fathers Vol. III,* 660-666. Also: John T. McNeill, *A History of the Cure of Souls* (New York: Harper & Brothers Publishing, 1951) 88-111; and, Michel Foucault, "About the Beginning of the Hermeneutics of the Self," *Political Theory* 21 (May 1993), 198-227.

[256] *The Ante-Nicene Fathers Vol. III,* 664.

Footwashing may be understood as *exomologesis,* a sacramental act that, by the power of the Holy Spirit, effects sanctification within the Christian community. John Christopher Thomas has written that

> ". . . footwashing functions as an extension of the disciples baptism in that it signifies continual cleansing from the sin acquired (after baptism) through life in a sinful world. This act then is a sign of continued fellowship with Jesus."[257]

Footwashing is a somatic expression of profound love and humility which offers an opportunity for the sinful to confess their offenses and receive forgiveness. James wrote, "Therefore, confess your sins to one another, and pray for one another so that you may be healed" (James 5:16). Too often, we have viewed confession of sin as a private matter—a matter of concern between the sinner and the Lord only. This individualistic view of repentance too often allows the sinful Christian to hide behind grace. Grace becomes a license to sin, and sinfulness is not remedied. If the purpose of confession and forgiveness is juridical only, that is, a divine declaration of pardon, then this "Jesus-and-me" religion will suffice. However, according to James, the confession of sin "to one another" is significant to healing, which should be understood in terms of restoration to wholeness. Secret sin often leads to personal anguish. The psalmist prayed, "When I kept silent about my sin, my body wasted away through my groaning all day long" (Psalm 32:3). The theologians of the Reformation taught the doctrine of the priesthood of the believer, but Martin Luther did not reject the practice of the sinner's confession to a minister of the church. He wrote:

> Private confession should be retained in the church, for in it consciences afflicted and crushed by the terrors of sin lay themselves bare and receive consolation which they could not acquire in public preaching . . . an approach to

---

[257] John Christopher Thomas, *Footwashing in John 13 and the Johannine Community* (Sheffield: Sheffield Academic Press, 1991), 150.

confession should be opened up so that they may seek and find consolation among the ministers of the church.[258]

The ultimate purpose of confession is sanctification. This means that the sinful Christian must tell the truth about oneself. Instead of hiding behind a false sense of grace, the penitent believer reveals oneself and is transformed by grace. This type of confession and forgiveness of sin takes place within the community of faith. The regular confession of sin in the presence of one's brothers and sisters offers an opportunity for the cleansing of guilt and sorrow. The sinner must seek forgiveness from and reconciliation with the offended individuals (Matthew 5:23-24). The church graciously responds and offers forgiveness. This is signified in footwashing.

Footwashing should be understood as a ministry of the high priestly office of Christ. The writer of Hebrews tells us that the priesthood of Jesus Christ is "eternal" and "unchangeable" and that "He always lives to make intercession" for His disciples (Hebrews 7:24-25). Within the community of Jesus' disciples, there had been a clash of egos and many examples of failure. The disciples found themselves ineffective in exorcising a demon. Jesus rebuked them for their faithlessness (Mark 9:17-19). James and John sought power, to be first in the Kingdom. This desire led to contention among the Twelve (Mark 10:35-41). Even as Peter confessed, "You are the Christ," he rebuked the Lord. Later, after insisting "I will never fall away," he denied that he knew the Lord three times (Matthew 16:12-22; 26:69-75). Judas betrayed the Lord (Matthew 26:47-49). Speaking of Judas' place at the table, John Chrysostom wrote, "Therefore Christ also repaid him who was about to betray Him with everything opposite. He washed his feet, convicted him secretly, rebuked him sparingly, tended him, allowed him to share His table and His kiss, and not even by these was he made better; nevertheless (Christ) continued doing His own part."[259] Chrysostom presents a view of Jesus as high priest who washes the feet of Judas in an effort to redeem him.

---

[258] Martin Luther. *Lectures on Genesis Chapters 31 to 37,* 1554. Quoted in: Thomas Oden, *Classical Pastoral Care, volume 2.* (Grand Rapids: Baker Book House, 1987), 135.
[259] *The Nicene and Post-Nicene Fathers Vol. XIV,* 262.

Augustine understood footwashing in terms of a spiritual journey along the way of salvation. Christians are sojourners in a corrupt world and often become corrupted. He wrote:

> The Truth declares that even he who has been washed has need still to wash his feet . . . in holy baptism a man has all of him washed . . . and yet, while thereafter living in this human state, he cannot fail to tread on the ground with his feet. And thus our human feelings themselves, which are inseparable from our mortal life on earth, are like feet wherewith we are brought into sensible contact with human affairs; and are so in such a way, that if we say we have no sin, we deceive ourselves, and the truth is not in us. And every day, therefore, is *He who intercedes for us, washing our feet:* and that we, too have daily need to be washing our feet, that is ordering aright the path of our spiritual footsteps . . . although the Church be also clean in respect of those who tarry on earth, because they live righteously; yet have they need to be washing their feet, because they assuredly are not without sin (emphasis mine).[260]

As high priest, Jesus washed the feet of all His disciples in spite of their failures. He washed their feet *because* of their failures, so they might be cleansed of sin.

The *way of salvation* begins with repentance and water baptism. Footwashing is a means of grace for subsequent cleansing. The Spirit, who graces the waters of baptism, also graces the waters of footwashing. Water baptism represents new birth, regeneration, and initial cleansing. Footwashing signifies the continuous cleansing of sanctification that is necessary for Christians who live in this corrupt age. This is affirmed in the testimony of early Pentecostals. In a report from a Church of God convention in Alabama, H.G. Rogers wrote:

> We surely had a good time. God was with us in giving out the word. Some were saved and some were blest in a wonderful way. On Sunday the saints met and partook of the Lord's Supper and washed feet. The Holy Ghost manifested

---

[260] *The Nicene and Post-Nicene Fathers Vol. VII*, 302.

Himself in a wonderful way. *One man was sanctified just after his feet were washed.* O, how it pays to obey God and be happy. On Monday there were twenty who followed the Lord in baptism. The Lord wonderfully blest them. (emphasis mine)[261]

Footwashing reminds us that the church is a community of grace where sinful Christians are to be welcomed and restored.

Jesus commanded that His disciples wash one another's feet. The disciples of Jesus can be a contentious group. This often provokes confrontation, but Jerome reminds us that ". . . our profession binds us to wash the feet of those who come to us, not to discuss their merits."[262] Feet are to be washed because they are dirty. Augustine wrote:

For what else does the Lord apparently intimate in the profound significance of this sacramental sign, when He says, "For I have given you an example, that ye should do as I have done to you;" but what the apostle declares in the plainest terms, "Forgiving one another, if any man have a quarrel against any: even as Christ forgave you, so also do ye"? Let us therefore forgive one another his faults, and pray for one another's faults, and thus in a manner be washing one another's feet. It is our part, by His grace, to be supplying the service of love and humility: it is His to hear us, and to cleanse us from all the pollution of our sins through Christ.[263]

Because each believer is "in Christ," a member of the one body of Christ, the one who washes the feet of another, does so as an extension of Christ the high priest. Tertullian said that to cast our sinful selves on the mercy of our fellow believers is to encounter the priestly care of Christ.

In a company of two is the church; but the church is Christ. When, then, you cast yourself at the brethren's knees, you are handling *Christ,* you are entreating *Christ.* In like

---

[261] H.G. Rogers, *The Evening Light and Church of God Evangel,* (June 1, 1910), 7.
[262] *The Nicene and Post-Nicene Fathers, Second Series, Vol. III,* 528.
[263] *The Nicene and Post-Nicene Fathers, Vol. VII,* 307.

manner, when they shed tears over you, it is *Christ* who suffers, *Christ* who prays the Father for mercy. [264]

In other words, to have our feet washed by a brother or sister in Christ is to have our feet washed vicariously by Christ.

Authentic Christian Ministry

Footwashing exemplifies authentic Christian ministry. Jesus said, "Truly, truly, I say to you, he who receives whomever I send receives Me; and he who receives Me receives Him who sent Me" (John 13:20). The footwashing of the disciples is performed in the context of their apostolic mission. Jesus is the Divine Servant, the disciples are servants of the Divine One, and as such are servants to the world. The apostle Paul twice used the metaphor of "feet" to speak of the proclamation of the gospel (Romans 10:15; Ephesians 6:15). The apostolic vestments of Christian service include shoes of peace and a garment of humility (Ephesians 6:15; 1 Peter 5:5). In speaking of the "body of Christ," Paul tells us that the church is comprised of many parts. Christ is the head of the body (Ephesians 5:23). As the head of the church, through the Holy Spirit, Christ has given to the church various ministries—apostles, prophets, pastors, teachers, evangelists; and various offices—deacon and bishop (1 Corinthians 12:28; Ephesians 4:11). These ministries and offices are the feet of the body. Christ as the head oversees and guides His church. The ministers and officers of the church carry the body and move the body under the direction of Christ. Clement of Alexandria understood the sacrament of footwashing as preparation for mission. Commenting on the anointing of Jesus' feet, Clement wrote,

> For the feet anointed with fragrant ointment mean divine instruction traveling with renown to the ends of the earth. . . the feet of the Lord which were anointed were the apostles, having, according to the prophecy, received the fragrant unction of the Holy Ghost. Those, therefore, who travelled over the world and preached the Gospel, are figuratively called the feet of the Lord . . . And the Savior Himself

---

[264] *The Ante-Nicene Fathers Vol. III*, 665.

washing the feet of the disciples, and dispatching them to do good deeds, pointed out their pilgrimage for the benefit of the nations, making them beforehand fair and pure by His power."[265]

Regarding the characteristics of those who present themselves for service to the church, *The Apostolic Constitutions*, a fourth century document that reflects ecclesiastical law and tradition, states:

> For when He had taken a towel, He girded Himself. Afterward He puts water into a basin; and as we were sitting at meat, He came and washed the feet of us all, and wiped them with the towel." By doing this He demonstrated to us His kindness and brotherly affection, that so we also might do the same to one another. If, therefore, our Lord and Master so humbled Himself, how can you, the laborers of the truth, and administrators of piety, be ashamed to do the same to such of the brethren as are weak and infirm? Minister therefore with a kind mind, not murmuring nor mutinying; for ye do not do it on the account of man, but on the account of God, and shall receive from Him the reward of your ministry in the day of your visitation.[266]

Among the greatest temptations for humans is that of power and authority. Power intoxicates and corrupts the human soul. One would hope that those who serve the church would not be so easily seduced, but we know that we are not immune. The first-century Corinthian church suffered from schism and turmoil. Many people within the church challenged and rejected the apostolic ministry of Paul. The leaders of this group were known as the "super-apostles" (2 Corinthians 11:5).[267] Much of the conflict between Paul and the super-apostles was due to their models of ministry. Paul's model of ministry was that of "weakness" and the "meekness and gentleness

---

[265] *The Ante-Nicene Fathers, Vol. II*, 254.

[266] *The Ante-Nicene Fathers, Vol. VII*, 432.

[267] The Greek phrase is *tōn uperlian apostolōn*. This is translated in the *New American Standard Bible* and the *New King James Version* as "the most eminent apostles." However, it is better translated as "super-apostles" as in the *New International Version, New Revised Standard Bible, English Standard Version, New American Bible,* and *New Jerusalem Bible.* Paul is not comparing himself with the original twelve, but with others who have usurped his ministry.

of Christ" (1 Corinthians 2:3; 2 Corinthians 10:1). The model of the super-apostles was that of triumphalism. The super-apostles commended themselves as men of divine power and boasted in their charismatic gifts. However, Paul was "unimpressive" and his preaching style was "contemptible"(2 Corinthians 10:10; 11:6). Paul's ministry was characterized by "weakness and fear," and he suffered from many bodily ailments, one of which was a "thorn in the flesh, a messenger of Satan."[268] When the members of the Corinthian church compared the two models of ministry before them, they favored the super-apostles. However, with all the apparent strengths of the super-apostles they lacked that which is necessary to establish an authentic Christian ministry, that is, a model of ministry that follows after the example of Jesus Christ. In fact, they were not super-apostles, but false apostles (2 Corinthians 11:13-15).

Authentic Christian ministry is not defined simply in terms of bold, charismatic leadership. Christian ministry is best defined in the willingness to lay all garments aside, and take up the towel and basin to wash the feet of God's people. Footwashing exemplifies authentic Christian ministry in that by participation in this sacrament, we embrace Christ's sufferings for the sake of the church. With Paul, we may proclaim, "Now I rejoice in my sufferings for your sake, and in my flesh I do my share on behalf of His body, which is the church, in filling up what is lacking in Christ's afflictions" (Colossians 1:24).

Washing Jesus' Feet

There are two texts that speak of Jesus' feet being washed: Luke 7:36-45 and John 12:1-8. In these stories, two women demonstrate their love for Jesus. Both events are interpreted as salvific. In John, Mary, the sister of Lazarus, anointed the feet of Jesus with perfume and wiped them with her hair. Mary was a righteous woman, a devoted disciple. She was accustomed to sitting at the Lord's feet and listening to His teaching. Once Jesus said, "Mary has chosen the good part, which shall not be taken away from her" (Luke 10:42). Her act of devotion filled the house with the fragrance of the

---

[268] 1 Corinthians 2:3; 2 Corinthians 12:7: Galatians 4:3.

perfume. Judas was offended by the extravagance of her gesture. But his offense was that of a distracted disciple who was unaware of the significance of the event he had witnessed. This occurred just before the Passover and was interpreted as preparation for the burial of the crucified Lord. In John 13, Jesus washed the feet of His disciples so that they might be cleansed and have life in Him. Among all of His disciples, only Mary had the prophetic insight to anticipate Jesus' self-sacrifice as the Lamb of God. She anointed and washed the feet that would carry our Lord to the cross.

In Luke, a prostitute anointed the feet of Jesus with expensive perfume, washed his feet with her tears, and wiped them with her hair. Simon the Pharisee was offended by her presence in his home. Jesus was not offended; He is the friend of sinners. The Lord responded to her gesture of devotion with forgiveness: "Your sins are forgiven . . . . Your faith has saved you. Go in peace" (Luke 7:48, 50). Ambrose saw this sinful woman as a wounded soul seeking healing from the Great Physician. Her tears represented the sorrows of repentance. Wiping His feet with her hair represented her putting "aside all the pomp of worldly trappings." Her kisses on His feet are expressions of deep devotion. By washing the feet of the Lord, she "wiped out the stench of her sin." Convicted by his own sinfulness, Ambrose offered a prayer of repentance: "I would that You, Lord Jesus, might reserve for me the washing off from your feet of the stains contracted since you walk in me! O that you might offer to me to cleanse the pollution which I by my deeds have caused on your steps!"[269] Ambrose understood that he lived "in Christ" and that Christ lived in him (Colossians 1:27). He was intensely aware of his sinfulness and understood that the sins of humanity had been imputed upon Christ. He sought an opportunity to wash the feet of Christ that, like the prostitute, he too might encounter the salvific peace of Christ.

An anonymous third-century bishop cited the story of the prostitute washing the feet of Jesus in his challenge against Novatian. Novatian was a schismatic presbyter of the church at Rome. He

---

[269] *The Nicene and Post-Nicene Fathers Second Series Vol. X*, 354.

opposed the restoration of bishops and priests who had lapsed during the persecution of Decian. The schism was no small matter, because it threatened the unity of the church and it implied that there was no remedy for postbaptismal sin. The bishop wrote:

> . . . to those who repent, and pray, and labor, restoration is possible . . . this is proved in the Gospel, where is described that woman who was a sinner . . . and stood at the Lord's feet, and washed His feet . . . Behold, the Lord grants the debt with His liberal kindness . . . behold Him who pardons sins; behold the woman who was a sinner penitent, weeping, praying, and receiving remission of her sins![270]

Footwashing signifies the restoration of the sinful. Christ identifies Himself with the stranger, the poor, the hungry, and the prisoner. He is the friend of sinners. When Christ returns in the power and glory of His kingdom He will say to His righteous sheep:

> Come, you who are blessed of My Father, inherit the kingdom prepared for you from the foundation of the world. For I was hungry, and you gave Me something to eat; I was thirsty, and you gave Me something to drink; I was a stranger, and you invited Me in; naked, and you clothed Me; I was sick, and you visited Me; I was in prison, and you came to Me . . . . Truly I say to you, to the extent that you did it to one of these brothers of Mine, even the least of them, you did it to Me (Matthew 25:34-36, 40).

The church is the body of Christ. Paul wrote, "Now you are Christ's body, and individually members of it (1 Corinthians 12:27). Just as Christ is the friend of sinners, also the church must be the friend of sinners. As we kneel to wash the feet of our Christian brothers and sisters, righteous and fallen, we wash the feet of the Lord. As we wash the feet of the stranger, the poor, and the prisoner, we wash the feet of the Lord.

---

[270] *The Ante-Nicene Fathers, Vol. V*, 660.

Service and Worship

The apostle Paul wrote to Timothy, the pastor of the church at Ephesus, regarding the qualifications for widows who wish to receive assistance from the church. He wrote:

> Do not let a widow under sixty years old be taken into the number, and not unless she has been the wife of one man, well reported for good works: if she has brought up children, if she has lodged strangers, *if she has washed the saints' feet*, if she has relieved the afflicted, if she has diligently followed every good work (1 Timothy 5:9-10, emphasis mine).

Many New Testament scholars believe that this reference to footwashing is to an act of hospitality common in the Ancient Near East, rather than to an act of worship in the Christian church. Further, it is assumed that since 1 Timothy was written about A.D. 65 and the Gospel of John was written about A.D. 90, any relationship to the footwashing in John 13 and 1 Timothy is doubtful. But this is not necessarily the case. Even if John was written in the late first century, there most certainly would have been an early oral tradition of Jesus washing the feet of His disciples. While it is apparent that Paul lists footwashing among other acts of hospitality, this does not exclude the possibility that Jesus' act of footwashing would have given the common act of footwashing greater significance. Would not the widows of the church seek to emulate the Divine Servant? Jesus used familiar rites to establish Christian sacraments. The Lord's Supper was established from the familiar elements of the Passover. As he raised the bread and cup, Jesus said, "This is my body . . . this is my blood." Baptisms and washings were common among Jewish religious practices. But Jesus said, "He who has believed and has been baptized shall be saved" (Mark 16:16). Footwashing, even as an act of hospitality, would have greater significance among Christians because of the example of Jesus. Ephraim the Syrian (fourth century) understood hospitality, including footwashing, in terms of Christian service *and* worship. He wrote:

> Has a poor man entered into thy house? God has entered into thy house; God dwells within thy abode. He, whom thou hast refreshed from his troubles, from troubles will

deliver thee. *Hast thou washed the feet of the stranger? Thou
has washed away the filth of thy sins.* Hast thou prepared
a table before him? Behold God eating [at it], and Christ
likewise drinking [at it], and the Holy Spirit resting [on it]:
Is the poor satisfied at thy table and refreshed? Thou hast
satisfied Christ thy Lord. He is ready to be thy rewarder; in
presence of angels and men He will confess thou hast fed
His hunger; He will give thanks unto thee that thou didst
give Him drink, and quench His thirst.[271]

Footwashing is presented as an act of hospitality in which the guest
is refreshed and the one who washes the feet experiences salvific
cleansing.

Augustine presented footwashing as a custom that was "generally
prevalent" and a commendable act of Christian humility. He quoted
the words of 1 Timothy 5:10 and wrote:

And wherever such is not the practice among the saints,
what they do not with the hand they do in heart . . . But it
is far better, and beyond all dispute more accordant with
the truth, that it should also be done with the hands; nor
should the Christian think it beneath him to do what was
done by Christ. For when the body is bent at a brother's feet,
the feeling of such humility is either awakened in the heart
itself, or is strengthened if already present.[272]

Footwashing is more than a common act of hospitality; more that
an act of humility; more than a metaphor for Christian service.
Augustine continued:

But apart from this moral understanding of the passage
[1 Timothy 5:10], we remember that the way in which we
commended to your attention the grandeur of this act of
the Lord's, was that, in washing the feet of disciples who
were already washed and clean, the Lord instituted a sign,
to the end that, on account of the human feelings that
occupy us on earth, however far we may have advanced in
our apprehension of righteousness, we might know that
we are not exempt from sin; which He thereafter washes

---

[271] *The Nicene and Post-Nicene Fathers, Second Series, Vol. XIII*, 334.
[272] *The Nicene and Post-Nicene Fathers Vol. VII*, 306.

away by interceding for us, when we pray the Father, who is in heaven, to forgive us our debts, as we also forgive our debtors.[273]

For Augustine, footwashing was a wonderful and profound sacramental symbol, a sign instituted by the Lord for the purpose of salvific cleansing.

Footwashing should be understood as Spirit-movement toward the altar. Ambrose provides a theological precedent for understanding footwashing as a sacramental encounter with the Holy Spirit. In *On the Holy Spirit,* he wrote:

> Let us come now to the Gospel of God. I find the Lord stripping Himself of His garments, and girding Himself with a towel, pouring water into a basin, and washing the disciples' feet. That heavenly dew was this water, this was foretold, namely, that the Lord Jesus Christ would wash the feet of His disciples in that heavenly dew . . . .
>
> I, then, wish also myself to wash the feet of my brethren, I wish to fulfill the commandment of my Lord, I will not be ashamed in myself, nor disdain what He Himself did first. Good is the mystery of humility, because while washing the pollutions of others I wash away my own.
>
> This, I say, is a divine mystery which even they who wash will enquire into. It is not, then, the simple water of the heavenly mystery whereby we attain to be found worthy of having part with Christ. There is also a certain water which we put into the basin of our soul. . . . It is the water of the message from heaven. Let, then, this water, O Lord Jesus, come into my soul, into my flesh, that through the moisture of this rain the valleys of our minds and the fields of our hearts may grow green. May the drops from Thee come upon me, shedding forth grace and immortality.[274]

Ambrose affirmed footwashing as an encounter with the Spirit of grace—"the water . . . from heaven"—who conveys "grace and immortality." He understood footwashing to be a powerful spiritual

---

[273] *The Nicene and Post-Nicene Fathers Vol. VII*, 306.
[274] *The Nicene and Post-Nicene Fathers, Second Series, Vol. X*, 95

experience in which sins were washed away and the soul was refreshed.[275]

Observance of Footwashing

In many Pentecostal churches, the observance of footwashing has traditionally been in conjunction with the celebration of the Eucharist. James L. Cross, suggested that the Lord's Supper and footwashing should be understood as a single sacrament in two parts. He wrote, "One is equally as binding as the other, and the serving of Communion is not enough in itself. There must of necessity also be the washing of the saints' feet."[276] This is a faithful representation of how the two sacraments were understood since the earliest days of the Church of God.

The Gospel of John presents footwashing within the theological context of water baptism *and* the Eucharist. Therefore, it follows that footwashing can rightly be observed in conjunction with both water baptism and the Eucharist, or it can even be observed as a sacrament in its own right. A proper understanding of footwashing must allow for multiple interpretations, none of which excludes the others. Footwashing is a sacrament that lends itself to a wide variety of occasions and experiences.

Footwashing may be observed in conjunction with the Lord's Supper as a sacrament of sanctification. Jesus washed the feet of His disciples because He wanted them to be "completely clean." Paul encouraged the believers at Corinth to examine themselves before the Table of the Lord. Footwashing in conjunction with the celebration of the Eucharist could be an excellent opportunity for brothers and sisters in the Lord to confess their sins to one another, embrace each other in the love of God, and allow the Holy Spirit to cleanse the sins of the community, as well as the sins of the individual.

Footwashing may be observed in conjunction with the Lord's Supper as a sacrament of commission. Because footwashing has been associated with the mission and ministry of the church, it would be

---

[275] *The Nicene and Post-Nicene Fathers, Second Series, Vol. X*, 321.
[276] James L. Cross, "The Lord's Supper and Feet Washing," *Church of God Evangel* (June 19, 1961), 9.

appropriate that the footwashing service be presented in terms of Christian mission. Christians must be reminded that our sanctuaries and auditoriums are places of rest and nourishment, but we must leave our places of worship to do the work of Christ. It is into the fields and highways that we are called. Footwashing should be a perpetual reminder that Christ expects our feet to become dirty from our travels throughout this world. The feet of holy men and women are the instruments by which the gospel is to be carried into our neighborhoods, hospitals, schools, prisons, and everywhere that lost and hurting people can be found. The apostle Paul exclaimed, "How beautiful are the feet of those who bring good news of good things!" (Romans 10:15). Each time we receive Christ in the Lord's Supper, we should be reminded of the Great Commission.

Footwashing should be observed at ordination ceremonies. Jesus washed the feet of His disciples and sent them into the world. Since footwashing exemplifies authentic Christian ministry it should be incorporated into public worship services in which men and women are affirmed and credentialed by the church for ministry. Ministerial candidates should station themselves at the altar, and before the congregation. There, at the altar, they present themselves as a "living and holy sacrifice, acceptable to God" (Romans 12:1). There the candidates are charged for ministry by their respective ordaining authority. Then these ministerial candidates should have their feet washed by their respective bishop, or ordaining council, as a commissioning act.

Footwashing should also be incorporated into services and ceremonies in which ministers are installed into new places of ministry. When pastors arrive at a new place of ministry, a footwashing ceremony should be preformed as an act of commission and dedication. New pastors should have their feet washed by the officer of installation, or by the leaders of the local church. This act would signify that the congregation has accepted their new pastor, and pledges their love, prayers, and support. In turn, pastors should wash the feet of the members of their new congregation as an act of devotion and service to them. Footwashing should be similarly incorporated into the installation services of regional bishops (superintendents, etc.) and denominational leaders. By doing so, ministers demonstrate that those who lead the church are in fact bond-servants of the church (Mark 10:42-45).

Several years ago, I was called to serve a congregation in which there had been much conflict between the congregational leaders and a series of pastors. Of course, as in most cases, fault and blame could be shared by many. After a few months, I called for a prayer meeting with the men of the church. About fifteen men joined me for a time of prayer. After prayer, I informed them that I wanted to wash their feet. I took the towel and basin and in turn washed each man's feet. When I concluded, the "leader" of these men stood and exclaimed, "In all my years in the church, I have never seen a pastor do this! You have washed our feet, now I will wash yours." The Holy Spirit moved in our hearts, and old hurts within that church began to be healed. There were more conflicts ahead, but the tone of the conversation changed. That night, adversaries became brothers.

Footwashing may be observed in conjunction with water baptism as a sacrament of confession and remission of postbaptismal sins. Whereas, water baptism is rightly understood as an unrepeatable act of initiation, footwashing should be repeated often as a sacrament of cleansing. Footwashing serves as a sign of grace that the fallen may be restored. Therefore, footwashing could be scheduled in conjunction with water baptismal services. After all baptismal candidates have been baptized "for the remission of sins," the pastor could issue a call for repentance and offer an opportunity for penitent sinners to come to the altar, confess their sins, and have their feet washed by the pastor or other congregational leaders. Ken Archer has written:

> As we wash each other's feet, we are reminded of our own shortcomings; yet we proleptically experience God's declaration—"your sins are forgiven." The community realizes it is a holy people and a royal priesthood. Communal holiness, wholeness, discipline, and discipleship are integral aspects of traveling on the *via salutis*.[277]

---

[277] Archer, "Nourishment for Our Journey," 92.

Of course, a similar service could be held apart from a baptismal service. Repentance and confession must become a significant part of any church that seeks a renewing encounter with the Spirit (Acts 3:19). Many times our worship is hindered because we grieve or quench the Holy Spirit (Ephesians 4:30; 1 Thessalonians 5:19). Further, the witness of Christ is diminished when the church fails to reflect the character of our Lord. Christ has called His church to be a model of unity and peace, but too often we have failed. Our Lord has commanded that we are to love and pray for our enemies, and He has called us to be "ambassadors of reconciliation" (2 Corinthians 5:20). In his Sermon on the Mount, Jesus said:

> . . . I say to you that everyone who is angry with his brother shall be guilty before the court; and whoever says to his brother, "You good-for-nothing," shall be guilty before the supreme court; and whoever says, "You fool," shall be guilty enough to go into the fiery hell. Therefore if you are presenting your offering at the altar, and there remember that your brother has something against you, leave your offering there before the altar and go; first be reconciled to your brother, and then come and present your offering (Matthew 5:22-24).

Our Lord has taught us that we can offer worship that is unacceptable. We cannot approach the altar of God with an acceptable sacrifice when our hearts are filled with anger and bitterness, or conflicts and schisms. Often, these conflicts involve entire communities and are grounded in ethnic, economic, and geopolitical issues. The church must transcend the conflicts of this world and be a prophetic people in whom the world may see the redemption of God. In this regard, footwashing can become a significant prophetic act in which the grace of God is conveyed and demonstrated.

Some years ago, I was pastoring a church in a small rural city of the American South. This city has a long history of racial tension. During a week of revival services, I scheduled a choir from a local African-American church to sing in our services. On this evening, the Spirit of the Lord was moving and everyone seemed to be enjoying the music of our guest choir. During the service, I was impressed by the Holy Spirit to wash the feet of my African-American colleague and brother. I sent for a towel and basin and asked permission to wash his feet. He agreed. As our two combined congregations watched, I bowed before my brother and washed his feet as a symbol of reconciliation between our two communities of faith. The weeks that followed were filled with much trouble for me and the church I served. When I washed the feet of my black brother, many of the members of the church became angry. The act of footwashing became a prophetic confrontation in that congregation. Many believers were forced to acknowledge their sin of racial prejudice, but they were unprepared to repent and be sanctified. Some months later, I resigned from that pastorate. About two years later, I received a telephone call from one of the congregational leaders of that church. During the course of our conversation, he informed me that several African-American families had been received into the membership of the church. The church was becoming a prospering multicultural congregation. He said, "It would not have happened without your example of reconciliation." Footwashing is a sacrament of grace that prophetically confronts the human heart so that our conflicts may be healed. Through the Spirit of grace, footwashing forms a sanctified community.

Footwashing may be observed in ceremonies in which fallen members and ministers are restored to fellowship. When a Christian falls into such sin that the discipline of the church requires that person to be excluded from membership, the whole body is injured. Likewise, when a pastor or other minister of the church falls into such sin, the integrity of the whole ministry is injured. Too often, the church fails in the ministry of restoration because of the pain associated with such events. At other times, restoration fails due to the unwillingness of the fallen minister (or member) to demonstrate humility and repentance. However, every effort should be made to effect healing and the restoration of integrity and fellowship. In many cases, such ethical failures become a public scandal. Because the failure is public, the work of restoration must likewise be public. The sacrament of footwashing could become an important element in the public restoration of the fallen. In such cases, those who are to be restored to fellowship and ministry should present themselves at the altar and before the assembled congregation. After a time of prayer, the presiding officer—a pastor, or bishop—would then perform the footwashing as a sign of forgiveness and restoration.

Footwashing may be observed as a sacrament of Christian unity. Through many years of service as pastor, I have had the pleasure of serving in various ecumenical ministerial associations. On many occasions I have been involved in planning special community services such as the National Day of Prayer, Holy Week observances, and Christian unity events. These community services are attended by Christians from various traditions. Sadly, many churches prohibit their members from sharing in Holy Communion among nonmembers. So, it is often difficult to conduct an ecumenical worship service that includes Holy Communion. I have often suggested that ecumenical services include the observance of footwashing. In most cases, this suggestion has been enthusiastically received. I remember one such service in which the local Catholic priest and Methodist pastor washed each other's feet. On another occasion, during a National Day of Prayer observance, about thirty pastors, representing various denominations, gathered on the steps of the county courthouse to publicly wash each other's feet. The observance of footwashing serves as a visible expression of the church as the fellowship of the Holy Spirit in which grace is extended to all brothers and sisters in Christ.

Hymns and Songs for the Occasion

Hymns and songs selected for the footwashing occasion should reflect the themes of journey, confession, cleansing, restoration, service, and mission. Classic hymns and songs for the occasion may be:

> William Hunter, James D. Vaughan, "**I Feel Like Traveling On**," *Church Hymnal* (Cleveland, TN: Pathway Press, 1951, 1979) 133.

> Sabine Gould, Arthur Sullivan, "**Onward Christian Soldiers**," *Church Hymnal*, 372.

> R.H. Cornelius, "**O, I Want to See Him**," *Church Hymnal*, 279.

Johnson Oatman, Jr., Charles H. Gabriel, "**Higher Ground**," *Hymns of the Spirit* (Cleveland, TN: Pathway Press, 1969) 269.

Unknown, "**Just a Closer Walk With Thee**," *Hymns of the Spirit*, 288.

Jack Campbell, Billy Campbell, "**Jesus Use Me**," *Hymns of the Spirit*, 286.

J. Edwin Orr, "**Cleanse Me**," *Hymns of the Spirit*, 277.

Unknown, "**I Have Decided to Follow Jesus**," *The Celebration Hymnal* (Word Music/Integrity Music, 1997) 602.

William J. Gaither, "**He Touched Me**," *The Celebration Hymnal*, 505

Contemporary hymns and songs appropriate to the observance of footwashing may be:

Russ Taff, Tori Taff, James Hollihan, "**We Will Stand**," *The Celebration Hymnal*, 417.

Richard Gillard, "**The Servant Song**," *The Celebration Hymnal*, 424.

Carman, "**I Will Serve the Lord**," *The Absolute Best*, Sparrow, 1993.

David Nasser, "**Restore to Me**," *Glory Revealed: The Word of God in Worship*, Reunion, 2007.

Chris Tomlin, "**Give Us Clean Hands**," *I Could Sing of Your Love Forever 2*, Sparrow, 2001.

Gary Sadler, Dan Dean, "**Pour My Love on You**," *Let My Words Be Few*, Sparrow, 2001.

Michael Card, "**The Basin and the Towel**," *Poiema*, Sparrow, 1994.

Donald Lawrence, "**Beautiful Feet**," *I Speak Life*, Verity, 2004.

Graham Kendrick, "**The Servant King**," *The Best Worship Songs Ever*, Virgin / EMI, 2004.

Noel Richards, "**You Laid Aside Your Majesty**," *The Best Worship Songs Ever*, Virgin / EMI, 2004.

Matt Redman, "**I Will Offer Up My Life**," *The Best Worship Songs Ever,* Virgin / EMI, 2004.

Footwashing Etiquette

In preparing for a footwashing service, one should be careful to preserve the dignity of the event. A few suggestions here are in order. First, it has often been the practice to separate the sexes in order to maintain modesty. This may be preferred, but it is possible to maintain modesty without separating the sexes into different rooms. A suggestion would be to prepare footwashing stations on either side of the sanctuary, near the altar. Men and women could participate in the footwashing service separately, yet together in the primary place of worship.

Many people have objected to participating in footwashing services due to issues of sanitation. They object to placing their feet into water that has been used by others before them. This objection can be easily overcome. The footwashing service will require an empty basin, a clean towel, and a pitcher of water. Instead of a basin filled with water to be used by all, an empty basin is placed under the foot of the worshiper. Then the water may be poured onto the worshiper's foot and collected in the basin. The process may be repeated to wash the second foot. Because of the nature of footwashing as a sacrament of humiliation, it would be proper that the pastor and congregational leaders of the church wash the feet of the congregation before their own feet are washed. This order of service is a reminder that the greatest among us is but a servant.

CHAPTER 7

The Anointed Touch: Anointing With Oil And Laying On Hands

Is anyone among you sick? Then he must call for the elders of the church and they are to pray over him, anointing him with oil in the name of the Lord; and the prayer offered in faith will restore the one who is sick, and the Lord will raise him up, and if he has committed sins, they will be forgiven him (James 5:14-15).

Sister Lemon of Whittier, who had been a sufferer for eighteen years and could receive no help from physicians, and had been bed-ridden for fourteen years of that time has been marvelously healed by the Lord through the laying on of hands and the prayer of faith. She has been walking to meetings. The opposers of the work cannot deny that a notable miracle has been performed through the mighty name of Jesus [*sic*].

—*The Apostolic Faith*[278]

During the time I was studying and preparing to write this material, I had a conversation with an instructor at a Pentecostal university. During our conversation, I said, "Pentecostals have always been sacramental in worship." He responded, "No, you're wrong. Pentecostals have never been sacramental." I countered, "Since the beginning of the movement, Pentecostals

---

[278] *The Apostolic Faith* (November 1906), 1.

have practiced anointing with oil and the laying on of hands. We have always believed that the grace of God is transferred through the laying on of hands." After a moment of silent thought he exclaimed, "You're right!"

The practice of anointing with oil and laying on hands is an excellent example of the embodied spirituality and sacramental nature of Pentecostalism.[279] Pentecostal spirituality is a physical spirituality. The Holy Spirit dwells within the believer; the Spirit fills the believer, and the believer often expresses these divine encounters with physical manifestations—dancing, shouting, clapping, and tongues speech. When Pentecostals pray for the sick, it is often expressed in the physical act of anointing the sick with oil and/or laying hands on the sick. The oil represents the presence and anointing of the Holy Spirit. Spirit-filled believers are laying on "holy hands." Sometimes handkerchiefs are anointed with oil and these "anointed cloths" are sent to the sick. In divine healing, the Spirit touches the body and effects physical healing. Healing is a sensory experience. The body is healed and all pain associated with the injury or disease ceases. The healed person *feels* better. This sacramental practice involves fellowship with the Spirit and the church, and the interaction between that which is of the Spirit and that which is physical.

Healing comes in a variety of ways, so there will be no attempt to argue that divine healing must be limited to a sacramental rite. I will suggest that the sacramental rite of the laying on of hands extends beyond the hope for healing, but is also a means whereby the sick and suffering encounter the comforting and sustaining Spirit of grace as death approaches.

---

[279] The primacy of prayer for the sick and healing in Pentecostal theology is demonstrated in the academic literature that has been produced by Pentecostal scholars. Three exhaustive works have been completed by Church of God scholars. See: Kimberly Ervin Alexander, *Pentecostal Healing: Models in Theology and Practice* (Blandford Forum, UK: Deo Publishing, 2006); John Christopher Thomas, *The Devil, Disease and Deliverance: Origins of Illness in New Testament Thought* (New York: Sheffield Academic Press, 1998); and John Fleter Tipei, *The Laying on of Hands in the New Testament* (Lanham, MD: University Press of America, Inc., 2009).

The Anointed Touch

In the Scriptures, anointing with oil and the laying on of hands are not always associated together. Throughout the Acts of the Apostles, there are many examples where apostles and elders laid their hands upon believers for healing and reception of the Holy Spirit, but anointing with oil is not mentioned. It may be that in the primitive church anointing with oil was so associated with the laying on of hands that Luke did not find it necessary to mention. However, it is certain that anointing with oil suggests some kind of touch. For the purposes of our discussion, we will assume that anointing with oil and the laying on of hands are related expressions of one sacramental rite—***the anointed touch***.

In the Orthodox tradition, this sacramental practice is called *euchelaion* (prayer oil). In the tradition of the Western church, this sacramental practice is called *unction, chrism,* or *chrismation.* These terms are derived from two Greek words: *chriō* and *chrisma. Chrisma* (not to be confused with *charisma*) is used in the Johannine Epistles to suggest the initial event of receiving the Spirit and the abiding presence of the Spirit: ". . . the anointing which you received from Him abides in you"(1 John 2:27). *Chriō* is used to speak of the anointing of the Spirit upon Jesus (Luke 4:18; Acts 10:38) and to the anointing of the Spirit upon the apostles and saints of the church(2 Corinthians 1:21).

The Anointed Touch in the Ministry of Jesus

The title *Christ* is from the Greek word *Christos* which means "anointed one." After Jesus was baptized in the Jordan River and the Spirit of God descended upon Him, He declared, "The Spirit of the Lord is upon Me, because He anointed Me to preach the gospel to the poor. He has sent me to proclaim release to the captives, and recovery of sight to the blind, to set free those who are oppressed, to proclaim the favorable year of the Lord" (Luke 4:18-19). The Holy Spirit empowered Jesus for ministry. But why would Jesus, who is the eternal Son, cosubstantial with the Father and the Spirit, need to be empowered for ministry? Paul wrote that Jesus "existed in the form of God . . . but emptied Himself" (Philippians 2:6-7). In the Incarnation, the eternal Son "emptied Himself" of divine power and authority, but never ceased to be cosubstantial with the Father and the Spirit. In Jesus Christ, we have the perfect union of full divinity and full humanity. So then, if Jesus "emptied Himself," how did He perform His ministry of miracles and deliverance? Luke answers that Jesus was "full of the Holy Spirit" (Luke 4:1) and went forth "in the power of the Spirit" (Luke 4:14). The author of Hebrews, quoting Isaiah, associates the anointing of the Spirit upon Jesus with the "oil of gladness."[280] The "oil of gladness" is God's remedy for the "mourning" and suffering of God's people. Because Jesus is anointed with the "oil of gladness," God's people can be redeemed, healed, and comforted. The sounds of suffering are replaced by the sounds of joy. When Jesus, the Anointed One, entered Jerusalem on Palm Sunday, He was greeted with the sounds of celebration: "Hosanna! Blessed is He who comes in the name of the Lord" (Mark 11:9).

Throughout the Gospels, Jesus' anointed touch transformed the lives of the suffering. A.J. Gordon wrote that Jesus is a person "in whom an abounding infectious health is present, so that it only needs the contact of a finger-tip that it may leap like the electric current to thrill and vitalize the sickly body."[281] The anointed touch of Jesus cleansed lepers, cooled fevers, restored sight to the blind, comforted the fearful, healed deaf ears, blessed children, strengthened the crippled, and raised the dead. Because of the power of His touch, people reached out to touch Him, or His garments, and were healed.[282] Jesus allowed even sinners to touch Him (Luke 7:39). After His resurrection, Jesus implored His doubting and fearful disciples, "See My hands and My feet, that it is I Myself; *touch Me and see*"

---

[280] Isaiah 61:1-3; Hebrews 1:9; see also Psalm 45:7.

[281] A.J. Gordon, "Who Healeth all Thine Iniquities, Who Healeth all Thy Diseases." *The Latter Rain Evangel* (May 1909), 14.

[282] Matthew 8:3, 15; 9:20-22, 29; 17:7; 20:34; 19:13-15; Mark 1:41; 3:10; 5:25-34, 41; 6:56; 7:32-35; 8:22-25; 10:13-16; Luke 5:13; 6:19; 7:14; 8:43-48; 13:11-13; 18:15; 22:51.

(Luke 24:39). Just before He ascended to Heaven, Jesus "lifted up His hands and blessed" His disciples in anticipation of Pentecost (Luke 24:49-50).

Jesus Christ is "the Anointed One." Anointed by the Holy Spirit, Jesus went forth "in the power of the Spirit." It is clear that the saving and healing power of Jesus—the anointing—was transferred to the suffering through His anointed touch. In some cases, Jesus is active—He reaches out to touch the suffering individual. In other cases, Jesus is somewhat passive—as He walks by, those who are suffering reach out to touch him, or his clothes. In all cases, there is a perceivable and physical transfer of power, and people are healed and delivered (Mark 5:30; Luke 6:19; 8:46). The Gospels insist "that Jesus' body was a source of power which could be released physically, through a touch accompanied by faith."[283] Even unbelievers were made to wonder at the miracles performed with the hands of Jesus (Mark 6:2).

The Anointed Touch in the Apostolic Church

All of the Gospels tell of Jesus commissioning His disciples to continue His redemptive work. The commissioning of the disciples involves divine empowerment. In the Gospel of John, the Holy Spirit is given at the bequest of the Son (John 14:16; 26; 16:7). Jesus is "the way, and the truth, and the life" (John 14:6), and the Spirit is the teacher of truth (John 14:26; 16:13-14). One of the primary works of the Spirit in the world is to "convict the world concerning sin . . . because they do not believe" in Jesus Christ. The Spirit's work also includes the declaration of righteousness and judgment (John 16:8-11). After the resurrection, Jesus "breathed on them and said to them, 'Receive the Holy Spirit. If you forgive the sins of any, their sins have been forgiven them; if you retain the sins of any, they have been retained'" (John 20:22-23).[284] Just as God

---

[283] John Fleter Tipei, *The Laying on of Hands in the New Testament*, 154.

[284] John's forgiveness and retention of sin is similar to Mark's commissioning statement: "He who has believed and has been baptized shall be saved; but he who has disbelieved shall be condemned" (Mark 16:16).

breathed life into Adam, Jesus Christ bestowed the breath of God—the Holy Spirit—upon and into His disciples. With the bestowal of the Holy Spirit, the disciples are given the authority to declare the forgiveness of sin, and also judgment upon those who do not believe. Many Protestants, fearing the taint of the Catholic practice of granting absolution, resist the implication of this text. While I too share that concern, in the pastoral context, there have been many times that a believer has confessed sin to me. In such cases, I have often quoted the words of 1 John 1:9: "If we confess our sins, He is faithful and righteous to forgive us our sins and to cleanse us from all unrighteousness." Then, I have offered my hand—the anointed touch—and led the penitent in a prayer of repentance. After the prayer, I have declared with great joy and the authority of the Holy Spirit, "Your sins are forgiven." On some occasions, a sinner has confessed sin to me, but without any sense of godly sorrow. In those cases, I have encouraged the sinner to repent, and often warned of divine judgment. Without an expression of genuine repentance, I have withheld the declaration of forgiveness. In both cases, the declaration of righteousness or judgment is ultimately the work of Christ and the Spirit.

In Matthew, Jesus said, "All authority has been given to Me in heaven and on earth. Go therefore . . . " (Matthew 28:18-19). Jesus' authority transcends that of the ancient scribal tradition, and even that of Moses. He challenged the authority of the scribal tradition with the words, "I say to you . . . " (Matthew 5:18-44). He is the enfleshed fulfillment of the Torah and the Prophets (Matthew 5:17). Jesus has authority to forgive sin, to heal all manner of disease, and subdue the power of demons.[285] Also, He has authority over the created order (Matthew 14:22-33). His authority was challenged by the chief priests and elders of Israel and mocked by the Roman authorities. Even the condemned criminals who were dying with Him mocked Jesus.[286] But the resurrected Jesus is vindicated by the Father and has been given all authority "in heaven and earth." Jesus

---

[285] Matthew 4:23-24; 8:1-34; 9:1-8, 32-35; 12:22; 14:14; 15:22-31; 17:14-18; 19:2; 21:14.
[286] Matthew 21:23; 27: 27-31, 39-44.

grants authority to His disciples so that His redemptive mission may continue to all the nations. They have been given "authority over unclean spirits" and commissioned to "heal the sick, raise the dead, cleanse the lepers, cast out demons" (Matthew 10:1-8). They are to "make disciples" by teaching and baptizing. As they do, they will often find that their authority will be questioned and mocked. With the grant of His divine authority, Jesus also assures His disciples of His presence to "the end of the age."

The apostolic practice of anointing the sick with oil is first mentioned in the Gospel of Mark:

> And He summoned the twelve and began to send them out in pairs, and gave them authority over the unclean spirits . . . They went out and preached that men should repent. And they were casting out many demons and *were anointing with oil many sick people and healing them* (Mark 6:7-13).

In Luke's story of the Good Samaritan, the Samaritan uses oil to treat the wounds of his patient (Luke 10:34). This is testimony to the ancient practice of using oil as a medicine. However, Mark's account of the apostolic practice of anointing with oil is different. It reflects the Old Testament tradition that oil is often associated with the endowment of the Holy Spirit.[287] John Christopher Thomas has written:

> The associations which oil had come to have with healing . . . suggest that its presence in Jesus' ministry and in the practice of the early church signified the power of God to heal. . . . Consequently, oil was a powerful reminder to the church that God was able to heal and that his healing powers were already being made manifest.[288]

The use of oil in Mark is associated with miraculous healing and charismatic endowment. The transference of power and authority through the anointed touch was normative in the apostolic church. Mark records Jesus' commissioning of His disciples in terms of charismatic manifestations and miraculous signs: "These signs will

---

[287] 1 Samuel 16:13; Psalm 89:20; Isaiah 61:1.
[288] Thomas, *The Devil, Disease, and Deliverance*, 28.

accompany those who have believed: in My name they will cast out demons, they will speak with new tongues; they will pick up serpents, and if they drink any deadly poison, it will not hurt them; they will lay hands on the sick, and they will recover" (Mark 16:17-18).[289] This seems somewhat unusual because Jesus laments that the unbelieving generation is seeking signs, and he warns of the signs and wonders of false prophets (Mark 8:11-12; 13:22). However, the words of Mark 16:17-20 correspond with the apostolic commission of Mark 6:7-13. The disciples are given authority over "unclean spirits," they are commissioned to preach, and the sick are healed. In both texts, charismatic signs are the confirmation of the preached word (Mark 16:20).

Luke offers two accounts. First, in the Gospel, Jesus tells the disciples that they will receive "the promise of My Father" and be "clothed with power from on high." He then lifts His hands to bless them (Luke 24:49-50). Then in Acts, Jesus said, "but you will receive power when the Holy Spirit has come upon you" (Acts 1:8). As Jesus ascended into Heaven, the "Anointed One" bestowed the "Anointing." The church, as the body of Christ, is empowered with the anointed touch of Jesus. Jesus' ministry of healing and salvation is continued through His anointed disciples. The transfer of anointing has its precedent in the Old Testament. Moses transferred his prophetic anointing to his successor, Joshua. "Now Joshua the son of Nun was filled with the spirit of wisdom, for Moses had laid his hands on him" (Deuteronomy 34:9). When Jesus lifted His hands to bless His disciples, He was acting in the Mosaic tradition. Also, Elisha received the prophetic mantle of his mentor, Elijah (2 Kings 2:9-22). Elisha had requested that "a double portion" of Elijah's spirit be bestowed upon him. As Elijah was being taken up to Heaven in a fiery chariot, his mantle (garment, or robe) fell so that Elisha received it. When Jesus told the disciples they would be "clothed with power from on high," He was drawing from the Elisha tradition. But even more

---

[289] It should be noted that the authenticity of the "long ending" of Mark (verses 9-20) is challenged by textual critics. Even so, the long ending is the received text, and even if it is a later redaction, it bears witness to the charismatic nature of the early Christian church.

significant is the promise of Joel 2:28: "I will pour out My Spirit on all mankind." Jesus is "sending forth the promise of the Father." In the words of the Pentecostal "full gospel"—Jesus is the Holy Spirit baptizer. Because of the Spirit's presence and empowerment, "at the hands of the apostles many signs and wonders were taking place among the people" (Acts 5:12). The anointed hands of the apostles have become the sacramental presence of the Anointed One—Jesus Christ.

The anointed touch in Acts is often associated with reception of the Spirit. Peter and John prayed for the Samaritan believers to receive the Spirit. "Then they began laying their hands on them, and they were receiving the Holy Spirit" (Acts 8:17). Saul was healed of blindness and filled with the Spirit as Ananias laid his hand on him (Acts 9:17). The believers at Ephesus received the Spirit as Paul "laid his hands upon them" (Acts 19:6). The anointed touch was also employed in commissioning various ministries in the church. When the apostles commissioned the first deacons, "after praying, they laid their hands on them" (Acts 6:6). When Barnabas and Saul were commissioned as apostles, the leaders of the church "prayed and laid their hands on them" and "sent them away" (Acts 13:3). Timothy received his pastoral call "through prophetic utterance with the laying on of hands by the presbytery" (1 Timothy 4:14). This is not to imply that reception of the Holy Spirit, or the *charismata*, requires the laying on of hands. Just as there are many instances when healings occurred without the anointed touch, there are also instances when the Holy Spirit was received without the anointed touch. So then, what is the purpose of the anointed touch in relation to reception of the Holy Spirit and confirmation of ministry? Remember, Luke tells us that just before Jesus ascended, He told His disciples of the promise of the Spirit and "He lifted up His hands and blessed them" (Luke 24:50). The gesture of lifting His hands corresponds to the promise of the Spirit. The blessing of Christ is the gift of the Holy Spirit. The transfer of anointing is implied and it expresses the continuity of Christ's presence with His disciples. Christ blessed His church with lifted hands. The church has become the healing hands of Christ extended to the world (Acts 4:30), and through the hands of His anointed servants, signs and wonders are performed (Acts 5:12). The lifted hands and blessing of the Anointed One are expressed throughout Acts with the anointed touch of Spirit-filled believers.

The anointed touch is also associated with prayer for the sick. It is implied in the healing of the lame man at the Beautiful Gate. Luke records that Peter "took him by the right hand and lifted him up" (Acts 3:7, *NKJV*). This is more than a helpful gesture. Peter, Spirit-filled and anointed, extended his hand to the lame man and "lifted him up." It seems that the healing of "his feet and ankles" corresponds to Peter's extended hand—the anointed touch. On the island of Malta, the shipwrecked Paul prayed for the father of Publius, who was afflicted with a fever and dysentery. "Paul went in to see him and after he had prayed, he laid his hands on him and healed him" (Acts 28:8). Many others on the island came to Paul to receive healing through the anointed touch. Furthermore, just as many were healed as they touched the garments of Jesus, in Acts we discover that the sick were carried into the streets and healed as Peter's shadow fell upon them (Acts 5:14-16). Also, handkerchiefs or aprons were carried from the body of Paul to the sick "and the diseases left them and the evil spirits went out" (Acts 19:11-12).

The anointed touch in James 5:14-15 reflects the apostolic practice in the writings of Mark and Luke. As we examine this text, we will focus on two Greek words used by James: *sōzō* and *egeirō*. James says, "the prayer offered in faith will restore (*sōzō*) the one who is sick" (5:15). The use of the word *sōzō* is interesting. Most English translations of the text translate *sōzō* as "save."[290] Some translate *sōzō* as "heal."[291] The various translations reflect the word's range of meaning. In the Septuagint, *sōzō* is most often translated "to keep" or "to save" and speaks to God's intervention. In the New Testament, *sōzō* reflects its use in the Septuagint. In the Gospels, Acts, and the

---

[290] *King James Version, New King James Version, New Revised Standard Version, American Standard Version, English Standard Version, Holman Christian Standard Bible, and the New American Bible.*

[291] *New Living Translation, Good News Translation.* The *New International Version* reads "will make the sick person well."

Pauline writings, *sōzō* is most often used to speak of salvation, that is, the forgiveness of sins and eschatological deliverance. In a few occasions *sōzō* refers to healing. The question is, "How did James intend for his audience to understand *sōzō*? Before we answer this question, let's consider the meaning of *egeirō*. James wrote, "The prayer offered in faith will restore the one who is sick, and the Lord will raise (*egeirō*) him up" (5:15). The Greek word *egeirō* is most often used to denote "resurrection" or "new life." And, sometimes it is used to denote "healing." So, what is James telling us about the significance of the anointed touch? If James had wanted to limit the anointed touch to healing, he could have used other common Greek words—*iaomai* (used in verse 16) or *therapeuō*—instead of *sōzō*. But James, following the example of his Lord, is addressing more than healing; he is also speaking about the forgiveness of sin (Mark 2:3-12). James, under divine inspiration, chose *sōzō* to reflect its use in the Septuagint, that is, the power of God to deliver, to save, to forgive, and to keep. Salvation is holistic, that is, God desires that the whole person—body, soul, spirit—be touched by God's saving power. Salvation is healing—being healed from the corruption and disease of sin. Ultimately, salvation is resurrection and glorification— eschatological deliverance from the corruption of this present age. The use of *sōzō* with *egeirō* could speak to the sick being healed and raised from the sick bed. It is more likely that James understands the anointed touch as signifying salvation in a broader sense. Is James speaking about a sacramental act of healing? Yes. He wrote, ". . . pray for one another so that you may be healed" (*iaomai*). Sick people often die. It seems that James is considering that possibility. So then, what is the significance of the anointed touch when the sick are not healed? Their sins are forgiven and they shall be saved, that is, raised up to new life. In other words, the sick may die, but those who die in Christ are confident in the resurrection. Paul declared, "But if the Spirit of Him who raised Jesus from the dead dwells in you, He who raised Christ Jesus from the dead will also give life to your mortal bodies through His Spirit who dwells in you" (Romans 8:11).

The anointed touch in James is an expression of a Christo-Pneumatic ecclesiology—Christ and the Spirit in fellowship with the church. Jesus said:

> I will ask the Father, and He will give you another Helper, that He may be with you forever; that is the Spirit of truth, whom the world cannot receive, because it does not see Him or know Him, but you know Him because He abides with you and will be in you. I will not leave you as orphans; I will come to you (John 14:16-18).

The sick should never suffer alone. The sick person calls for the "elders of the church." This suggests that the sick believer is too sick to travel, possibly close to death. So, the church responds to the call and comes together with the sick believer. The sick believer is to be "anointed with oil," which signifies the presence of the Holy Spirit, in "the name of the Lord"—Jesus Christ. The church gathered together is to offer the prayer of faith. The sick person calling for the elders of the church is an act of faith. The elders' anointed touch "is the visible confession of confidence in the power of Christ to make whole."[292] James presents the gathered church, sick and well, in fellowship with the Holy Trinity. The Son and the Spirit are present as the two hands of the Father. The praying church is a community of healing and care which is expressed in the anointed touch and becomes a sacramental means of grace to the suffering.

The power and authority of the church is wholly derived from Christ and the Spirit—the Anointed One and the Anointing. The power and authority of Jesus is unique. Because of the intra-Trinitarian relationship between the Son and the Spirit, Christ is anointed by the Spirit in a unique manner that cannot be ontologically shared.[293] The elders (*presbýteroi*) of the church represent those who are anointed, that is "full of the Spirit and of wisdom" (Acts

---

[292] A.J. Gordon, *The Latter Rain Evangel* (May 1909), 14.

[293] Augustine wrote, "Christ, therefore, is the Anointed. He is peculiarly anointed, pre-eminently anointed; wherewith all Christians are anointed, He is pre-eminently anointed. . . . For all the holy ones are His fellows, but He in a peculiar sense is the Holy of Holies, peculiarly anointed, peculiarly Christ. *The Nicene and Post-Nicene Fathers Vol. VII*, 52.

6:3) and "righteous" (James 5:16). Because of the healing powers associated with the apostles and elders of the apostolic church, many pagans believed them to be gods (Acts 14:11-13). But James likens the elders to the prophet Elijah who "was a man with a nature like ours" (James 5:17). In other words, the elders of the church are not divine. However, in relationship with Christ, believers may be filled with the Holy Spirit and anointed for ministry. As believers exercise the anointed touch in the apostolic church, they are acting as "petitioners and mediators of divine power."[294] Anointed believers act "in the name of Jesus" and in the power of the Holy Spirit. Further, there is no intrinsic power in the various media used in healing—Peter's shadow, Paul's handkerchiefs, or anointing oil. The healing power always proceeds from God. God is free to use various substances as symbols of God's power, and even to use them as a medium, or channel, to transfer God's power.[295] Therefore, the prayer of faith and the anointed touch are sacramental means of grace. Through the prayers of anointed and faithful believers the presence of Christ and the Spirit is manifested and those who are suffering are comforted, healed, and made confident in the hope of the resurrection. "The effective prayer of a righteous man can accomplish much" (James 5:16).

The Anointed Touch in the Early Church

In the tradition of the church, the anointed touch represents the anointing of the Holy Spirit. Irenaeus referred to the Holy Trinity as the Father who anoints, the Son who is anointed, and the anointing who is the Spirit.[296] Theophilus of Antioch explained that Christians are followers of the Anointed One; therefore, "we are called Christians on this account, because we are anointed with the oil of God."[297] Clement of Alexandria wrote that the feet of Jesus, "anointed with fragrant ointment," represented the apostles who "received the

---

[294] Tipei, *The Laying on of Hands in the New Testament*, 154.
[295] Tipei has written that "the author's intention is to tell his readers that the healings and exorcisms . . . are precisely the effect of these 'mediating sub-stances' on the sick people" (146).
[296] *The Ante-Nicene Fathers Vol. I*, 446.
[297] *The Ante-Nicene Fathers Vol. II*, 92.

fragrant unction of the Holy Ghost."[298] John Chrysostom said that the Holy Spirit is the "precious ointment" received in baptism. He wrote:

> There is, if you desire it, a precious ointment and a fragrance, with which you might anoint your soul; not brought from Arabia, or Ethiopia, nor from Persia, but from heaven itself; purchased not by gold, but by a virtuous will, and by faith unfeigned. Buy this perfume, the odor of which is able to fill the world. It was of this the Apostles savored. "For we are (he says) a sweet savor, to some of death, to others of life." . . . With this we are anointed at our Baptism, then we savor sweetly of it; but it must be by our care afterwards that we retain the savor.[299]

In the early church, the anointed touch was commonly associated with water baptism. Candidates for baptism received a double anointing. They were anointed with "the Oil of Exorcism" immediately prior to baptism and they were anointed with "the Oil of Thanksgiving" immediately afterwards. The oil used in the baptismal anointing is called "sanctified oil."[300] Tertullian says that even as the anointing oil is applied to the body, that its effect is spiritual.[301] This practice was canonized in the fourth century in the *Constitution of the Holy Apostles*. In preparation for baptism, the bishop would offer a prayer of blessing so that God might "sanctify the oil in the name of the Lord Jesus, and impart to it spiritual grace and efficacious strength." The baptismal candidate was then anointed with the "holy oil" which represented "the participation of the Holy Spirit."[302] The anointed touch included the laying on of hands (also

---

[298] *The Ante-Nicene Fathers Vol. II*, 253.
[299] *The Nicene and Post-Nicene Fathers Vol. XIII*, 415.
[300] Hippolytus writes: "When the elder takes hold of each of them who are to receive baptism, he shall tell each of them to renounce, saying, 'I renounce you Satan, all your service, and all your works.' After he has said this, he shall anoint each with the Oil of Exorcism, saying, 'Let every evil spirit depart from you.'" *On The Apostolic Tradition*, 110-114.
[301] *The Ante-Nicene Fathers Vol. III*, 672.
[302] *The Ante-Nicene Fathers Vol. VII*, 469, 476.

called the "imposition of hands"), usually by the bishop. Following the apostolic practice found in Acts, it was believed that the Holy Spirit was conferred upon the candidate by the anointed touch.[303]

How did the sacramental practice of anointing the sick with oil become associated with water baptism? The evidence suggests that the convergence of anointing with oil and water baptism occurred very early in the life of the church. First, as we have demonstrated earlier, reception of the Holy Spirit was associated with water baptism. In the same manner that the Spirit descended upon Jesus at baptism, it was expected that all believers would receive the Spirit when they were baptized "in the name of the Father, and of the Son, and of the Holy Spirit." Likewise, anointing with oil was associated with the anointing of the Spirit. Water and oil were symbols of the cleansing and healing power of the Holy Spirit. This practice represents the ancient understanding of Jesus as Savior and the nature of salvation. Clement of Alexandria offered a brief synopsis: "the Word of the Father, who made man, cares for the whole nature of His creature; the all-sufficient Physician of humanity, the Savior, heals both body and soul."[304] For these early Christians, the healing of the body was a sign of eschatological redemption. Justin wrote, "All things which the Savior did, He did . . . to induce the belief that in the resurrection the flesh shall rise entire. For if on earth He healed the sicknesses of the flesh, and made the body whole, much more will He do this in the resurrection, so that the flesh shall rise perfect and entire.[305] Irenaeus insisted that human salvation was for the healing of the flesh and is culminated in the resurrection of the body.

> For the Maker of all things, the Word of God, who did also from the beginning form man, when He found His handiwork impaired by wickedness, performed upon it all kinds of healing. . . . He did once for all restore man sound and whole in all points, preparing him perfect for Himself unto the resurrection. For what was His object in healing

---

[303] *The Ante-Nicene Fathers Vol. III*, 672; *Vol. V*, 668; *Vol. VII*, 412, 415, 477; et al.

[304] *The Ante-Nicene Fathers Vol. II*, 210.

[305] *The Ante-Nicene Fathers Vol. I*, 295.

[different] portions of the flesh, and restoring them to their original condition, if those parts which had been healed by Him were not in a position to obtain salvation? For if it was [merely] a temporary benefit which He conferred, He granted nothing of importance to those who were the subjects of His healing. Or how can they maintain that the flesh is incapable of receiving the life which flows from Him, when it received healing from Him? For life is brought about through healing, and incorruption through life. He, therefore, who confers healing, the same does also confer life; and He [who gives] life, also surrounds His own handiwork with incorruption.[306]

One of the most prominent titles for Jesus in these early writings is "Physician." Origen wrote, "God the Word was sent, indeed, as a physician to sinners."[307] The Incarnation meant that the eternal Word of the Father assumed human flesh and that which is assumed is healed. Healing and salvation are two aspects of the same divine work. Salvation is understood as the healing of sin and its corrupting effects on the body. Therefore, when the new convert is presented for water baptism, the convert is anointed with oil because salvation is understood as the healing of the body and soul. Theophilus exhorted;

Entrust yourself to the Physician, and He will couch the eyes of your soul and of your heart . . . . But before all let faith and the fear of God have rule in thy heart, and then shalt thou understand these things. When thou shalt have put off the mortal, and put on incorruption, then shall thou see God worthily. For God will raise thy flesh immortal with thy soul; and then, having become immortal, thou shalt see the Immortal, if now you believe on Him . . . [sic][308]

---

[306] *The Ante-Nicene Fathers Vol. I*, 539.
[307] *The Ante-Nicene Fathers Vol. IV*, 488. In an earlier document, Ignatius wrote, "There is one Physician who is possessed both of flesh and spirit; both made and not made; God existing in flesh; true life in death; both of Mary and of God; first possible and then impossible—even Jesus Christ our Lord." *The Ante-Nicene Fathers Vol. I*, 52.
[308] *The Ante-Nicene Fathers Vol. II*, 91.

The anointed touch was not limited to water baptism. The early church continued the practice of anointing the sick. Sozomen, the fifth century church historian, tells the story of a group of monks who were being persecuted for their Nicene doctrine by the Arian bishop, Lucius. About the same time that Lucius' soldiers arrived to arrest the orthodox monks, a lame man was brought for prayer. The monks anointed the lame man with oil "and commanded him in the name of Christ, whom Lucius persecuted, to arise and go to his house" and "he suddenly became whole."[309] As a result of the miracle, the Arians were embarrassed, and the monks' Nicene faith was vindicated. Jerome wrote a biography of Hilarion, a fourth-century ascetic, who was filled with the Spirit and known for miracles. One of the miracles attributed to Hilarion is the healing of the daughter and son-in-law of a holy woman named Constantia. Jerome tells us that the two were "saved from death" because Hilarion anointed them with oil.[310] John Cassian tells the story of Abbot Paul who was stricken with paralysis over his whole body. In his great affliction, such "goodness proceeded from him that when sick persons were anointed with the oil which had touched . . . his body, they were instantly healed of all diseases."[311] Accounts of anointing the sick with oil are not common in the writings of the early fathers. But there are only two accounts of the practice in the New Testament. Even though it may be rarely attested, the anointed touch was a sacramental practice associated with healing throughout the early centuries of the church.

There are other instances in which the anointed touch was administered in the early church. Clement of Alexandria offers a brief mention in which the dead are anointed.[312] Although Clement may be referring to customary funerary rites, the context suggests that he is implying a sacramental anointing. Also, the anointed

---

[309] *The Nicene and Post-Nicene Fathers Second Series Vol. II*, 358.
[310] *The Nicene and Post-Nicene Fathers Second Series Vol. VI*, 314.
[311] *The Nicene and Post-Nicene Fathers Second Series Vol. XI*, 372.
[312] *The Ante-Nicene Fathers Vol. II*, 254.

touch was administered as a rite of reconciliation in the restoration of heretics and apostates to the church in lieu of rebaptism.

By the twelfth century, the rite of anointing and laying on hands had evolved into the Roman Catholic sacrament of "extreme unction" or "last rites." Although healing continued to be associated with the sacrament, it was commonly associated as a means of salvation for those who were at the point of death. The Council of Trent defined the sacrament as an anointing that "is to be used for the sick, but especially for those who are dangerously ill as to seem near death." However, with the reforms of Vatican II, the sacrament is no longer called "extreme unction," but "anointing of the sick" and is commonly observed in the pastoral care of the sick.[313]

The practice of anointing with oil in the Protestant church was a casualty of the Reformation. Martin Luther rejected the practice as sacramental, partly because its scriptural mandate is found in the letter of James, which he infamously considered to be an "epistle of straw." Luther and John Calvin considered the practice to be obsolete, limited to the apostolic age. Calvin wrote:

> Did this ministry, which the apostles then performed, still remain in the Church, it would also behoove us to observe the laying on of hands: but since that gift has ceased to be conferred, to what end is the laying on of hands? Assuredly the Holy Spirit is still present with the people of God; without his guidance and direction the Church of God cannot subsist. For we have a promise of perpetual duration, by which Christ invites the thirsty to come to him, that they may drink living water (John 7:37). But those miraculous powers and manifest operations, which were distributed by the laying on of hands, have ceased. They were only for a time.

The Reformers understood "sacrament" as that which is instituted by Christ himself. They understood the biblical practice to be a sacrament of healing, and since there was little evidence of

---

[313] *The New Dictionary of Theology* s.v "Anointing of the sick."

any miracle associated with extreme unction, it was an empty rite. They ridiculed the sacrament of extreme unction. In Calvin's words, the anointed touch was a "fictitious sacrament" and a "hypocritical stage-play."[314] Although a few Protestant groups have occasionally practiced the rite, in most Protestant churches it is considered a vestige of Roman Catholic sacramentalism.

The Anointed Touch—
A Pentecostal Sacrament

The proclamation that "Jesus is our Healer" is essential to the Pentecostal way of salvation (Isaiah 53:4-5; 1 Peter 2:24). The Pentecostal doctrine of divine healing in the Atonement is not a novel concept—it faithfully represents the teaching of the early church. Jesus is savior and the Great Physician. W.J. Seymour wrote, "Sickness and disease are destroyed through the precious atonement of Jesus . . . a body that knew no sin and disease was given for these imperfect bodies of ours."[315] "Through Jesus, we are entitled to health and sanctification of the soul and body."[316] W.C. Stevens proclaimed that "Christ's vicarious assumption of human sickness is the same as that employed in the case of sins." He explained:

> While our mortal life contracts disease, Jesus' life banishes disease. Contagious disease is dangerous to us, but the life of Jesus is destructive to disease. The very life of Jesus is of healing virtue. It is immortality touching mortality with a foretaste of the coming redemption. No child of God can afford to be living in mortality without these sippings of the life to come. The experience of the Spirit's quickening in our mortal flesh brings literal bodily immortality nigh to our consciousness and it puts us in advance touch with "the power of the age to come."[317]

---

[314] John Calvin, *Institutes of the Christian Religion*, IV, xix, 6, 18.
315 W.J. Seymour, "The Precious Atonement." *The Apostolic Faith* (September 1906), 2.
[316] "Salvation and Healing." *The Apostolic Faith* (December 1906), 2.
[317] W.C. Stevens, "The Cross and Sickness." *The Pentecostal Evangel* (August 23, 1924), 6-7.

Alex Boddy wrote that believers may have "divine health" through union with the "life-giving Christ" and the Holy Spirit who is "the indwelling Divine Life." "If any man is in Christ he is a new creation— the old nature passes away, all things become new. We believe that this is true of the body as well as of the soul."[318] Throughout his writings Boddy says, "the oil follows the blood," that is, Pentecost follows Calvary.

> The outpouring of the Blood at Calvary (together with the Resurrection) is the preparation for a true "Pentecost" for each one. The Blood of Jesus Christ, God's Son, cleanses us from all sin. Then the Holy Ghost is glad to come, and free to come. He comes (1) as the Holy Anointing OIL from above (I John ii., 20-27); (2) As the Presence which is as a Consuming FIRE (Heb. xii., 29) burning up all the chaff. (Jesus baptizes with the Holy Ghost and with Fire – Matt. iii., 11). Then He also comes as Living WATER, now that Jesus is glorified (John vii., 35). Out of the Spirit-baptized shall flow rivers of Living Water. Hallelujah! [sic][319]

Boddy's theology reflects the Christo-Pneumatic emphasis of Pentecostal spirituality. The Father's two hands—Christ and Spirit— are extended to touch the suffering of humanity.

The healing of the body is a blessing of sanctification. "A sanctified body is one in perfect health, through faith in God. It does not mean we could not get sick, but we are maintained in health by faith."[320] Although all sickness is a result of the corruption of sin, the sickness of a saint should not be interpreted as evidence of willful disobedience. After all, Job was blameless, but suffered.[321] Some

---

[318] Alex A. Boddy, "Health in Christ." *Confidence* (August 1910), 175-179. Likewise, C.H. Waddell wrote that believers receive "Divine healing" and "Divine health" as they partake of the "Divine life" of Jesus. He insisted that the believer must "partake of the living person of our Lord Jesus Christ through the Holy Ghost." "How to Receive Divine Healing," *The Christian Evangel* (February 8, 1919), 2.

[319] Alex A. Boddy, "Faith in His Blood." *Confidence* (August 1911), 189.

[320] *The Apostolic Faith* (January 1907), 1; and (January 1908), 4.

[321] *The Evening Light and Church of God Evangel* (July 11, 1914), 1.

Pentecostals taught that Christians should trust God with healing, and therefore faithful believers would not use medicine. What was the "divine prescription" for the sick? "Jesus is all the medicine you need."[322] How do believers receive divine healing? "James gives us explicit directions as to what we should do when we get sick (James 5:14)."[323] Will all believers be healed? Yes, said some Pentecostals, suggesting that failure to receive healing was a sign of weak faith. But others offered a more biblically balanced perspective. One pastor wrote that "in every case of sickness we can come to Jesus . . . the redemption of our body is already completed by the death and resurrection of Jesus, but the full redemption of our body can only become our possession when our Savior comes again."[324] The healing of the body is an eschatological sign that anticipates the resurrection of the body. Pentecostals believe that "living in the fullness of God" is more important than divine health for the body.[325] Many believers testified to receiving the baptism in the Holy Spirit as they sought to be healed.

The practice of praying for the sick by anointing with oil and laying on hands has been central to Pentecostal faith and practice. In an early letter, A.J. Tomlinson wrote,

> Hundreds have received the Baptism with the Holy Ghost and spoken in tongues as they did on the day of Pentecost. . . . when the altar calls were made hundreds and even thousands were moved by the Spirit to seek salvation or the Baptism with the Holy Ghost. Streaks of fire have been witnessed by observers. Wonderful demonstrations of the Spirit in many different ways [sic]. *I am not able to tell the numbers that have received healing for their bodies as we*

---

[322] *The Evening Light and Church of God Evangel* (April 15, 1910), 7.
[323] A.J. Tomlinson, "Healing in the Atonement." *The Evening Light and Church of God Evangel* (December 1, 1910), 1-2. Also, "Sickness and Health" *Church of God Evangel* (July 11, 1914), 1.
[324] "What Shall we Preach to the Sick?" *Confidence* (April 1915), 73.
[325] Sam C. Perry, "How to Get Healed." *The Church of God Evangel* (February 3, 1917), 3.

anointed them with oil, prayed for and laid our hands on them (emphasis mine).[326]

Pentecostals proclaimed "the full gospel." For early Pentecostals, the anointed touch was essential because it was "the Bible way." It occurred with great frequency in Pentecostal worship services and camp meetings. Early Pentecostal periodicals are filled with the testimonies of the faithful who were healed in the name of Jesus through the means of the anointed touch.

Early Pentecostal sacramental teaching followed the Protestant model of two (or three) sacraments. Most early Pentecostal creeds listed the "ordinances" or "sacraments" of the church as water baptism and the Lord's Supper. Many included footwashing. Because most early Pentecostals were anti-Catholic and anti-liturgical, it did not occur to them to view anointing and laying on of hands as a formal sacrament of the church. However, in faith and practice the anointed touch was a prevalent Pentecostal sacrament. Many early Pentecostal creeds included prayer for the sick by anointing and laying on of hands in connection with an affirmation of divine healing. The first issue of *The Apostolic Faith* listed the teachings of W.J. Seymour and the Apostolic Faith Movement.[327] The teachings include the three Pentecostal works of grace—justification, sanctification, and baptism in the Holy Spirit—and "seeking healing." Among the Scripture references to support the doctrine of healing are, Mark 16:16-18 and James 5:14. Both of these passages prescribe laying on hands in offering prayer for the sick. The earliest creedal statement of the Church of God (Cleveland, Tennessee) offers a list of "teachings that are made prominent" with accompanying Scriptural citations.[328] The sacramental teachings include:

- Water baptism by immersion—Matthew 28:19; Mark 1:9-10; John 3:22-23; Acts 8:36-38.

---

[326] A.J. Tomlinson, "Missionary Evangelism" (December 31, 1908). *Church of God Publications 1901-1923 DVD.* Cleveland, TN: Dixon Pentecostal Research Center, 2008.
[327] "The Apostolic Faith Movement." *The Apostolic Faith* (September 1906), 2.
[328] *The Evening Light and Church of God Evangel* (August 15, 1910), 3.

- Divine Healing Provided for All in the Atonement— Psalm 103:3; Isaiah 53:4-5; Matthew 8:17; James 5:14-16; 1 Peter 2:24.
- The Lord's Supper—Luke 22:17-20; 1 Corinthians 11:23-33.
- Washing the Saints' Feet—John 13:4-17; 1 Timothy 5:9-10.

Again, James 5:14-15 is given in support of the doctrine of divine healing. The anointed touch is essential to the doctrine of divine healing. The Pentecostal "full gospel" includes all sacramental practices that were blessed by Christ and practiced by the apostles. This sacramental practice was a sign that the Pentecostal church was a restoration of apostolic faith. George Holmes expressed the Pentecostal view of the anointed touch when he wrote, "This ordinance to the Church is surely as binding as those of Communion and baptism. If it were not God's intention to heal, this ordinance would be superfluous."[329]

In the New Testament, the Spirit-anointed elders were charged with praying for the sick. In the early church, only baptized believers were permitted to anoint the sick because it was expected that they received the Spirit at baptism. Likewise, early Pentecostals believed that Spirit-baptized believers are a "channel through which the Spirit may operate to do the works of Jesus Christ."[330] This expresses the sacramental nature which is essential to Pentecostal spirituality. The church is a visible and physical expression of the extended hands of Jesus Christ to those who are suffering. This Pentecostal spirituality is beautifully expressed in a song by Vep Ellis:

> Let me touch Him, let me touch Jesus. Let me touch Him as He passes by; then when I shall reach out to others, they shall know Him, they shall live and not die.

---

[329] George E. Holmes, "Why I believe in Divine Healing." *The Pentecostal Evangel* (July 19, 1959), 6. Also, an earlier unsigned article refers to "the ordinance of anointing with oil." "The Anointing Oil." *The Pentecostal Evangel* (July 20, 1929), 5.

[330] Sam C. Perry, "There are Other Things as Well." *The Church of God Evangel* (May 11, 1918), 3.

There's a river, a river flowing, from within and to cleanse my soul; and the flow sets my life to glowing, Holy Spirit, more than silver and gold.

Oh, to be His hand extended, reaching out to the oppressed, let me touch Him, let me touch Jesus, so that others may know and be blessed.[331]

Early Pentecostals were sacramental, and when it was considered to be "the Bible way," they could even be somewhat liturgical. Because of their sincere desire to be apostolic in faith and practice, proper biblical order was important. But proper biblical order always meant the presence of the Holy Spirit. The Church of God *Book of Doctrines* offered the usual manner by which the anointed touch was administered:

The sick one calls upon the elders of the church to pray for his healing. (The elders in this case are considered any that are leaders in the church service—faithful brethren or sisters.) They anoint with oil (usually olive oil), by dropping a few drops from a bottle on the head of the sick one. This is done with the prayer of faith. Frequently, the evil spirit must be rebuked from the sick one's body—just as in Matthew 8:28-34 out of whom Jesus cast the evil spirits—and then deliverance comes. Oftentimes the evil spirit is rebuked by the Holy Ghost in unknown tongues.[332]

The anointed touch is presented as a charismatic sacrament. It is more than a form, or a liturgical practice. The Holy Spirit is present and often speaks. Also, just as the early church exorcised demons with the baptismal anointing, Pentecostals often rebuked evil spirits that might be the cause of disease. Pentecostals call this "Holy Ghost order." This is a form of godliness in which the power of God is affirmed and demonstrated in physical manifestations, including a healed body.

---

[331] V.B. "Vep" Ellis, "Let Me Touch Him." *Hymns of the Spirit* (Cleveland, TN: Pathway Press, 1969), 284.
[332] *Book of Doctrines*, 93-94.

Alex Boddy published a "form of procedure" for administering the anointed touch. He wrote, "Pouring a few drops of olive oil into his left palm, the Elder prays that God will graciously sanctify the oil: and that He will use it as a channel of spiritual blessing to the sufferer for Christ's sake, also as a symbol of consecration to His blessed service, and a token of the coming of the Holy Ghost."[333] Boddy presents the anointed touch in a sacramental manner that is reminiscent of the early church. Through the prayer of the elder, the oil is to be sanctified by the Spirit of grace and becomes "a channel of spiritual blessing." The anointing oil is touched by the divine Anointing. The oil signifies the participation of the Holy Spirit. Not only could anointed men and women be channels of God's grace, but anointed oil was a "means of grace" as well.

Following the traditions of the Scripture and the early church, Pentecostals have always associated the Holy Spirit with oil.

> "He anointeth my head with oil, my cup runneth over." The oil of the Holy Ghost is poured upon our heads, and when we get filled, it will run over, that we may help others . . . when the oil of the Holy Ghost overflows, it will saturate and thrill and fill with the power of God other souls.[334]

The baptism of the Holy Spirit is "the Holy Anointing Oil" from above.[335] The church, which is the body of Christ, must be anointed with "the blessed oil of the Holy Ghost."[336] Donald Gee wrote that the Pentecostal church is "well lubricated" by the oil of the Spirit. He exclaimed, "I bless God for the oil. Hallelujah for the Oil!"[337]

The anointed handkerchief was another "means of grace" by which the sick may be healed. Oil was often used to anoint handkerchiefs so that they could be sent to the sick. Sometimes, sick individuals

---

[333] Alex A. Boddy, "The Anointing with Oil." *Confidence* (April-June, 1922), 21.
[334] *The Apostolic Faith* (September 1907), 2.
[335] Alex Boddy, "Faith in His Blood." *Confidence* (August 1911), 189. Sam C. Perry, "The Baptism of the Holy Ghost." *The Church of God Evangel* (April 8, 1916), 3.
[336] Mrs. B.L. Shepherd, "Jewel Joints." Church of God Evangel (February 21, 1920), 3.
[337] Donald Gee, "The Anointing." *The Pentecostal Evangel* (August 17, 1935), 2.

would send a handkerchief to the church to be anointed and returned. This practice was common among Pentecostals from Azusa Street in Los Angeles to those in the Appalachian Mountains of Tennessee and North Carolina, and throughout the world. W.J. Seymour wrote that "Handkerchiefs are sent in to be blest, and are returned to the sick and they are healed in many cases."[338] This practice was one of the signs of the restoration of the apostolic church.[339] A.J. Tomlinson reported that Pentecostals were "practicing the Bible way of healing." He continued:

> The common way now is by sending request by wire and letter, and by sending handkerchiefs and aprons. We pray for the sick every day, but on Sunday about 12:30 we have from twenty to forty handkerchiefs to pray over besides a number of requests. When this time comes we spread the handkerchiefs out on the altar and the saints gather around and prayers are offered up in the earnestness of our souls. We are often reminded of the experience of the apostles . . . . We think of every handkerchief representing a sick person. . . . And oh, how the saints pray! Then, as we cannot get to the people and anoint them and lay our hands on them we lay our hands on the handkerchiefs and anoint them and send them to be placed on the sick ones. Many have sent us good news of instantaneous healing when the handkerchief touched the body, while others have stated that they began to amend that very hour. And either way God gets the glory.[340]

There have been hundreds of healing testimonies printed in various Pentecostal publications. Here I will offer just two of the "good reports" that were printed in the *Church of God Evangel*. Sister Mary Davis wrote:

> I am still praising God for healing in my body. I was very low and Sister Blake sent my handkerchief to Brother Tomlinson for the saints there to pray over and anoint with

---

[338] W.J. Seymour, "Beginning of World Wide Revival." *The Apostolic Faith* (January 1907), 1.

[339] "In Denver, Colorado." *The Apostolic Faith* (May 1907), 1.

[340] A.J. Tomlinson, "Healing for the Body." *The Church of God Evangel* (June 10, 1922), 1.

oil in the name of Jesus. When the handkerchief returned
I was completely healed of consumption. Glory to God
forever.[341]

Sister Laura Williams said:

> I want to testify of His wonderful healing power. I had a
> large growth on my head for twenty-seven years and last
> winter it hurt so bad that I asked the good Lord to heal my
> head. About the middle of February it burst and commenced
> running very bad. So in July I sent a handkerchief to Brother
> Tomlinson, for him and the saints to pray over it anointing
> it with oil. When it came back I wore it on my head for a few
> nights and the place was healed wonderfully. I thank and
> praise the Lord for it.[342]

Did early Pentecostals believe that healing grace was transferred
through the anointed touch? Can the anointed human hand, anointed
oil, or an anointed handkerchief be a channel through which the
power of God touches and heals the sick? Well, yes and no. The
primary concern of Pentecostal theology is that every believer can
have a direct and unmediated encounter with Christ and the Spirit.
W.J. Seymour insisted, "We are not divine healers any more than
we are divine saviors. Healing is done through Almighty God."[343]
Concerning the anointing oil, J.T. Butlin wrote, "There is no healing
power in the oil itself, and if a patient thinks too much of the oil
as a means of healing, he will be disappointed. It is the Lord who
heals."[344] These Pentecostals were adamant that divine healing is
provided in the atonement of Jesus Christ and through the power of
the Holy Spirit. Also, they were utterly committed to obedience to
the Holy Scriptures. As we have observed, Pentecostal spirituality
is often manifested in physical actions. Yes, divine healing is the
salvific work of Christ and Spirit; but it also involves the "prayer

---

[341] Mary Davis, "Was Healed of Consumption." *The Church of God Evangel* (November 26, 1921), 3.

[342] Laura Williams, "Great Healing Power." *The Church of God Evangel* (December 31, 1921), 2.

[343] *The Apostolic Faith* (October 1906), 4.

[344] J.T. Butlin, "The Anointing of the Sick for Healing." *The Pentecostal Evangel* (August 23, 1924), 4.

of faith" and the anointed touch. Here we discover the major distinction between Roman Catholic and Pentecostal sacramental teaching. For Pentecostals, sacraments are not *ex opera operato*, or, "by virtue of the act itself." In Roman Catholic thought, as long as grace is not resisted, grace is conveyed. The role of faith is somewhat passive. Pentecostals insist that sacraments require faith and the "effective prayer" of the righteous (James 5:16). The role of faith is active—even efficacious. Sacraments are charismatic, that is, they require the direct mediation (presence) of Christ and the Spirit. For Pentecostals, sacraments are efficacious when they are observed in faithful obedience to the Scriptures by the sanctified church where Christ and the Spirit are present. This spirituality represents the Father (the Anointer) embracing humanity, and all creation, with His two hands—Christ (the Anointed One) and Spirit (the Anointing). The Word became flesh. The Spirit is poured out upon all flesh. Flesh is of the created order. Jesus Christ is the perfect union of humanity and divinity. The Spirit baptizes and anoints all who are in Christ. Also, the Spirit moves and rests upon all creation. Therefore, saving and healing grace can be conveyed in the waters of baptism and footwashing, through the bread and cup of Holy Communion, and through anointed hands, oil, and handkerchiefs.

"The Gift of God"

> Now when Simon saw that the Spirit was bestowed through the laying on of the apostles' hands, he offered them money, saying, "Give this authority to me as well, so that everyone on whom I lay my hands may receive the Holy Spirit." But Peter said to him, "May your silver perish with you, because you thought you could obtain the gift of God with money! You have no part or portion in this matter, for your heart is not right before God. Therefore, repent of this wickedness" (Acts 8:18-22).

Once, I was watching a prominent Charismatic evangelist on a Christian network preach a message on salvation and healing. As he preached, I listened attentively. I thought, *He's really doing a good job presenting the gospel.* Then, he gave the altar call. He said, "If you're ready to receive from God, come now and sow your $1000 seed faith gift into our ministry." I wish I could say that I was surprised, but I was not. This is all too common in contemporary Pentecostal and Charismatic churches. And frankly, it is appalling. Salvation and healing are the *free* gifts of God. Jesus paid it all!

Simon Magus was a notorious Samaritan magician who heard the preaching of Philip, believed on Christ and was baptized (Acts 8:13). Because of his preconversion experience in the magical arts, he was "constantly amazed" at the "signs and great miracles" that were taking place at the hands of the apostles and elders of the church. He was seduced by power and offered money to the apostles so that he might receive the power of the Spirit. Peter's rebuke was harsh. "May your silver perish with you." Previously, Peter had pronounced judgment upon Ananias and Sapphira because they had lied to the Holy Spirit (Acts 5). They died at the feet of Peter. Simon was offered the possibility of repentance, but was sternly warned of impending eternal destruction.[345] Peter declared, "Your heart is not right before God."

Jesus warned of the corrupting influence of power and money.

> No one can serve two masters; for either he will hate the one and love the other, or he will be devoted to one and despise the other. You cannot serve God and wealth (Matthew 6:24).

> Not everyone who says to Me, "Lord, Lord," will enter the kingdom of heaven, but he who does the will of My Father who is in heaven will enter. Many will say to Me on that day, "Lord, Lord, did we not prophesy in Your name, and in Your name cast out demons, and in Your name perform many miracles?" And then I will declare to them, "I never knew you; depart from Me, you who practice lawlessness" (Matthew 7:21-23).

Likewise, Paul said that leaders in the church should be "free from the love of money" (1 Timothy 3:3). He explained, "For the love of money is a root of all sorts of evil, and some by longing for

[345] The Greek word translated as "perish" is *apōleia* and is associated with eternal destruction in the New Testament (Matthew 7:13; John 17:12; Romans 9:22; Philippians 1:28; 2 Thessalonians 2:3; 2 Peter 2:1; Revelation 17:8, 11).

it have wandered away from the faith and pierced themselves with many griefs" (1 Timothy 6:10).

Just as Peter had discerned the greed of Ananias' heart, he discerned the "intent" of Simon's heart. Simon Magus' love of power and money had produced in him "the gall of bitterness" and "the bondage of iniquity." Indeed, he had wandered from the faith. In the tradition of the church, Simon is remembered as the first heretic. Also, his name is associated with the scandal of power and greed within the church. The crime of "simony" is defined as buying the holy offices of the church. Simon was not the last believer to be scandalized by the love of money.

In 1517, Pope Leo X offered indulgences, a pardon of temporal punishment, to all who would give money in support of the construction of St. Peter's Basilica. To put this in the language of the contemporary Pentecostal/Charismatic Movement, if believers would "plant a seed faith gift" in support of St. Peter's, then their sins would be forgiven. In effect, God's grace was for sale. Johann Tetzel, a German Dominican friar, was appointed commissioner for the Pope and authorized to sell indulgences throughout Germany. Tetzel preached, ". . . all who confess and in penance put alms into the coffer according to the counsel of the confessor, will obtain complete remission of all their sins."[346] Like a wolf, Tetzel preyed upon the despair of God's lambs, enriching himself as well as the coffers of the Pope. It was Tetzel's activity that stirred the passions of Martin Luther. Luther denounced the practice of selling indulgences. He wrote, "It is certain that when the penny jingles into the money-box, gain and avarice can be increased, but the result of the intercession of the Church is in the power of God alone."[347] According to Luther, salvation, and pardon from sin, could not be purchased because "the just shall live by faith." Salvation and healing are the free and gracious acts of God. With Luther's protest, the Protestant Reformation was launched.

---

[346] Hans J. Hillerbrand, *The Reformation (New York: Harper and Row*, 1964), 41-46.
[347] Martin Luther, *Disputation of Doctor Martin Luther on the Power and Efficacy of Indulgences: October 31, 1517*, electronic ed. (Bellingham, WA: Logos Research Systems, 1996), 95 Theses #28.

The Roman Catholic Church eventually recognized the error. After the Council of Trent, Pope Pius V issued a decree that forbade the granting of indulgences associated with any financial transaction.

The Pentecostal Movement has been scandalized by the "prosperity gospel." The love of money has corrupted Pentecostal and Charismatic churches from pulpit to pew. It seems that the new sacramental element is coin and currency. A relationship with God is presented in terms of a contractual agreement between business partners. The anointing and grace of God have become commodities that are auctioned to the highest bidder. Charismatic men and women who proclaim the message of Jesus Christ have cheapened that which is more desirable than the finest gold. In the process, their anointing has become "a ring of gold in a swine's snout" (Proverbs 11:22). It may be that, like Simon Magus, the Pentecostal/Charismatic Movement will perish with our silver.

This much is certain. The substance of the kingdom of God is not the perishable wealth of this present age. The gift of God cannot be obtained with money. The price of human redemption has been paid with the blood of God's dear Son. God the Father has extended his two hands—Son and Spirit—to save and heal all who will respond in sincere faith. Rich and poor alike have the same access to the throne of grace. Luther was right. The righteous by faith shall live!

The Anointed Touch—Dying in the Faith

As we have seen, Pentecostals have been praying for the sick since the beginning of the movement. There have been many testimonies of miraculous healings. But, not all have been healed. Many have continued to suffer and eventually succumb to the disease that afflicted them. Among Pentecostals, there has existed a tension between the "prayer of faith" for the sick and the fact that many have died in spite of the faithful prayers of the saints. Kimberly Alexander has demonstrated this tension among early Pentecostals. The editors of *The Pentecostal Evangel* refused to print obituaries.

The editors of the *Church of God Evangel* chose to print obituaries. Alexander has written:

> The obituaries often tell the story of the suffering of the saint, the prayers that were offered over time, the ups and downs of seeming victory and then relapse and final words of the dying person, often accompanied by worship of God. These obituaries reveal what is stated elsewhere; *a person was to die in the faith as they had lived in the faith* (emphasis mine).

> These Pentecostals seemed to be able to hold in tension God's will to heal and his will not to heal. Prayer for healing could be offered for those who were suffering until the last breath . . . . And then one could rejoice that "they had safely landed on the other shore."[348]

Here we must return to the earlier exposition of James 5:14-15. Remember, James speaks of the anointed touch in terms of the *possibility* of healing and the *certainty* of the resurrection. As the author of Hebrews reminds us, "it is appointed for men to die once" (Hebrews 9:27). Even those who have been healed will face death. But death can be faced in faith and in confidence of the resurrection. So, the task before the Pentecostal pastor is to minister the anointed touch to the sick and dying. With this tension in mind, I would like to share a pastoral experience.

Larry was not a religious person. His family attended church, but he had little use for religion. Larry struggled with the concept of faith. He was a strong man and had worked with his hands for years. He had a hard time believing in something he couldn't see. One day he experienced some pain in his side, so he went to the doctor. The news wasn't good. Larry was diagnosed with cancer. Surgery was scheduled to remove a cancerous kidney, and I visited with him in the hospital and prayed for his healing and the success of the surgery. After the surgery, he discovered that the cancer had moved to his colon and liver. There was no cure. I spoke with Larry on many occasions about the condition of his soul. Many times he

[348] Alexander, *Pentecostal Healing*, 112-113, 170.

reminded me, "Preacher, I'm not afraid of death." He was a veteran of the Vietnam conflict, and he often shared his near death experience. If he could live through that horror, he thought that facing death couldn't be worse.

One day I invited Larry to help me with a project at my home. I knew that he wasn't well, but I also knew that he would be happy to get out of the house and work with his hands. Over two days, we worked and talked. On the first day, we talked about life, family, his illness, and his impending death. Again, he reminded me that he was not afraid. On the second day, I began to talk earnestly to Larry about his soul. Again, I heard that familiar response, "Preacher, I'm not afraid to die." This time I responded, "That's fine, Larry. But you need to be *prepared* to die." He stared at me for a minute, and replied, "Yea, I reckon so."

Over the next several weeks, I visited Larry at his home. His illness was progressing, and he was getting weaker. I continued to talk to Larry about being prepared to die. In one of our conversations, I discovered that Larry didn't really believe in "life after death." He told me that he would live in the memories of his family. I responded, "Larry, that's not good enough. There has to be more." I shared with him the hope of Christian faith—the resurrection of the body. On another occasion, he told me that even though he wasn't afraid to die, he didn't want his family to have to watch his suffering. I said, "Larry, I'll make a deal with you. If you promise to be prepared to die, I'll pray that God will grant you a quick death." That may seem strange, but even as Larry struggled with faith, he understood reality. He knew he was dying. He replied, "Preacher, I'll make that deal with you." After each visit, I would offer my hand and pray for him. Larry accepted the Lord Jesus.

About three weeks before he died, I visited Larry. As we sat together, I could see that he was in great pain. He said, "Preacher, I've got a lot to thank God for, but if this gets any worse, I won't be thanking God for anything." I replied, "Larry, there is a comfort that God brings to us in our darkest times, and I am confident that God will grant you that comfort." Then I took his hand and prayed for him. After that, the more he suffered, the more comforted and peaceful he became. God's grace proved sufficient.

One Sunday night, just after church, I received a call from Larry's wife, Brenda. Larry was in great pain and needed prayer. Several men from the church accompanied me to Larry's home. He was sitting in his reclining chair, suffering and struggling with the torments of his disease. We gathered around him, anointed him, and prayed for him. After prayer we talked and offered our love and support to Larry and his family. Days later, Larry died. But he died in the Faith. Many times, we prayed for Larry. We prayed for healing, for comfort, for peace, and for his salvation. James said, ". . . and the prayer offered in faith will restore the one who is sick, and the Lord will raise him up, and if he has committed sins, they will be forgiven him" (5:15). Each time we prayed for Larry, he encountered the grace of God in the anointed touch of believers. Larry was restored. Many times during his illness, the Lord restored his soul and comforted him in the presence of his enemies—cancer and mortality. Because Larry faced death in faith, "the Lord will raise him up."

The anointed touch can be a powerful practice in the pastoral care of the sick and terminally ill. The wise pastor will always offer comfort and hope. Yes, there is hope in healing, and some will be healed. However, the goal of salvation is the resurrection. The presence of the elders is a demonstration of the church's care for those who suffer. The prayers and anointed touch of the elders is sacramental—a means of grace—to the suffering. Jesus said, "For where two or three have gathered together in My name, I am there in their midst" (Matthew 18:20). All who are suffering, sick, or dying need the presence of the praying church. The praying church brings to the suffering and dying the presence of the risen Lord.

Afterword

"Or what woman, if she has ten silver coins and loses one coin, does not light a lamp and sweep the house and search carefully until she finds it? When she has found it, she calls together her friends and neighbors, saying, 'Rejoice with me, for I have found the coin which I had lost!'" (Luke 15:8-9).

Ironic as it may seem, renewal movements often look back for inspiration and guidance as they engage the future. This is especially true for those who seek reformation, or revival, within the Christian church. Renewal movements seek to *recover* something that has been lost. The Pentecostal Movement was birthed as sincere believers sought to recover the apostolic faith. The heart of Pentecostal spirituality is an encounter with the Holy Trinity.

There are many challenges that face Pentecostal churches as we transition into the second century of the movement. Many of these challenges are not unlike the difficulties of the early church in the second and third centuries; or the challenges of other renewal movements throughout the history of the church. From time to time, the church loses a treasure. The parable of the lost coin teaches us that we must be very careful to guard the treasures with which we have been blessed. The woman had ten coins. Early Pentecostals inherited a rich deposit of Christian tradition.

The first great treasure is the revelation of God as Holy Trinity. Human redemption is accomplished as God the Father embraces us with God's two hands—Son and Spirit. This divine embrace lifts us out of the corruption of this present age and places us in heavenly places. We must be careful to preserve this treasure of the faith. From the perspective of a Pentecostal, it seems that all too often the church has presented God the Father with one hand (Christ) reaching out to humanity, but the other hand (Spirit) is tied behind God's back. As we move into a postmodern (and post-Christian) world, there is another concern, that is, the tendency to present God with God's right hand (Christ) somewhat diminished. The Spirit is sometimes presented as working outside of the Holy Trinity, as if God's left hand is unaware of the right hand. In other words, the Spirit without Christ, can lead humans to salvation. This does not reflect the apostolic faith. The Pentecostal "full gospel" affirms the ancient Christian faith that the Son and the Spirit are one with the Father. The Father's salvific embrace is fully expressed in the Incarnation and Pentecost. Salvation is receiving Christ and the Holy Spirit. Pentecostal spirituality is Christo-Pneumatic.

Another treasure is the church—redeemed humanity in fellowship with the Holy Trinity. The church is the "body of Christ" and the "fellowship of the Holy Spirit." The church is our mother, from whom we receive nourishment and nurture. She is to be honored. There are many challenges presently before us as it relates to our understanding of the church. Some Christians don't even like the term. They claim there is too much negative historical baggage associated with the term. It is because of the church's baggage that the Spirit continuously works to renew the church. A full hearing of the church's history will reveal its sins, but also its glory. For Pentecostals, the church is essential in God's redemptive plan. The church is the dwelling of the Holy Spirit and is empowered by the Spirit for mission. So, instead of deconstructing the church, we should seek to renew her. Pentecostal spirituality is expressed as a Christo-Pneumatic ecclesiology.

The sacraments are salvific treasures. The sacraments are visible and physical expressions of God's redemptive work in our lives. Sacraments call us to the altar so that we may present our bodies to God as a "living and holy sacrifice." Sacraments tell the story of redemption. As we participate in sacramental worship, we are washed and cleansed, we are nourished and healed, and we confess and are forgiven. As I have demonstrated, early Pentecostals enthusiastically embraced the sacraments. The "full gospel" means that the whole counsel of God's Word is to be proclaimed and practiced. As we seek to make church "relevant," we have witnessed the inclusion of liturgical dance, living drama, and even mime in worship services. I embrace these forms of visual worship. However, the sacraments should not be viewed as archaic, or incidental, forms of worship. Worship must be more than entertainment. Worship must be a transformative encounter with God. The sacraments are the physical means of this encounter. Pentecostalism is a Christo-Pneumatic ecclesiology that is expressed in a physical spirituality.

The woman had ten coins, but lost one. She was not satisfied with the nine remaining coins. She sought to recover the lost coin. If we are to be faithful to our Pentecostal heritage, we must never allow any treasure of the "full gospel" to be lost. Just as our Pentecostal patriarchs and matriarchs sought to recover an encounter with the Holy Spirit, we must be diligent to search the house for any lost treasure. Pentecostal pastors must hold fast to their role as the primary teachers and worship leaders of the church. We must be students of the Scriptures, searching the Scriptures for every salvific treasure. This is an ongoing task that is essential to the renewal of the church. The sacraments have become the lost treasure of many Pentecostal churches. We have treasures remaining. However, we must not be satisfied until we recover all lost treasures. Then we can rejoice.

Select Bibliography

Books

Admission to the Lord's Supper: Basics of Biblical and Confessional Teaching. A Report of the Commission on Theology and Church Relations of the Lutheran Church—Missouri Synod. St. Louis: The Lutheran Church—Missouri Synod, 2000.

Alexander, Kimberly Ervin. *Pentecostal Healing: Models in Theology and Practice*. Blandford Forum, UK: Deo Publishing, 2006.

Archer, Kenneth J. *A Pentecostal Hermeneutic for the Twenty-First Century: Spirit, Scripture and Community* (Journal of Pentecostal Theology Supplemental Series). London and New York: T. & T. Clark, 2004.

Bartleman, Frank. *Azusa Street*. South Plainfield, NJ: Bridge Publishing Inc., 1980.

Beasley-Murray, G.R. *Baptism in the New Testament*. London: Paternoster Press, 1972, 1997.

Blumhofer, Edith L. *Restoring the Faith: The Assemblies of God, Pentecostalism, and American Culture*. Chicago: The University of Illinois Press, 1993.

Bonhoeffer, Dietrich. *The Cost of Discipleship*. New York: Simon and Schuster, 1995.

Book of Common Prayer. New York: Oxford University Press, 1990.

Book of Doctrines. Cleveland, TN: Church of God Publishing House, 1922.

Book of General Instructions for the Ministry and Membership. Cleveland, TN: Church of God Publishing House, 1927.

Book of Minutes: A compiled history of the work of the General Assemblies of the Church of God. Cleveland, TN: Church of God Publishing House, 1922.

Braaten, Carl E. *Mother Church: Ecclesiology and Ecumenism*. Minneapolis: Augsburg Fortress Press, 1998.

Bradshaw, Paul F., Maxwell Johnson, L. Edward Phillips. *The Apostolic Tradition: A Commentary* (Hermeneia). Minneapolis: Augsburg Fortress Publishers, 2002.

263

Bromiley, G.W. ed. *Zwingli and Bullinger.* (Library of Christian Classics). Louisville: Wesminster John Knox Press, 1953, 2006.

Bulgakov, Sergius. *The Bride of the Lamb.* Grand Rapids: Eerdmans Publishing Co., 2002.

_____. *The Comforter.* Grand Rapids: Eerdmans Publishing Co., 2004.

Burgess, Stanley M. and Gary B. McGee, editors. *Dictionary of Pentecostal and Charismatic Movements.* Grand Rapids: Zondervan Publishing House, 1988.

Burgess, Stanley and Eduard M. Van Der Maas, eds. *The New International Dictionary of Pentecostal and Charismatic Movements.* Revised and expanded edition. Grand Rapids: Zondervan Publishing House, 2002.

Catechism of the Catholic Church, 2nd edition. Washington, DC: United States Catholic Conference, 1994, 1997.

Chan, Simon. *Pentecostal Theology and the Christian Spiritual Tradition.* Sheffield: Sheffield Academic Press, 2000.

_____. *Liturgical Theology: The Church as Worshiping Community.* Downers Grove, IL: IVP Academic, 2006.

Collins, Raymond F. *First Corinthians* (Sacra Pagina). Collegeville, MN: The Liturgical Press, 1999.

Confession of Faith in a Mennonite Perspective. Scottdale, PA: Herald Press, 1995.

Congar, Yves. *I Believe in the Holy Spirit.* New York: Crossroad Herder Publishing, 1999.

Conkin, Paul K. *Cane Ridge: America's Pentecost.* Madison, WI: The University of Wisconsin Press, 1990.

Cox, Harvey. *Fire From Heaven.* New York: Addison-Wesley Publishing Company, 1994.

De Arteaga, William. *Forgotten Power: The Significance of the Lord's Supper in Revival.* Grand Rapids: Zondervan, 2002.

Dix, Gregory Dom. *The Shape of the Liturgy.* New York: Continuum, 2003.

Dudley, Martin and Geoffrey Rowell, eds. *The Oil of Gladness: Anointing in the Christian Tradition.* Collegeville, MN: The Liturgical Press, 1993.

Faupel, William D. *The Everlasting Gospel: The Significance of Eschatology in the Development of Pentecostal Thought.* Sheffield: Sheffield Academic Press, 1996.

Fee, Gordon D. *God's Empowering Presence: The Holy Spirit in the Letters of Paul.* Peabody, MA: Hendrickson Publishers, 1994.

Ferguson, Everett. *Baptism in the Early Church: History, Theology, and Liturgy in the First Five Centuries.* Grand Rapids: Eerdmans Publishing Company, 2009.

Fox, Robin Lane. *Pagans and Christians.* New York: Alfred A. Knopf, Inc., 1989.

General Assembly Minutes 1906-1914: Photographic Reproductions of the First Ten General Assembly Minutes. Cleveland, TN: White Wing Publishing House, 1992.

George, Timothy. *Theology of the Reformers.* Nashville: Broadman Press, 1988.

Hartin, Patrick J. *James.* (Sacra Pagina). Collegeville, MN: The Liturgical Press, 2003.

Hillerbrand, Hans J. *The Reformation.* New York: Harper and Row, 1964.

Holmes, Michael W., ed. *The Apostolic Fathers, 2nd Edition.* Trans. J.B. Lightfoot and J.R. Harmer. Grand Rapids: Baker Book House, 1989.

Hughes, Ray H. *Church of God Distinctives.* Cleveland, TN: Pathway Press, 1968.

Hippolytus. *On The Apostolic Tradition.* Trans. Alistair Stewart-Sykes. New York: St. Vladimir's Seminary Press, 2001.

Jacobsen, Douglas. *Thinking in the Spirit: Theologies of the Early Pentecostal Movement.* Indianapolis: Indiana University Press, 2003.

Jeffrey, Peter. *A New Commandment: Toward a Renewed Rite for the Washing of Feet.* Collegeville, MN: The Liturgical Press, 1992.

Jernigan, John C. *From the Gambling Den to the Pulpit: A Short Autobiography of John C. Jernigan.* Rev. ed., 1939.

John Paul II. *The Holy Spirit in the Life of the Church and the World.* Boston: Pauline Books and Media, 1986.

Johnson, Luke Timothy. *The Letter of James.* The Anchor Bible. New York: Doubleday, 1995.

Kodell, Jerome. *The Eucharist in the New Testament.* Collegeville, MN: The Liturgical Press, 1988.

Komonchak, Joseph A., Mary Collins, and Dermot A. Lane, eds. *The New Dictionary of Theology*. Wilmington, DE: Michael Glazier Inc., 1987.

Kydd, Ronald A.N. *Healing through the Centuries: Models for Understanding*. Peabody, MA: Hendrickson Publishers, 1998.

LaCugna, Catherine Mowry. *God for Us: The Trinity and Christian Life*. San Francisco: HarperCollins, 1991.

Land, Steven J. *Pentecostal Spirituality: A Passion for the Kingdom*. Sheffield: Sheffield Academic Press, 1993.

Macchia, Frank D. *Baptized in the Spirit: A Global Pentecostal Theology*. Grand Rapids: Zondervan, 2006.

McDonnell, Kilian and George T. Montague. *Christian Initiation and Baptism in the Holy Spirit: Evidence From the First Eight Centuries*. Collegeville, MN: The Liturgical Press, 1991.

McDonnell, Kilian. *The Baptism of Jesus in the Jordan: The Trinitarian and Cosmic Order of Salvation*. Collegeville, MN: The Liturgical Press, 1996.

_____. *The Other Hand of God: The Holy Spirit as the Universal Touch and Goal*. Collegeville, MN: The Liturgical Press, 2003.

McNeill, John T. *A History of the Cure of Souls*. New York: Harper & Brothers Publishing, 1951.

Milavec, Aaron. *The Didache: Faith, Hope, and Life of the Earliest Christian Communities, 50-70 C.E.* New York: The Newman Press, 2003.

Moltmann, Jürgen. *The Church in the Power of the Spirit*. San Francisco: HarperCollins Publishers, 1991.

Niederwimmer, Kurt. *The Didache: A Commentary* (Hermeneia). Minneapolis: Fortress Press, 1998.

Oden, Thomas. *Classical Pastoral Care, Vol. 2*. Grand Rapids: Baker Book House, 1987.

_____. *Systematic Theology, Vol. 3: Life in the Spirit*. Peabody, MA: Prince Press, 1998.

Palamas, Gregory. *The Triads*. Trans. Nicholas Gendle. New York: Paulist Press, 1983.

Pelikan, Jaroslav. *The Emergence of the Catholic Tradition*. Chicago: The University of Chicago Press, 1971.

_____. *The Spirit of Eastern Christendom (600-1700)*. Chicago: The University of Chicago Press, 1977.

_____. *The Growth of Medieval Theology (600-1300)*. Chicago: The University of Chicago Press, 1980.

Peritti, Frank. *The Oath*. Nashville: WestBow Press, 1995.

Ramirez, Frank. *He Took a Towel: Sermons and Services for Communion and Feetwashing*. Lima, OH: CSS Publishing Company, 2000.

Robertson, Edwin. *The Shame and the Sacrifice*. New York: Macmillian Publishing Company, 1988.

Root, Michael and Risto Saarinen, eds. *Baptism and the Unity of the Church*. Grand Rapids: Eerdmans Publishing Co., 1998.

Rogers, Eugene F. Jr. *After the Spirit: A Constructive Pneumatology From Resources Outside the Modern West*. Grand Rapids: Eerdmans Publishing Co., 2005.

Rordorf, Willy. *The Eucharist of the Early Christians*. New York: Pueblo Publishing Company, 1978.

Schoedel, William R. *Ignatius of Antioch: A Commentary on the Letters of Ignatius of Antioch* (Hermeneia). Philadelphia: Fortress Press, 1985.

Skarsaune, Oskar. *In the Shadow of the Temple: Jewish Influences on Early Christianity*. Downers Grove, IL: InterVarsity Press, 2002.

Stoffer, Dale R. *The Lord's Supper: Believers Church Perspectives*. Scottdale, PA: Herald Press, 1997.

Stronstad, Roger. *The Prophethood of All Believers*. Sheffield: Sheffield Academic Press, 1999.

The Book of Common Prayer. New York: The Church Hymnal Corporation, 1979.

The Book of Worship. Nashville: The United Methodist Publishing House, 1965.

Thomas, John Christopher. *Footwashing in John 13 and the Johannine Community*. Sheffield: Sheffield Academic Press, 1991.

_____. *The Devil, Disease and Deliverance: Origins of Illness in New Testament Thought*. New York: Sheffield Academic Press, 1998.

Tipei, John Fleter. *The Laying on of Hands in the New Testament*. Lanham, MD: University Press of America, Inc., 2009.

Tomlinson, A.J. *The Last Great Conflict.* Cleveland, TN: Press of Walter E. Rodgers, 1913.

Volf, Miroslav. *After Our Likeness: The Church as the Image of the Trinity.* Grand Rapids: Eerdmans Publishing Co., 1998.

Wacker, Grant. *Heaven Below: Early Pentecostals and American Culture.* Cambridge, MA: Harvard University Press, 2001.

Wainwright, Geoffrey and Karen B. Westerfield Tucker, editors. *The Oxford History of Christian Worship.* Oxford: Oxford University Press, 2006.

Warrington, Keith. *Pentecostal Theology: A Theology of Encounter.* London: T&T Clark, 2008.

Webber, Robert E., ed., *The Services of the Christian Year.* The Complete Library of Christian Worship, Vol. 5. Nashville: Star Song Publishing Group, 1994.

_____. *The Sacred Actions of Christian Worship.* The Complete Library of Christian Worship, Vol. 6. Nashville: Star Song Publishing Group, 1994.

_____. *Ancient-Future Time: Forming Spirituality Through the Christian Year.* Grand Rapids: Baker Book House, 2004.

_____. *Ancient Future Worship: Proclaiming and Enacting God's Narrative.* Grand Rapids: Baker Books, 2008.

Wenger, John C. *Complete Writings of Menno Simons: Circa 1496-1561.* Scottdale, PA: Herald Press, 1956.

White, James F. *The Sacraments in Protestant Practice and Faith.* Nashville: Abingdon Press, 1999.

White, L. Michael and O. Larry Yarbrough, eds. *The Social World of the First Christians. Essays in Honor of Wayne A. Meeks.* Minneapolis: Fortress Press, 1995.

Williams, J. Rodman. *Renewal Theology: Vol. 3. The Church, the Kingdom, and Last Things.* Grand Rapids: Zondervan Publishing House, 1992.

Wright, N.T. *The New Testament and the People of God.* Minneapolis: Fortress Press, 1992.

_____. *Jesus and the Victory of God.* Minneapolis: Fortress Press, 1996.

_____. *Justification: God's Plan and Paul's Vision.* Downers Grove, IL: InterVarsity Press, 2009.

Yong, Amos. *The Spirit Poured Out on All Flesh: Pentecostalism and the Possibility of Global Theology*. Grand Rapids: Baker Academic, 2005

Periodicals

Anderson, W.G. "The Fight Is On." *Church of God Evangel* (April 20, 1918), 4.

Archer, Kenneth J. "Nourishment for our Journey: The Pentecostal *Via Salutis* and Sacramental Ordinances." *Journal of Pentecostal Theology* 13 (October 2004), 79-96.

_____. "A Pentecostal Way of Doing Theology." *International Journal of Systematic Theology* 9 (July 2007), 301-314.

Baker, Elizabeth V. "The Gospel and the Kingdom." *Trust* (Feb. 1914).

"Baptism May Mean Martyrdom." *The Pentecostal Evangel* (November 13, 1920).

Bell, E.N. "Baptized Once for All." *Weekly Evangel* (March 27, 1915), 1, 3.

_____. "Scriptural Varieties on Baptismal Formula." *Weekly Evangel* (July 3, 1915).

_____. "The Lord's Supper." *The Christian Evangel* (July 12, 1919).

Boatwright, D.C. "Water Baptism." *Church of God Evangel* (22 October 1949).

Boddy, Alex A. "Health in Christ." *Confidence* (August 1910).

_____. Faith in His Blood. *Confidence* (August 1911).

_____. The Holy Ghost for Us. *The Weekly Evangel* (September 1, 1917).

_____. The Anointing With Oil. *Confidence* (April-June, 1922).

Bowers, James. "A Wesleyan-Pentecostal Approach to Christian Formation." *Journal of Pentecostal Theology* 6 (1995), 55-86.

Brogdon, Turner. "Report of a Georgia Meeting." *Church of God Evangel* (August 20, 1921).

Buckalew, J.W. *The Evening Light and Church of God Evangel* (October 15, 1910).

Buckalew, Mattie. "The Church of God—A Visible Organization." *Church of God Evangel* (July 17, 1920).

Butlin, J.T. "The Anointing of the Sick for Healing." *The Pentecostal Evangel* (August 23, 1924).

Chan, Simon. "Mother Church: Toward a Pentecostal Ecclesiology." *Pneuma: The Journal for the Society of Pentecostal Studies* 22.2, 177-208.

Coulter, Dale M. "The Development of Ecclesiology in the Church of God." *Pneuma* 29 (2007), 59-85.

Cox, William A. "The Lord's Table." *The Pentecostal Evangel* (May 25, 1929).

Cross, James L. "The Lord's Supper and Feet Washing." *Church of God Evangel* (June 19, 1961).

Culpepper, E.B. "The Church of God—Is Visible or Invisible, Which?" *Church of God Evangel* (July 5, 1919).

Davis, Mary. "Was Healed of Consumption." *The Church of God Evangel* (November 26, 1921).

Downey, C.W. "The Gospel of the Kingdom." *The Word and Witness* (March 20, 1914).

Ellis, J.B. "The Church Literal or Invisible." *Church of God Evangel* (June 10, 1916).

Everett, John W. "Healing at the Communion Table." *The Pentecostal Evangel* (February 18, 1968).

Executive Presbytery. "Preliminary Statement Concerning the Principles Involved in the New Issue." *Word and Witness* (June 1915).

Flower, J. Roswell. "The Broken Bread: A Meditation on the Lord's Supper." *The Pentecostal Evangel* (April 2, 1932).

_____. "The Lord's Supper." *Word and Witness* (August 1915).

Foucault, Michel. "About the Beginning of the Hermeneutics of the Self." *Political Theory* 21 (May 1993), 198-227.

Frodsham, Stanley H. "Baptism." *The Christian Evangel* (June 28, 1919).

Gee, Donald. "The Anointing." *The Pentecostal Evangel* (August 17, 1935).

_____. "Baptism and Salvation." *The Pentecostal Evangel* (March 22, 1953).

Gordon, A.J. "Who Healeth all Thine Iniquities, Who Healeth all Thy Diseases." *The Latter Rain Evangel* (May 1909), 14.

Holmes, George E. "Why I believe in Divine Healing." *The Pentecostal Evangel* (July 19, 1959).

Hubbell, Mrs. E. S. "Efficiency." *Church of God Evangel* (June 13, 1914).

Hughes, Jesse P. "Is the Church of God Losing Her Power?" *Church of God Evangel*, (January 17, 1920).

Hughes, Ray H. "Until Men Are Ready for His Soon Coming." *Church of God Evangel* (22 Oct 1973).

_____. "The Church and Your Pentecostal Experience." *Church of God Evangel* (May 12, 1975).

Jernigan, John C. "The Church of God From a Bible Standpoint." *Church of God Evangel* (May 27, 1922).

Kärkkäinen, Veli-Matti. "The Church as the Fellowship of Persons." *PentecoStudies*, vol. 6, no. 1, 2007, pp. 1-15.

Kerr, D.W. "The Message of the Sacrament." *The Weekly Evangel* (October 28, 1916).

Knight, Cecil B. "Communion: A Sign and a Seal." *Church of God Evangel* (22 March 1971).

Looney, W.A. "Revival Report." *Church of God Evangel* (October 2, 1920).

"Letter of a Baptist Preacher to His Wife Describing a Pentecostal Meeting at Durant, Fla." *The Evening Light and Church of God Evangel* (July 1, 1910).

Macchia, Frank D. "Tongues as a Sign: Towards a Sacramental Understanding of Pentecostal Experience." *Pneuma: The Journal of the Society for Pentecostal Studies* 15, (Spring 1993) 61-76.

Mallough, Don. "The Twofold Meaning of Communion." *The Pentecostal Evangel* (29 January 1956).

Marks, I.H. "Report from Ft. Myers, Florida." *Church of God Evangel* (October 30, 1915).

McDonnell, Kilian. "Communion Ecclesiology and Baptism in the Spirit: Tertullian and the Early Church." *Theological Studies* 49 (1988) 671-693.

Olsen, Ted. "What Really Unites Pentecostals?" *Christianity Today* (December 2006).

Perry, Sam C. "The Church." *Church of God Evangel* (September 15, 1912).

_____. "Spiritual Life and Power." *The Church of God Evangel* (February 2, 1913).

_____. "The Baptism of the Holy Ghost." *The Church of God Evangel* (April 8, 1916).

_____. "There are Other Things as Well." *The Church of God Evangel* (May 11, 1918).

Richardson, Thomas J. "Theocratic Government." *Church of God Evangel* (July 7, 1923).

Roberson, Beatrice. "Testimony." *Church of God Evangel* (August 25, 1923).

Rogers, H.G. "Report on the Convention." *The Evening Light and Church of God Evangel* (June 1, 1910).

Sexton, E. A. "College vs. Gifts of the Spirit." *The Bridegroom's Messenger* (October 1, 1907).

Seymour, W.J. "The Precious Atonement." *The Apostolic Faith* (September 1906).

_____. "Salvation and Healing." *The Apostolic Faith* (December 1906).

_____. "Beginning of World Wide Revival." *The Apostolic Faith* (January 1907).

_____. "Pentecost in Winnipeg, Manitoba." *The Apostolic Faith* (June to September, 1907).

_____. "The Ordinances Taught By Our Lord." *The Apostolic Faith* (September 1907).

_____. "The Principles of the Doctrine of Christ." *The Apostolic Faith* (October 1907).

_____. "The Baptism of the Holy Ghost." *The Apostolic Faith* (May 1908).

Shepherd, Mrs. B.L. "Report on Revival." *Church of God Evangel* (July 7, 1917).

_____. "Jewel Joints." *Church of God Evangel* (February 21, 1920).

Spurling, R.G. "The Church." *The Evening Light and Church of God Evangel* (March 15, 1910).

Stevens, W.C. "The Cross and Sickness." *The Pentecostal Evangel* (August 23, 1924), 6-7.

Stockton, R.E. "Education and the Church of God." *The Faithful Standard* (November 1922).

Taylor, G.F. *The Pentecostal Holiness Advocate* (May 22, 1930).

Thomas, John Christopher. "Pentecostal Theology in the Twenty-First Century." *Pneuma: The Journal of the Society for Pentecostal Studies* 20:1 (Spring 1998), 3-19.

_____. "Healing in the Atonement: A Johannine Perspective." *Journal of Pentecostal Theology 14.1* (2005), 23-39.

Thornhill, J.L. "The Church of God—The Pillar and Ground of the Truth." *The Church of God Evangel* (April 28, 1923).

Tomlinson, A.J. "Apology for Above Title." *The Evening Light and Church of God Evangel* (March 1, 1910).

_____. "Fourth of July at Tabernacle." *The Evening Light and Church of God Evangel* (July 15, 1910).

_____. *The Evening Light and Church of God Evangel* (September 15, 1910).

_____. "Christ, Our Law-Giver and King." *The Evening Light and Church of God Evangel* (November 1, 1910).

_____. "Obedience to Jesus." *Church of God Evangel* (May 5, 1917).

_____. "Promptness in Obedience." *Church of God Evangel* (October 6, 1917).

_____. "Warriors for Jesus." *Church of God Evangel* (July 13, 1918).

_____. "The Government of God." *Church of God Evangel* (June 14, 1919).

_____. "Healing for the Body." *The Church of God Evangel* (June 10, 1922).

Trussell, E.R. "The Lord's Supper." *Confidence* (April 1915).

Volf, Miroslav. "Materiality of Salvation: An Investigation in the Soteriologies of Liberation and Pentecostal Theologies." *Journal of Ecumenical Studies*, 26:3, (summer) 1989.

Waddell, C.H. "How to Receive Divine Healing." *The Christian Evangel* (February 8, 1919).

Williams, Laura. "Great Healing Power." *The Church of God Evangel* (December 31, 1921).

ELECTRONIC MEDIA

Archer, Kenneth J. "The Spirit and Theological Interpretation: A Pentecostal Strategy." *Cyberjournal for Pentecostal-Charismatic Research* 16 (January 2007). Internet: http://www.pctii.org/cyberj/cyber16.html.

Calvin, John. *The Institutes of the Christian Religion.* Trans. Henry Beveridge. Oak Harbor, WA: Logos Research Systems, Inc., 1997.

Church of God Publications 1901-1923 DVD. Cleveland, TN: Dixon Pentecostal Research Center, 2008.

Evans, P.W. "Sacraments in the New Testament." London: (The Tyndale New Testament Lecture, 1946).The Tyndale Press, 1946. Internet: http://www.theologicalstudies.org.uk/pdf/sacraments_evans.pdf.

Luther, Martin. *Disputation of Doctor Martin Luther on the Power and Efficacy of Indulgences: October 31, 1517,* electronic ed. Bellingham, WA: Logos Research Systems, 1996.

_____. *The Larger Catechism.* Albany, OR: Ages Software, 1997.

Parmentier, Martin. "Water Baptism and Spirit Baptism in the Church Fathers." *Cyberjournal for Pentecostal-Charismatic Research* 3 (January 1998). Internet: http://www.pctii.org/cyberj/cyber3.html.

Ravetz, Tom. "Patristic Theology of the Efficacy of the Eucharist." *Journal for the Renewal of Religion and Theology* 3 (September 2008). Internet: http://www.renewtheology.org/archive.htm.

Roberts, Alexander, James Donaldson, and A. Cleveland Coxe, eds. *The Ante-Nicene Fathers: Translations of the Writings of the Fathers Down to A.D. 325.* Oak Harbor, WA: Logos Research Systems, 1997.

Smith, James K.A. "Thinking in Tongues." *First Things* (April 2008). Internet: http://www.firstthings.com/article.php3?id_article=6173

The Pentecostal Holiness Advocate 1917-1924 CD. Oklahoma City: International Pentecostal Holiness Church, 2005.

Schaff, Philip, editor. *The Nicene and Post-Nicene Fathers, First Series.* Oak Harbor, WA: Logos Research Systems, 1997.

_____. *The Nicene and Post-Nicene Fathers, Second Series.* Oak Harbor, WA: Logos Research Systems, 1997.

_____. *History of the Christian Church.* Oak Harbor, WA: Logos Research Systems, 1997.

Verheyen, Boniface, trans. *The Holy Rule of St. Benedict.* 1949 edition. Internet: http://www.kansasmonks.org/RuleOfStBenedict.html

Wesley, John. *Sermons on Several Occasions.* Grand Rapids: Christian Classics Ethereal Library. Public Domain.

_____. *The Works of John Wesley, 3rd edition.* Albany, OR: Ages Software, 1997.

Wright, N. T. "Worship and the Spirit in the New Testament" (2008). Internet: www.ntwrightpage.com/Wright_Yale_Worship_Spirit.htm

fOR ⲘORE INfORⲘATION

Daniel Tomberlin
http://www.pentecostalsacraments.com

Center for Pentecostal Leadership and Care
http://www.cplc.cc

5957952R0

Made in the USA
Charleston, SC
26 August 2010